D0546340

yeast

The Practical Guide to Beer Fermentation

Chris White with Jamil Zainasheff

A Division of the
Brewers Association
Boulder, Colorado

Brewers Publications
A Division of the Brewers Association
PO Box 1679, Boulder, Colorado 80306-1679
BrewersAssociation.org

© Copyright 2010 by Brewers Association

All rights reserved. No portion of this book may be reproduced in any form without written permission of the publisher. Neither the authors, editor nor the publisher assume any responsibility for the use or misuse of information contained in this book.

Printed in the United States of America.

10 9 8 7 6 5 4

ISBN: 0-937-381-96-9
ISBN-13: 978-0-937381-96-0

Library of Congress Cataloging-in-Publication Data

White, Chris, 1968-
 Yeast : the practical guide to beer fermentation / by Chris White with Jamil Zainasheff.
   p. cm.
 Includes bibliographical references and index.
 ISBN-13: 978-0-937381-96-0
 ISBN-10: 0-937381-96-9
 1. Brewing. 2. Yeast. 3. Fermentation. I. Zainasheff, Jamil, 1961-
II. Title.

 TP580.W45 2010
 641.8'73--dc22
                        2010029741

Publisher: Kristi Switzer
Technical Editor: William L. Pengelly, Ph.D.
Copy Editing and Index: Daria Labinsky
Production & Design Management: Stephanie Johnson
Cover and Interior Design: Julie Korowotny
Cover Illustration: Alicia Buelow
Interior Images: White Labs unless otherwise noted

table of contents

Part Two: Biology, Enzymes, and Esters

Part Three: How to Choose the Right Yeast

Part Five: Yeast Growth, Handling, and Storage

Part Six: Your Own Yeast Lab Made Easy

Acknowledgements

This is a book I wanted to write for a long time. I've written about yeast, spoken about yeast, and worked with yeast every day for what seems like forever. I wanted to put that information and more into one source. I began to write the book three years ago with my brother, Mike White. We put a lot of material together, but it was still missing something. When Jamil Zainasheff came into the project, the book really began to take shape. Jamil added a lot of information and a professional touch. He is not only a great writer and brewer but also a good friend. The Brewers Association was a natural place for me to publish the book; Ray Daniels was very helpful in the beginning, then Kristi Switzer took over and has done a great job. I want to thank the people who contributed or reviewed material: Neva Parker, Lisa White, Troels Prahl, Mike White, Sharon Fernandez, Liz Strohecker, Lee Chase, Yuseff Cherney, Dan Drown, and Craig Duckham.

I also want to thank the many people who have supported the book, given me information, or helped in other ways: Jamie Reyes, John Schulz, Tomme Arthur, Jack White, Justin Crossly, Saskia Schmidt, John White, Tobias Fischborn, Graeme Walker, Sharon Heredia, Jay Prahl, Meg Falbo, Pam Marshall, Michael Lewis, Randy Mosher, Betsy Komives, Barbara Maisonet, Joanne Carilli–Stevensen, Lyn Kruger, the Maynard A. Amerine Viticulture & Enology Room at the University of California at Davis Shields Library, where I did most of my writing, Chris Boulton and David Quain for their great yeast book *Brewing Yeast & Fermentation* and personal discussions, *Brew Your Own* magazine, *Zymurgy* magazine, and *New Brewer* for some of the articles I have written, twenty-twos at Sudwerk Brewery, the many homebrewers and commercial brewers, who have taught me so much, and of course my supporting and loving parents, Eric and Gina White.

−Chris White

I could not have completed this book without the love, assistance, and support of my family: I do love them more than beer or brewing, but they never ask me to prove it. They know how hard I work on these books and how it takes away from family time as the deadline nears. For this book, they even put up with Dad furiously editing and writing during the family vacation to Disneyland. While my children, Anisa and Karina, are very supportive, my wife, Liz, goes much further and even helps edit all of my writing. I know my wife does not believe me when I tell her, "Dear, all homebrewers have their own yeast lab," but I really appreciate that she lets me spend money on and take up space with a lab, anyway. Yes, I know, I lead a charmed life.

Besides my family, this book would not exist without the help of many dear friends. I would especially like to thank Peter Symons for his dedication to reviewing every last word with a critical eye and letting me know where I went astray or had outdated information. I cannot express how strong the support and feedback of John Palmer, John Tull, Gordon Strong, and Gary Angelo has been, not only to this book, but to all of my writing and beer thinking.

Thank you also to those who believed I had the knowledge and ability to get this book done, especially Ray Daniels, Kristi Switzer, Chris White, and Justin Crossley.

A special thank you to Samuel Scott. Even though he was in the middle of moving, he found the time to create some great photos for the book. Then I asked for more, and he sent those, too.

As usual, there are so many others who helped with information, photos, or support. I avoid listing them, not because their contributions were less significant, but rather my memory is shoddy and I know I would accidentally leave someone off the list.

And thank you my friends, my brewing brothers and sisters, you have shared your beers, your homes, your knowledge, and most important to me, your friendship. I am forever grateful.

–Jamil Zainasheff

Portions of the text were previously published in *Zymurgy* and *Brew Your Own* magazines.

You can find the latest version of the Beer Judge Certification Program Style Guidelines at the BJCP website, www.bjcp.org.

Foreword

"We brewers don't make beer, we just get all the ingredients together and the beer makes itself."

— Fritz Maytag

"Beer does not make itself properly by itself. It takes an element of mystery and of things that no one can understand."

— Fritz Maytag

I've always liked these two quotes, as I believe they perfectly illustrate the mysteries of fermentation, the least understood and often the most neglected part of the brewing process. If you read beer recipes provided on various brewing websites and in brewing books, you'll see that much attention is paid to things like grain bills, and more significantly these days, to hop bills. Yeast seems a bit like an afterthought, and maybe that's because it has been that way throughout much of history.

Read historical brewing books and you will find plenty of references to malting, malt quality, hop growing, hop quality, and even water quality. These processes were well understood fairly early in the game. But because most brewers believed fermentation was a spontaneous process, there are virtually no references to yeast in historical texts. This despite the fact the brewers realized how critical yeast is to the brewing process, calling yeast "godisgood," "berme," and "yeste." Yeast is often only mentioned in passing in recipes and procedural texts. Even the first version of the German purity law, Reinheitsgebot, failed to include yeast as an ingredient in beer. And on the occasions that yeast *is* explored thoroughly in historical texts, it's a tough read, because the information is painfully inaccurate.

What is even more amazing is that despite this lack of knowledge, understanding, or willingness to address the inclusion of yeast as a vital ingredient, brewers knew yeast was important, and they knew fairly early on that they had to harvest yeast and repitch it to the next fermentor to ensure the successful transformation of wort to beer. Yeast strains have survived for hundreds, if not thousands, of years, and have been successfully maintained and carefully selected to become the multitude of wonderful strains that are available to brewers everywhere today. Throughout history brewing processes evolved that favored the maintenance of yeast strains. Techniques such as top cropping, repitching, lagering, and seasonal brewing to maintain good fermentation temperature were all developed to ensure complete fermentations and delicious beer, despite brewers having no real understanding of what yeast was and how it worked. Even as recently as the late 1800s, after Louis Pasteur proved that fermentation is a result of metabolism by yeast, a living organism, brewing literature was chock-full of "marketing speak" references to yeast: "yeast must be of the *highest quality*," "yeast must be *excellent*," "yeast must be *exceptionally fine*," all of which really mean nothing, but do give the appropriate impression that the brewer treats his yeast with care.

Yeast research started in the late 1600s, shortly after the invention of the microscope, but really took off in the late 1700s and early 1800s. Several scientists came up with theories that were close to what we now know as reality, postulating that yeast were single-cell organisms and were responsible for alcoholic fermentation, but no one really landed on the key fact that yeast were metabolizing sugars to produce alcohol and carbon dioxide. In the late 1830s, yeast research was focusing in on the fact that yeast cell activity was the source of alcohol and CO_2 production. This promising thread of research was derailed slightly by the publishing of the following derogatory description of cellular fermentation by organic chemists Liebig and Wohler, who favored chemical reaction as the explanation for fermentation:

... Incredible numbers of small spheres are seen, which are the eggs of animals. When placed in sugar solution, they swell, burst, and animals develop from them, which multiply with inconceivable speed. The shape of these animals is different from any of the hitherto described 600 species. They have the shape of a Beindorf distilling flask (without the cooling device). The tube of the bulb is some sort of a suction trunk, which is covered inside with fine long bristles. Teeth and eyes are not observed. Incidentally, one can clearly distinguish a stomach, intestinal tract, the anus (as a pink point), and the organs of urine excretion. From the moment of emergence from the egg, one can see how the animals swallow the sugar of the medium and how it gets into the stomach. It is digested immediately, and this process is recognized with certainty from the elimination of excrements. In short, these infusoria eat sugar, eliminate alcohol from the intestinal tract and CO_2 from the urinary organs. The urinary bladder in its filled state has the shape of a Champagne bottle, in the empty state it is a small bud. After some practice, one observes that inside a gas bubble is formed, which increases its volume up to tenfold; by some screwlike torsion, which the animal controls by means of circular muscles around the body, the emptying of the bladder is accomplished. ... From the anus of the animal one can see the incessant emergence of a fluid that is lighter than the liquid medium, and from their enormously large genitals a stream of CO_2 is squirted at very short interval . ... If the quantity of water is insufficient, i.e., the concentration of sugar too high, fermentation does not take place in the viscous liquid. This is because the little organisms cannot change their place in the viscous liquid: they die from indigestion caused by lack of exercise (Schlenk, 1997).

Fortunately, some researchers continued on, and cell theory became more gradually accepted through the groundbreaking work of Pasteur. And groundbreaking it was; it completely changed the whole brewing industry. Pasteur traveled from brewery to brewery in the late 1800s and offered his services to inspect their yeast cultures, and gave the breweries a passing or failing grade. The story of Pasteur's influence on the Carlsberg brewery is well documented later in this book, but Pasteur didn't stop there; he traveled throughout Europe. When Pasteur indoctrinated the

English brewers of the late 1800s on the importance of yeast, they hired chemists as senior level staff members. These brewing chemists became highly sought after and also became the highest-paid members of the brewery staffs.

As the field of biochemistry has grown, larger breweries have adopted scientific techniques to better understand their yeast strains. When I worked at Anheuser-Busch, we tracked yeast fermentation by-products like diacetyl, pentanedione, acetoin, and acetaldehyde at regular points throughout the lagering process. These maturation factors were quick indications of how healthy the yeast and fermentations were. But despite all the technology and research available, yeast still remains mysterious and unpredictable in many ways, and monitoring fermentations remains a very reactive type of situation. It wasn't uncommon for a team of experts from St. Louis to hop on a plane and visit a brewery that was having a problem with its yeast or its fermentations, arriving with the dreaded statement, "We're from Corporate, and we're here to help."

I remember a discussion we had as brewers at Anheuser-Busch several years ago regarding how much yeast contribute to the final flavor of beer. In general, the consensus was that yeast was responsible for nearly 80 to 90 percent of the flavor in an American lager. All you have to do is taste wort and beer side by side to understand the importance of yeast's contribution to beer flavor. And if you consider the three flagship beers from the big three American lager brewers, which are brewed to the same style and use similar ingredients, you'll realize the beers taste markedly different when compared side by side. And that difference is primarily due to yeast.

In a craft beer the impact of yeast on the final beer flavor may not be quite as pronounced, due to the increased quantities of specialty malts and hops, but I know at Stone Brewing Company we have fermented several worts with both our house ale strain and with Belgian yeast, and the beers taste nothing alike. In some cases we weren't able to tell they came from the same wort, which we always found amazing.

So realistically, yeast can be the most active flavor ingredient in the brewing process, and it is certainly the most temperamental ingredient in beer. Yeast possess a tough combination of characteristics for a brewer to manage. As any experienced brewer knows, you must treat your yeast with the utmost care, or the beer can end up tasting horrible.

Chris White and Jamil Zainasheff have taken on the daunting task of explaining yeast and fermentation to us brewers. One of the difficulties in writing a comprehensive book on yeast and fermentation is that every yeast strain reacts differently to similar external conditions. Any brewer who has switched jobs or yeast strains knows that the conditions that make one strain perform well don't always work for the next strain. It's an inexact science, trying to manage this living organism and getting it to behave the way we want it to. Our job as brewers is to manage our yeast, keep it "happy" so that it only produces the flavor compounds we want in our beer, and not any of the "bad" flavors that yeast tend to produce when they are stressed.

Chris and Jamil have done a great job addressing these difficulties in this book. They have included loads of sound information and techniques that will work for brewers at all levels, from beginning homebrewers to production brewers at any sized brewery. Included are fantastic tips for working with all kinds of yeast strains and beer styles, introducing new strains, and how to use best brewing and lab practices to keep your yeast healthy and your beer tasting great. And even through the "dreaded" organic chemistry and biochemistry sections, the authors manage to keep the information conversational, which will allow brewers with varied educational backgrounds to take this information and use it effectively to improve their fermentations and their beer quality.

I hope everyone enjoys this book as much as I did. I think it's a must for every brewer's bookshelf. Welcome to the wonderful, mysterious, and complex world of brewer's yeast!

Mitch Steele
Head Brewer/Production Manager
Stone Brewing Company

Introduction

Yeast is critical to beer, which makes it critical to brewers. Whether brewers fully realize it or not, yeast function involves much more than converting sugars into alcohol. More than any other fermented beverage, beer depends on yeast for flavor and aroma. Our goal was to write a yeast book that focused on the brewer's perspective, and we quickly realized that there are just as many perspectives about yeast as there are brewers. While one brewer may have an interest in exploring native fermentation with wild yeast, another is concerned with maintaining a pure culture and minimizing unusual flavors, and yet another wants to know every detail of yeast biochemistry. In the end, we did our best to cover as much information as possible from a practical brewer's view.

This is not a book for the highly successful regional or larger brewer who already has multiple labs and a doctorate in microbiology. This is a book for those who are in the early stages of their love of yeast and what it can do for their beer. And when we use the word "brewer," we are talking not just about professionals but also hobbyists. Home-brewers (who call themselves craft brewers in some parts of the world) love the process of making beer as much as their professional counterparts do. Just like professional brewers, they range from eccentric to highly scientific, but all share a passion to create something out of nothing. Of course, brewing successfully on a professional level takes a great deal of dedication and financial risk that homebrewers can avoid. Whether you are a professional or hobbyist, brewing great beer requires both an artistic flair and, at times, the ability to think like an engineer. In fact, engineers seem to enjoy homebrewing more than most and have a passion for taking the hobby to its limit. Perhaps this is why many professional brewers began as homebrewers. They wanted to take their creativity and passion to the public.

From the beginning, we decided that this would not be a yeast biology book. It is not a book on the basics of brewing, either. You should already know how to brew, and if you do not, get yourself a copy of *How to Brew* by John Palmer and come back to this book later. If your passion is for yeast biology, there are many fine yeast science books available as well. In some cases, we do discuss what is happening within the cell wall, but only to show how it affects your beer. We wanted to write a book that was accessible and useful for brewers of all experience levels. We cover yeast information from the basics to some advanced procedures and even beyond to some areas for further study. One thing we know about brewers is that they always want to know more, so we hope this book satisfies your interest, stretches your horizons, and has you thinking about yeast every time you think about beer.

Fermentor vs. Fermenter

Fermenter or fermentor, which is right? You see both words used interchangeably, but technically that is not correct. In this book we follow the differentiation found in many dictionaries:

We use fermentor when talking about a fermentation vessel, such as a cylindroconical fermentor.

We use fermenter when talking about the yeast itself, such as, "WLP001 is a strong fermenter."

About Chris White

I have a peculiar resume. I graduated with a doctorate in biochemistry, but instead of joining a regular laboratory, I have spent my professional life immersed in the yeast and fermentation business.

The history of beer and yeast has been a fascinating subject for me since my college days, for many reasons. In the early 1990s I developed a passion for homebrewing while an undergraduate at University of California, Davis. My introduction to this fascinating world came through Michael Lewis' Brewing and Malting Science course. I started homebrewing there and continued homebrewing while pursuing a Ph.D. degree from the University of California, San Diego. My thesis involved an industrial yeast, *Pichia pastoris*, which I had the fortune to work with in its early development. *Pichia pastoris* is now widely used in biotechnology. While wonderful in the science world, *Pichia pastoris* makes beer that tastes something like sweaty socks, so I started collecting brewing yeast strains from breweries and yeast banks worldwide. I experimented with these in my homebrewing, and at the same time, a surge of new breweries opened in San Diego. Pizza Port Brewing, Ballast Point Brewing, Stone Brewing, and AleSmith all got started in the early 1990s, which gave me an opportunity to understand the needs of professional brewers. I founded White Labs Inc. in San Diego in 1995. The company's focus was large-volume liquid yeast cultures, based on technology that I learned with *Pichia pastoris* and later modified to meet the special needs of *Saccharomyces cerevisiae* brewing yeast.

Today, White Labs yeast is sold in homebrew shops and to professional breweries, and is also used in other industries, including winemaking. The thrill for me in those early years, and still today, was getting yeast of the highest quality to homebrewers and professionals. In this book I hope we show you how to maximize your fermentation experience by getting the most out of what can with good measure be called the most important ingredient in beer – the yeast.

About Jamil Zainasheff

"The yeast is strong within you."

— Karina Zainasheff to Anisa Zainasheff

Since the age of eight, I have had an interest in foods that involve fermentation or similar processes such as bread, cheese, kimchi, and yogurt. Sourdough bread cultures fascinated me, and I quickly realized that the conditions I provided to the culture made a difference in the quality and flavor of the bread I made from it.

So it seems strange to me now that during the 1980s, as a biochemistry undergraduate at the University of California at Davis, the extent of my beer knowledge was centered around which day of the week was dollar beer night at the local watering holes.

It was not until later, when my wife, Liz, got me started with a Mr. Beer kit, that I added alcoholic beverages to my list of fermentation interests. I started brewing, but through no fault of the kit, I had little initial success. I did have one advantage, though. While I had missed out on learning about beer, wine, or yeast like so many of my friends at UC Davis, I did gain a passion and talent for learning that I could put to use. I read everything I could find on brewing, and I asked many questions to those around me. I already knew that yeast was probably the key to making perfect beer, and by learning how to better work with yeast, my beer improved.

I became obsessed with making the best beer possible and entered many competitions to get objective feedback on beer quality. I would alter recipes, techniques, and yeast variables one at a time, until I understood what effect my actions had on the results. As my knowledge grew, I felt I should behave like those who helped me by sharing that knowledge. This is what led me to hosting shows on the Brewing Network and writing about brewing. My friend John Palmer got me started down the book path with our collaboration on *Brewing Classic Styles,* and when presented with a chance to work on a book about yeast with Chris White, I felt like it was an opportunity I could not pass up. Writing an authoritative book of this scope was challenging, but I think we succeeded in capturing a lot of the information that I used to take my beers from insipid to award winning. My hope is that this book inspires readers to have a passion for yeast as much as they do for beer. As my daughter Karina so eloquently put it, I hope the yeast will be strong within you, and you will use that passion to make advances in your own beer quality as well.

1

The Importance of Yeast and Fermentation

A Brief History of Yeast

Some historians believe that civilization developed from a desire to drink beer. They speculate that the transition from hunter-gatherer to farmer, and the beginning of civilization, was to grow crops to make beer. Of course, those early brewers could not have made beer without yeast. No yeast, no beer. No beer, no civilization. Therefore, we really have yeast to thank for all our modern-day conveniences and tasty beer.

Thousands of years ago in Mesopotamia, nobody understood that the naturally occurring yeast on soil and plants was critical to creating fermentation. Ancient brewers and winemakers relied on these natural yeast sources to inoculate their fermentations. For most of history, fermentation was a divine mystery. An offering set before a shrine and prayed over for several days would transform into an intoxicating beverage. Brewing implements became family heirlooms. They began to call the froth that would magically appear on the surface of the beer "godisgood," and they reverently transferred it to another vessel to begin another fermentation. Researchers believe that brewers started reusing yeast from batch to batch in the twelfth century, beginning the process of yeast domestication. Brewers and drinkers wanted beer that tasted better

and had a longer shelf life. Brewers reused the yeast from successful batches and discarded the yeast from bad batches, unknowingly putting selective pressure on the yeast.

Before microscopes allowed us to see yeast, no one knew exactly what happened during fermentation. When the Bavarians created the Reinheitsgebot beer purity law in 1516, making it illegal to brew beer containing anything other than water, barley malt, and hops, they left yeast off the list of ingredients because they did not know it existed.

In 1680, more than a century after the purity law went into effect, Anton van Leeuwenhoek was first to observe, through a microscope, that yeast was composed of small, interconnected elements. Interestingly, he did not realize that it was alive. At that time, the most commonly accepted theory of fermentation was that it was a spontaneous process—a chemical reaction promoted by contact with the air—and the yeast was a chemical by-product.

Another century later, in 1789, Antoine-Laurent Lavoisier described the chemical nature of fermentation as parts of sugar turning into carbon dioxide and alcohol. Yet scientists still did not make the connection between yeast and this conversion of sugar into ethanol. It was not until the mid-1800s that Louis Pasteur established that yeast was a living microorganism. This opened the gates for precisely controlling the conversion of sugar into alcohol. It also led to the creation of a separate field of study called biochemistry. The advances made, as direct or indirect results of beer research, led to our understanding of how cells work and laid the groundwork for many other breakthroughs in scientific research.

It is not exaggerating to suggest Pasteur made the greatest advances of anyone in the history of beer, and that these breakthroughs and others led to some important advances for the whole of civilization. His studies into beer and wine fermentation paved the way for his later work on anthrax, rabies, cholera, and other afflictions, which led to the development of the first vaccines.

When Pasteur started working with beer fermentation in the 1860s, most people believed yeast was not the causative agent of fermentation. Beer is a complex soup of material, containing protein, nucleic acids, bacteria, yeast, and much more. Scientists knew yeast was part of the mix, but they regarded it as a by-product of the fermentation. They

believed spontaneous generation catalyzed by air caused fermentation. The spontaneous generation theory held that yeast and bacteria were created spontaneously in fermentation. At the time, the theory that living cells could carry out fermentation was too "biological." Scientists had still not perfected their sterilization techniques, and this was one reason the spontaneous generation theory persisted. After all, if a scientist believed he sterilized a medium, yet it still contained cells that would later multiply, it would appear that spontaneous generation was the answer.

Pasteur did not believe this. Pasteur drew on his study of wine and did not believe there was enough air present to explain the growth of the yeast population during fermentation. He designed a simple experiment that would put an end to the theory of spontaneous generation.

Today we know Pasteur's experiment as the "swan neck" fermentation. He filled a swan neck flask with a sterilized mineral medium. Pasteur was fortunate to have used a medium with a pH that was acidic enough to stay sterile in his experiment. In fact, some of the flasks he prepared still remain sterile to this day.

Air can enter, but the swan neck traps any dust, which carries yeast and bacteria. Since the dust cannot reach the medium, there is no fermentation. If air was all that was required for fermentation, fermentation would still proceed, but it does not. Only when the flask is tipped can liquid enter the neck, taking up bacteria and yeast, and fermentation can start.

This was a controversial idea, and Pasteur would spend the next fifteen years conducting experiments to prove certain aspects. He also worked with different sugars, including those from fruits. By 1879 his theory was firmly in place and he wrote, "… we need no longer say, 'we think,' but instead, 'we affirm,' that it is correct," concerning alcoholic fermentation and yeast.

This was important for many reasons beyond academic value. Once you know the cause of something, you can better control the process that causes it. Beermaking went from something that was magical, with the brewer having little control, to something that the brewer could control simply by understanding yeast.

Pasteur understood right away. He not only proved what yeast was doing, he theorized that the bacteria and other yeast present were the cause of off-flavors. After all, the goal of his original work was to discover how to prevent the "disease of beer."

Some breweries adopted his ideas and began cleaning their yeast cultures and breweries. One such brewery was Carlsberg in Denmark. Carlsberg Laboratories, under the direction of Emil Christian Hansen, isolated the first lager yeast strain and brought it into the brewing world on November 12, 1883. Its scientific name was *Saccharomyces carlsbergensis* or *Saccharomyces uvarum* (now *S. pastorianus*), but most brewers call it "lager yeast." Hansen was also the first to develop pure culture techniques, techniques that we still use today in microbiology laboratories. It was these techniques that allowed Carlsberg Laboratories to isolate the pure lager yeast culture. Not only was Hansen able to grow this new lager yeast in pure form, he was also able to store it for long periods on a combination of wort and agar. This combination of isolating pure cultures and long-term storage allowed brewers to transport lager yeast all over the world, and soon after, lager brewing overtook ale brewing worldwide.

Why did lager beer become so popular? At the time that Hansen isolated lager yeast, most ale fermentations still contained some wild yeast

Figure 1.1: Busts of Louis Pasteur (left) and Emil Christian Hansen (right) decorating the old Carlsberg brewery in Copenhagen. Photos courtesy of Troels Prahl.

and bacteria. The resulting beer, even if it was acceptable at first, had a short shelf life before it went bad. For many people, unless they worked in a brewery, the first clean-tasting beer they had was probably a lager beer. Lager beer was also fermented cool, which suppressed the growth of wild yeast and bacteria. Therefore, lager beer had a longer shelf life, which meant a larger distribution area and increased sales. It is possible that many breweries switched to lager brewing because they saw it as an opportunity to increase their sales. Today, with modern pure culture techniques and good hygiene practices, ale is just as contamination free, but mass-market lager beer continues to thrive. Is it marketing or is the flavor more appealing for today's beer drinker?

Why Fermentation Is So Important

We think of the brewing process as divided into two stages or phases: the hot side and the cold side. The hot side is the cooking (or brewing) process, which takes place in the brew house. The hot side involves recipe design, milling, mashing, and the boiling of the wort and hops. The product of the hot side, the hopped wort, provides the food for yeast in the second phase, the cold side.

The cold side begins as the brewer cools the wort, adds yeast, and fermentation takes place. Depending on the recipe, the yeast will metabolize roughly 50 to 80 percent of the wort extract, with the remainder being protein, dextrins, and other nonmetabolized compounds. Karl Balling's work showed that yeast convert 46.3 percent of the extract into carbon dioxide, 48.4 percent into ethanol, and 5.3 percent into new yeast mass (De Clerck, 1957). Even though these numbers add up to 100 percent, they ignore one very important aspect of fermentation: While metabolizing the extract, yeast cells also produce hundreds of other compounds. These compounds exist in very small amounts, the sum total of which is less than 1 percent of the mass of the metabolized extract, but they contribute enormously to flavor, and indeed contribute what is the essence of beer. The types and amounts of these flavor compounds are by no means constant and can vary enormously depending on yeast health, growth rate, sanitation, and other factors.

Brewers can easily avoid or correct many of the issues that come up on the cold side of the process through sanitary wort production and creating an optimal environment for yeast. With mastery of the cold side, we gain better control over the flavors, aromas, appearance, and textures of our beer. It is this, the cold side and how the brewer manipulates it, which is the primary focus of this book.

Improving Fermentation Quality

So, if the yeast side is so important, what can we do to make it better? The first step is to recognize when there is a problem with the yeast. While a cat can cry out when it is hungry or hurt, yeast cannot vocalize. Yet we can detect many of their cries for help by looking, listening, tasting, smelling, and feeling. Yes, feeling. Get to know your yeast in every way possible. Become a yeast whisperer, if you can. Start by learning how the yeast performs when the beer tastes great. Take notes on fermentation and measure every variable you can. Get some yeast out of the tank at different stages and inspect it. Once you know how it performs, keep an eye out for changes in attenuation, off-flavors, sluggish fermentation, and changes in flocculation. Set up a dedicated area of your brewery or home for your own basic lab. With a few simple tools, you can learn even more using tests such as forced fermentation and mutation plates.

You need to get into the habit of counting your yeast. At the very least, measure the volume or weight of the yeast you pitch every time you brew. Measure their viability on a regular basis, also. Using the same number of cells at the same level of viability every time is important in developing consistent beer.

The yeast strain you use is also critically important to everything related to fermentation. Like people, each strain has a distinct personality. In fact, successive generations of the same yeast family will have their own unique attributes, whether related to fermentation temperature, oxygen requirements, or level of attenuation. In the end, perhaps the most important factor in good fermentation is preventing contamination from competing with your yeast.

You cannot accomplish any of this on the hot side. Other than the boil, fighting contamination all happens on the cold side. If you control the cold side with consistent pitching rates, if you understand your yeast's behavior, and if you keep it very clean, you have an opportunity for cold side success and an excellent probability of making great beer.

The Basics of Good Fermentation

What exactly happens during fermentation? When yeast ferments a solution, a transformation occurs from a sugary substance to an alcoholic one, with the added benefit of lower pH and vital beer flavor compounds. A low pH gives fermented products added protection against harmful bacteria, and the flavor compounds (esters, high molecular weight alcohols, sulfur compounds, and many more) add the characteristics that make beer taste the way it does. If you were simply to add pure ethanol to wort or grape juice, it would not taste like beer or wine, because it would be lacking those critical fermentation by-products.

What do we need for fermentation to take place? Many books detail the biochemistry of the yeast cell, but this is not a yeast biology book. For the brewer, good fermentation is more about what you need to do and what equipment you need than it is about what is going on inside a yeast cell. It takes very little besides yeast and a suitable sugary liquid for fermentation to occur. However, for fermentations to work well and achieve the flavors, aromas, and mouthfeel we want, we need the right sugars, healthy yeast, nutrients, controlled temperatures, and equipment to monitor the progress of fermentation—in short, we need a controlled fermentation.

Yeast

The most important part of fermentation is the yeast. Yeast convert sugar to alcohol, carbon dioxide, and other compounds that influence the taste of fermented foods and beverages. Yeast do this in order to make energy and gain material for reproduction. They do not care that you are trying to make great beer.

What kind of yeast do we need? Ah, this is where it gets interesting. Lots of yeast can convert sugar into alcohol, but you will want to use a strain that creates the best flavors for your beer. Sometimes history chooses a strain for you. It could be a yeast strain brought to the brewery a hundred years ago, or it may be a strain specified in a recipe, for stylistic accuracy. If you have the flexibility to choose, you might do your own research on the best strain to use or get advice from a supplier or brewing colleague.

Regardless of which strain you select, it must be in good health and pitched at the correct quantity for optimal fermentation. If you purchase yeast from a laboratory, the lab often guarantees a certain level of purity and can provide quantities necessary to pitch directly into your brew. If you are purchasing a less than pitchable amount or growing up your own yeast from a slant or plate, pay particular attention to the viability, vitality, and purity of the yeast culture throughout your process.

Sugar

Yeast feed on sugars to create alcohol, but the sugar sources and their complexity will result in varied fermentation conditions. Most brewers know that the type of sugars created in the mash, present in malt extract, or added to the kettle or fermentor affect the fermentability of the wort. As a general rule, simpler sugars are more fermentable than longer chain, more complex sugars. One thing many brewers do not know is that the type of sugars present can also affect fermentation flavors. For example, fermentation of wort high in glucose produces beers with higher than normal concentrations of esters (particularly ethyl acetate, which tastes like adhesive or solvent, and isoamyl acetate, which tastes like banana). Conversely, wort high in maltose results in lower concentrations of these esters. The higher the starting gravity, the more pronounced this effect.

The source of the sugars can also affect fermentation through differences in nutrients and flavor precursors. While the most common source for beer is malted barley, brewers around the world use many different starches. For instance, sorghum is quite popular in Africa, and it is gaining interest in North America as an alternative ingredient for consumers with wheat allergies. Brewers also utilize wheat, corn, rice, and preprocessed sugars and syrups.

Adding an adjunct starch such as rice or corn to the mash still results in the same types of sugars (mostly maltose), since the same malt enzymes that convert the malted barley will convert the adjunct starches. The concern when using large portions of nonbarley malt is that the adjunct starch often lacks the same nutrients and flavor precursors as barley malt, thus affecting fermentation and the flavor of the beer.

Oxygen

Oxygen is a critical factor in yeast growth, and it is often the limiting factor. Yeast use oxygen for sterol synthesis. The yeast use sterols to keep the cell walls pliant, which is important to cell growth and overall cell health.

Prior to fermentation, aerating the chilled wort is necessary to promote yeast growth. We consider 8-10 ppm oxygen the minimum level, with the amount of oxygen necessary varying by yeast strain and other factors, including specific gravity. Beers with higher yeast demands, such as lagers and high-gravity beers, tend to require more oxygen.

Contrary to what many brewers believe, it is possible to overoxygenate your wort when using pure oxygen. If you provide an overabundance of oxygen, too much growth can occur, creating an overabundance of fermentation by-products and resulting in a less than ideal fermentation character.

Nutrients

Yeast cells need 100 percent of their essential vitamins and minerals (nutrients) to make it through a fermentation properly nourished and to be ready to work again another day, much the same way humans do.

An all-malt wort is an excellent source of nitrogen, minerals, and vitamins. It supplies most of the vitamins yeast need for proper fermentation, such as riboflavin, inositol, and biotin. Yeast also require several key minerals, such as phosphorus, sulfur, copper, iron, zinc, potassium, calcium, and sodium. As the yeast take up minerals and vitamins from wort, they begin to manufacture the enzymes necessary for growth and fermentation. We can easily improve the health and performance of yeast by ensuring they have the proper levels of nutrients. If you are reusing yeast, this is especially important for continued yeast health. Several commercially available yeast nutritional supplements make it easy to ensure the wort contains the proper minerals and vitamins for yeast health.

Fermentation Systems

Different fermentation systems create vastly different results. Traditionally, brewers used large, open fermentation vessels, which were advantageous for several reasons. One is that they offered brewers the ability to harvest yeast for many, many generations, because brewers could scoop the yeast from the surface. These vessels are still quite popular in England. Many years ago brewers would ferment beers with a combination of native yeast and the brewer's yeast, reused from batch to batch. You can still find those kinds of beers today, although most modern beers are made with single strains.

However, these large, open fermentation vessels are not without their own set of issues. They can be difficult to clean, and they are not as sanitary as modern, closed fermentation equipment. Most brewers today use fermentation vessels with cone-shaped bottoms, which have their own advantages and drawbacks. These vessels offer clean-in-place technology and excellent temperature control, but extremely tall fermentors can put additional stress on yeast. The increased partial pressures of gasses in solution can affect yeast performance and the flavor of the beer. Homebrewers have the advantage of time and economic freedom, so they can utilize everything from open fermentors to smaller versions of commercial cylindroconical fermentors.

Temperature Control

Temperature control is essential for consistent, high-quality beer. This is far more important than the difference between stainless conical fermentors and plastic buckets. One of the most critical things to take away from this book is the importance of fermentation temperature on the quality of the beer. When a problem arises, and it is not a contamination problem, the first place to look is the temperature of the beer throughout all phases of fermentation, from pitching through final conditioning. High or low temperatures affect the production of many off-flavor precursors at the beginning of fermentation. Temperature also affects the yeast's ability to reduce many off-flavor compounds at the end of fermentation. Large, uncontrolled temperature swings produce poor results, especially when the batch sizes are small. The smaller the batch size, the more rapidly it is affected by changes in ambient temperature.

Fermentation Monitoring

Monitoring equipment and methods can range widely in cost and complexity. A brewer can achieve a lot with something as simple as the power of observation, a thermometer, and a few basic manual tests. Larger commercial breweries often invest in sophisticated computer testing systems.

The most important measurements during fermentation (in order of precedence) are temperature, specific gravity, pH, oxygen, and carbon dioxide. The important thing to note is the need for regular measurements and monitoring the progress of fermentation. You should keep logs, and part of every log should include detailed notes on how much yeast you pitched, its source, its viability, the gravity and pH of the beer, beer volume, temperatures, and daily progress notes. It is through your rigorous attention to fermentation that you will spot problems early on, perhaps saving considerable cost in lost product.

2

Biology, Enzymes, and Esters

Yeast Biology

We said this is not a biology book, but we do need to understand a little biology to best work with this tiny organism. Taxonomists have classified yeast as part of the fungus kingdom. Other kingdoms include bacteria, animals, and plants. Most of the organisms in the fungus kingdom, such as molds and mushrooms, are multicellular, but yeast is a single-cell organism. This means that yeast do not have forms of protection that multicellular organisms have, such as a skin. Yet these little single-cell organisms are surprisingly resilient, making up in numbers and rapid replication what they lack in protection.

A single yeast cell is about 5 to 10 microns in size and round to ovoid in shape. A yeast cell is ten times larger than bacteria but still too small to be seen by the naked eye. In fact, it takes more than ten yeast cells to equal the diameter of one human hair. A small, visible yeast colony on a Petri dish contains at least 1 million cells.

There are more than 500 species of yeast, and within each species are thousands of different yeast strains. We find yeast all over the world—living in soil, on insects and crustaceans, on animals, and on plants. In the early days, taxonomists classified yeast as part of the plant kingdom. Look at any piece of ripe fruit and you can be certain that yeast is all over it. Yeast can travel on dust, and air currents carry yeast to new areas. The yeast settle on just about every surface, anxious to find more sugars to ferment so they can multiply. Look at that sunshine streaming in through the brewery window. Do you see the dust particles? There is a good chance they are carrying native yeast, and bacteria, too, just waiting for an opportunity to land in your beer. Most brewers do not want native yeast in their beer, and they call these wild yeast. But what about a second brewer's yeast strain that accidentally winds up in our beer? We consider any yeast that is not in the brewer's control to be a wild yeast, and we will use that definition for the rest of this book. However, when most people speak of wild yeast they are usually referring to strains that aren't brewer's yeast.

Brewers, winemakers, and distillers use a few very specific species of yeast for their products. The brewer's genus is *Saccharomyces*, which is derived from Latinized Greek and means "sugar fungus." There are two main species of brewer's yeast, ale and lager: *S. cerevisiae* (ale yeast) and *S. pastorianus* (lager yeast). Taxonomists go back and forth about whether *S. pastorianus* is a member of the *S. cerevisiae* species or is its own species. Currently they consider them as separate, and this agrees with the brewing world. Lager yeast has gone by other names in the past, *S. uvarum* and *S. carlsbergensis*. Winemakers most commonly use either *S. cerevisiae* or *S. bayanus*, and it is interesting to note that lager yeast appears to have evolved through the rare hybridization of those two species (Casey, 1990).

Genetics of *S. cerevisiae*

A gene encodes a protein, and yeast has about 6,000 genes. We know this because yeast was the first eukaryotic organism to have its entire genome sequenced, by an international community of scientists in 1996. Genes are part of chromosomes, and yeast has sixteen different chromosomes. In comparison, bacteria have one chromosome, and human cells have twenty-three. Normally, yeast and human cells are diploid, which means that they contain two copies of each chromosome; haploid cells contain only a single copy of each chromosome.

Yeast in the wild is usually diploid and contains thirty-two chromosomes, two copies of each of the sixteen chromosomes. Yeast form spores in the wild, which is a key part of their mating cycle. This mating between wild yeast cells leads to evolutionary change and is good for yeast diversity and health. However, we as brewers want consistency from yeast, not diversity and rapid genetic change. Fortunately for us, brewers of the past worked diligently, selecting and reusing yeast to the point that brewer's yeast eventually lost the ability to form spores and lost the ability to mate. Losing the ability to mate seriously curtailed evolutionary change, and today brewers can count on yeast to be more consistent batch to batch. In addition, brewer's yeast developed more than two copies of each gene, an occurrence known as polyploidy. Although copies of a chromosome are not necessarily isogenic (identical), the beauty of polyploidy is that a mutation in one gene does not incapacitate the cell; the yeast has multiple copies of the gene to make the needed protein product. Polyploidy in brewer's yeast is possibly the result of brewers applying evolutionary pressure by only selecting the yeast that behaved like the last batch for re-use.

Yeast genetics determine whether a cell is an ale yeast or lager yeast. Genetics also determine everything else about a cell. Even though we know the DNA (deoxyribonucleic acid) sequence for *S. cerevisiae,* we do not yet know what each gene does. It is small differences in genotype expression and environment that determine the yeast's phenotype. The phenotype is every characteristic of the cell: what sugars it eats, what it produces, what nutritional and oxygen demands it has. Scientists are looking at ways to see which genes are active at any given time, but so far, this has resulted in little help for brewers. Brewers today still rely on the same techniques as brewers from the past: looking at what yeast does during fermentation (phenotype) in order to determine the identity, condition, performance, and purity of the yeast.

Yeast Cell Structure

Cell Wall. The cell wall is a thick, mostly carbohydrate barrier that surrounds the cell. A yeast cell wall is like a wicker basket protecting its contents. Polysaccharides, proteins, and lipids constitute up to 30 percent of the cell's dry weight. Approximately 10 percent of the protein is stuck into the cell wall. There are three cross-linked layers. The inner layer is a chitin layer, composed mostly of glucans; the outer layer is mostly mannoproteins; and the intermediate layer is a mixture of the two (Smart, 2000).

When a yeast cell clones itself and makes a new daughter cell, it creates a permanent scar in the cell wall, called a bud scar. A bud scar is composed

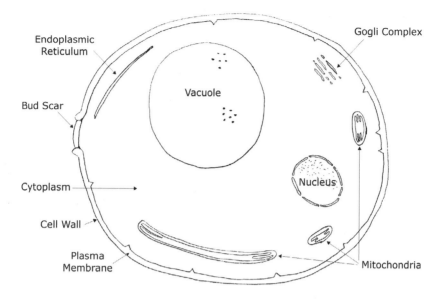

Figure 2.1: Simplified diagram of yeast cell structure.

mostly of chitin, the same material found in the exoskeletons of insects (Boulton and Quain, 2001). Bud scars are sometimes visible under light microscopy. During a single fermentation cycle, brewer's yeast usually bud only a few times, but in a laboratory setting, they can bud up to fifty. Generally, the average ale yeast cell will not bud more than thirty times over its lifetime (in multiple fermentation cycles), and lager yeast will bud only twenty times before they are unable to bud further.

Plasma Membrane. The plasma membrane, or cell membrane, is a lipid bilayer between the cell wall and the inside of the cell. This semi-permeable membrane determines what gets in and out of the cell, also providing additional environmental protection. Lipids, sterols, and proteins make up this membrane and give it fluidity, flexibility, and the ability to bud to form a new daughter cell.

Yeast require molecular oxygen to put double bonds in fatty acids and to control the level of fatty acid saturation. The saturation level determines the ease and extent of hydrogen bonding that can occur between fatty acids and determines their melting point. In lipids, the level of saturation controls the extent to which hydrogen bonding can occur between the hydrophobic tails of lipids.

Membrane fluidity is necessary for proper membrane function. Lipid bilayers are by their nature fluid, and that fluidity is determined by the extent to which the lipids bind one another. By controlling the level of saturation in their lipid membranes, yeast are able to maintain proper membrane fluidity at different temperatures, such as the brewer's desired fermentation temperature. Without proper aeration yeast are unable to control membrane fluidity through to the end of fermentation, leading to stuck fermentations and off-flavors.

Cytoplasm. A lot happens in the cytoplasm, which is everything inside the plasma membrane except the nucleus. The intracellular fluid, known as the cytosol, is a complex mixture of substances dissolved in water. Most importantly, the cytosol contains the enzymes involved in anaerobic fermentation. These enzymes enable the cell to convert glucose into energy as soon as it enters the cell. Specialized organelles, such as vacuoles, contain proteases. Proteases are enzymes that break down long proteins into short fragments and in some cases break off necessary amino acids. Yeast also store glycogen, an energy storage carbohydrate, in the cytoplasm. With the aid of a light microscope and iodine staining, a brewer can see the stored glycogen (Quain and Tubb, 1983).

Mitochondria. Aerobic respiration takes place in the mitochondrion. Mitochondria have a double membrane, which is where the conversion of pyruvate (a metabolic compound) to carbon dioxide and water (aerobic respiration) occurs. Even in brewer's yeast, where little to no aerobic

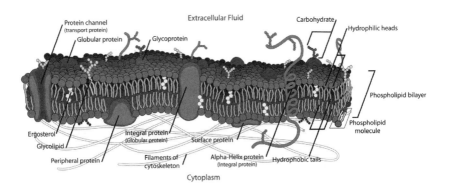

Figure 2.2: Detail of yeast cell plasma membrane.
Illustration courtesy of Mariana Ruiz.

respiration occurs during fermentation, mitochondria are still present and important to the health of the cell. Mitochondria contain a small amount of DNA with codes for a few mitochondria proteins. The cell makes some sterols here, and this is where the formation and utilization of acetyl-CoA, which is an intermediate compound for many metabolic pathways, occurs. Petite mutants, cells with impaired mitochondria, often create off-flavors such as phenol and diacetyl (see pp. 229).

Vacuole. The vacuole is a membrane-bound structure that stores nutrients. This is also where the cell breaks down proteins. Brewer's yeast has large vacuoles, large enough for us to see them by light microscopy. However, abnormally large vacuoles are a sign of stress.

Nucleus. The nucleus stores the cell DNA. A lipid membrane, similar to the plasma membrane, envelops the cell nucleus. Eukaryotic cells, such as yeast and human cells, use this organelle as the "nerve center." The DNA in the nucleus stores information for the cell. The cell uses mRNA to transfer the information out into the cytoplasm to use in protein synthesis.

Endoplasmic Reticulum. The endoplasmic reticulum is a network of membranes, and is usually where the cell manufactures proteins, lipids, and carbohydrates. There is very little endoplasmic reticulum in brewer's yeast.

Metabolism

Individual yeast cells do not grow significantly larger during their life-time. However, they do get a little larger as they age. Generally, when we talk about yeast growth, we are referring to the process of making new yeast cells. When we say the yeast is growing, we mean the yeast population is increasing in number. Yeast can derive the energy and nutrients for growth through several different pathways, though some are easier and more beneficial to the yeast than others.

Upon inoculation into wort, the cells first utilize their glycogen reserves and any available oxygen to revitalize their cell membranes for optimal permeability and transfer of nutrients and sugars. The cells rapidly absorb oxygen and then begin to pick up sugar and nutrients from the wort. Some of these compounds easily diffuse across the cell membrane and some require yeast transport mechanisms. Because yeast utilize some sugars more easily than others, they take up sugar in a specific order,

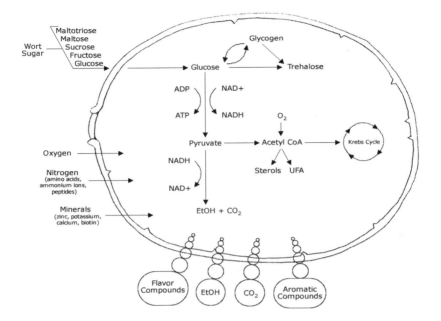

Figure 2.3: Sugar, oxygen, nitrogen, minerals enter the cell. Ethanol, carbon dioxide, and flavor/aroma compounds leak out.

with simpler sugars first: glucose, fructose, sucrose, maltose, and then maltotriose. Most of the sugar in a typical all-malt wort is maltose, with lesser amounts of glucose and maltotriose. Yeast take glucose into the cell through facilitated diffusion, without expending any metabolic energy. It is so easy for yeast to utilize glucose that the presence of glucose actually suppresses the yeast's ability to utilize maltose and maltotriose. All brewer's yeast can utilize maltose, but not all of them can utilize maltotriose to the same extent. The ability to utilize different sugars, the relative proportions of sugars in the wort, and the nutrients present in the wort determine much of the yeast's metabolism. The yeast's metabolism in turn determines the rate of fermentation and the degree of attenuation.

The uptake of oxygen happens rapidly, with the yeast usually depleting wort oxygen levels within 30 minutes of inoculation. In nature, yeast sitting on top of a pile of rotting fruit have lots of oxygen they can use to consume sugar. This is aerobic growth, which is the most effective way for an organism to get the greatest amount of energy out of a sugar molecule. However, there are times and environments where oxygen is limited. Consuming sugar in an oxygen-free environment leads to anaerobic growth. Louis Pasteur coined the term "anaerobic fermentation" in the 1860s, to describe the ability of yeast to grow when oxygen deprived.

Alcohol

One of the most important things yeast do for fermented beverages is produce alcohol. Whether the industry likes to admit it or not, without alcohol, and its effect on humans, beer and wine would be mere regional cultural beverages, like the soft drink malta. Worldwide, people consume alcoholic beverages in large quantities because they contain alcohol. The overall equation that describes yeast's conversion of sugar to ethanol is:

$$\text{Glucose} + 2 \text{ ADP} + 2 \text{ phosphate} \rightarrow 2 \text{ ethanol} + 2 \text{ CO}_2 + 2 \text{ ATP}$$

There are many individual steps in this equation, but we can split the equation into two main parts: glucose to pyruvate, then pyruvate to ethanol. The first part is the breakdown of one glucose molecule into two pyruvate molecules in this reaction:

$$\text{Glucose} + 2 \text{ ADP} + 2 \text{ NAD+} + 2 \text{ P}_i \rightarrow 2 \text{ Pyruvate} + 2 \text{ ATP}$$
$$+ 2 \text{ NADH} + 2 \text{ H+}$$

This occurs inside the cell, in the intracellular fluid called the cytosol. Enzymes in the cytosol catalyze this reaction and the other metabolic reactions that follow. Not all pyruvate ends up as ethanol. It has two possible paths: enter a mitochondrion and get broken down to CO_2 and water (aerobic respiration), or stay in the cytosol, where the cell converts it to acetaldehyde and then ethanol.

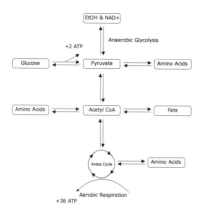

Figure 2.4: Pathways from glucose.

Which path would you prefer, water or ethanol? Well, yeast would rather not make ethanol and they only produce it under special conditions, such as high sugar levels or very low oxygen levels. Yeast get more energy from converting pyruvate into water and CO_2 in the presence of oxygen. To make yeast produce ethanol we need anaerobic fermentation.

The main reason yeast cells prefer aerobic respiration is that it enables them to get the maximum energy out of a molecule of glucose. During anaerobic fermentation, when they produce ethanol, yeast only get 8 percent as much energy from each molecule of glucose. It is easy to see why a yeast culture is able to bud more daughter cells with oxygen available. So why do yeast produce ethanol at all, if it is so inefficient? Because being able to produce ethanol gives them a way to survive in one more environment: an anaerobic environment.

Yeast rely on the co-enzyme nicotinamide adenine dinucleotide (NAD+ and NADH) for reduction-oxidation reactions (where nicotinamide adenine dinucleotide either accepts or donates electrons) and as an enzyme substrate. Yeast use NAD+ in the initial breakdown of glucose. If there is oxygen, the pyruvate from this step goes to the mitochondria, where it enters the Krebs cycle. The Krebs cycle produces an energy-rich compound called adenosine triphosphate (ATP). ATP is important to the cell, because it provides the cell with energy for protein synthesis and DNA replication, which is critical for population growth. If the cell is without oxygen, the pyruvate from that step does not go through the Krebs cycle. This leads to a buildup of pyruvate, no energy (in the form of ATP), and no more NAD+. Actually, many steps make up this sequence, but the bottom line is that without NAD+ you cannot get to the creation of pyruvate and ATP. The yeast need to "get NAD+ back" when there is no oxygen, and they do it the following way.

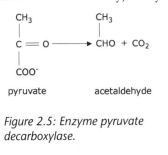

Figure 2.5: Enzyme pyruvate decarboxylase.

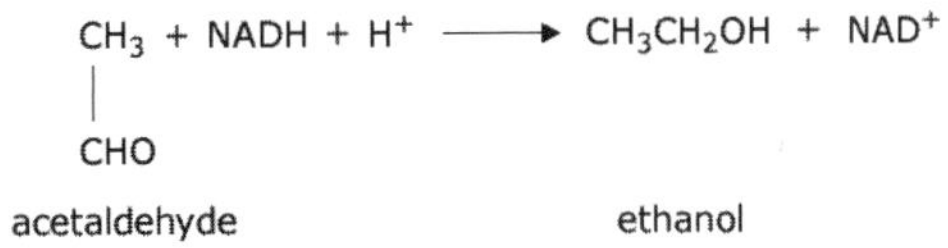

Figure 2.6: Enzyme alcohol dehydrogenase.

A two-step reaction of pyruvate to ethanol generates the required NAD+.

While the yeast are not exactly happy about producing ethanol, at least they can

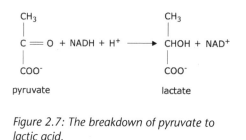

$$CH_3 \qquad\qquad\qquad CH_3$$
$$|\qquad\qquad\qquad\qquad |$$
$$C = O + NADH + H^+ \longrightarrow CHOH + NAD^+$$
$$|\qquad\qquad\qquad\qquad |$$
$$COO^- \qquad\qquad\qquad COO^-$$
pyruvate   lactate

Figure 2.7: The breakdown of pyruvate to lactic acid.

limp along. As the yeast make ethanol, it diffuses outside the cell. This is possibly a defense mechanism, since ethanol is toxic to many other organisms. In fact, as the alcohol level increases it becomes toxic to the yeast themselves. The better the health of the yeast, the better they are able to tolerate the alcohol and finish fermentation.

This change in the glucose conversion pathway under oxygen-limiting conditions is very similar to what happens to human cells when they lack oxygen. During heavy exercise, oxygen is limiting to muscle cell activity. Our muscle cells need energy to stay alive, and they need to regenerate NAD+, so in oxygen-poor conditions they break down pyruvate to lactic acid in one step.

Catalyzed by the enzyme lactic dehydrogenase, the cells are able to generate the NAD+ they need. The only reason our muscles do not make ethanol instead is that human cells lack the enzyme pyruvate decarboxylase.

There is another way yeast will ferment anaerobically and still produce ethanol: the Crabtree effect. This is very important to brewing. If there is a high-enough glucose concentration, even in the presence of oxygen, yeast produce ethanol (anaerobic fermentation). Brewer's wort always contains more than the 0.4 percent glucose required for the Crabtree effect, so fermentation always results in alcohol, even with oxygen present. The fact is that the concentration of glycolytic enzymes is so high that during wort fermentation yeast produce ATP faster by glycolysis alone than they do by oxidative phosphorylation. The problem with oxygen exposure during fermentation is not the loss of ethanol, but rather the activation of metabolic pathways that produce off-flavors. For example, beer fermentations exposed to oxygen have higher concentrations of acetaldehyde, due to oxidation of ethanol into acetaldehyde.

Flocculation

Flocculation is the almost magical ability of yeast to clump together. It is an important and desirable characteristic unique to brewer's yeast, as it helps them to rise to the top or sink to the bottom of the fermentor. Near the end of fermentation, single cells aggregate into clumps of thousands of cells. Different strains have different flocculation characteristics. Some strains flocculate earlier and tend not to attenuate as much, while others do not flocculate as readily and tend to attenuate more. Flocculating too early tends to result in a beer that is underattenuated and sweet. However, when yeast fail to flocculate entirely, it results in a beer that is cloudy with a yeasty taste.

Most wild yeast strains do not flocculate well and remain in suspension for extended periods. In nature, most yeast cells do not want to drop out of suspension, because in suspension they have nutrients and sugar available to them. All yeast will eventually drop out of a liquid with the help of gravity, but this can take months, and most brewers do not have that kind of time. In fact, it was selective pressure by brewers over many centuries that improved flocculation in brewer's yeast. By harvesting yeast from either the bottom or top of the fermentor for repitching, brewers left behind the yeast cells that did not flocculate well. The yeast left behind in the beer did not get the chance to replicate in the next batch, removing them from the population. The flocculent yeast strains we use today are descendents of that process of selective pressure.

Scientists have studied the biochemistry of flocculation for many years, and even today, the exact mechanism is still debated. Cell wall composition is a key factor in the ability of adjacent cells to stick to each other. Yeast have a thick cell wall made up of protein and polysaccharides with a net negative surface charge due to phosphates in the cell wall. The extent of the negative charge depends on the yeast strain, phase of growth, oxygen availability, starvation, generation number, dehydration, and cell age (Smart, 2000). Yeast cells are also hydrophobic due to exposure of hydrophobic peptides (Hazen and Hazen, 1993). The degree of hydrophobicity is dependent on yeast strain, phase of growth, ability to form chains, starvation, generation number, flocculation onset, and fibril formation (Smart, 2000). Yeast cell walls also have mannoproteins, proteins with large numbers of mannose groups attached, to help regulate cell shape, porosity, and cell-cell interactions, including those involved in flocculation.

The primary determinant of flocculation is the yeast strain itself. Each yeast strain has its own unique DNA sequence, which determines the exact set of proteins displayed on the cell surface. These minute differences in cell wall composition play a key role in flocculation behavior and determine the degree of flocculation for a strain. Factors that influence the degree of flocculation include the original gravity of the wort, temperature of fermentation, pitching rate, and initial oxygen content. Keep in mind anything that affects the health and growth rate of the yeast affects flocculation.

Flocculation Degree	Notes
High	Start to flocculate by day 3-5 Sometimes need to rouse the yeast Higher levels of diacetyl and lower attenuation Good for malty ales
Medium	Start to flocculate by day 6-15 Ideal for ales Clean, balanced flavor production Also called "powdery"
Low	Fail to begin to flocculate by day 15 Most wild yeast are low flocculators Good for *hefeweizen*, Belgians Makes filtering difficult

Figure 2.8: Differences in flocculation classification.

Brewers classify yeast as high, medium, or low flocculators (Figure 2.8). Ale strains span each category, while lager strains are predominantly medium flocculators. For example, those strains marketed as English/London ale strains are often high flocculators. Centuries of top cropping in Britain have selected for highly flocculent yeast. Interestingly, even though centuries of top cropping has made those strains so flocculent, in recent times brewers have put selective pressure on them to make them better bottom croppers. Today they are just as flocculent, but often they are also excellent bottom croppers.

Those yeasts marketed as California/American ale strains are most often medium flocculators, and *hefeweizen* strains are good examples of low flocculators. While high flocculation quickly results in clear beer, filtering can clarify a beer even more quickly, so a brewer willing to filter can use a strain with almost any level of flocculation.

A high flocculator begins to clump in three to five days. When it drops to the bottom of the fermentor, it forms a solid, compact yeast cake. In fact, some strains are so flocculent that they can form tight plugs that block openings and clog valves. Homebrewers working with small fermentors sometimes swirl the yeast cake to maintain fermentation activity, but even so, the yeast cake only breaks down into large chunks. Producing a fully attenuated beer with high flocculators can require special attention, such as rousing the yeast back into the beer. Even with such measures, highly flocculent strains usually result in lower attenuation and increased levels of diacetyl and esters.

Medium flocculators tend to produce "cleaner" beers with lower levels of diacetyl and esters. Because the cells stay in suspension longer, they attenuate the beer more and reduce diacetyl and other fermentation compounds to a greater degree. In a commercial brewery, they are slightly more difficult to work with than high flocculators, because they often require filtering for a quick turnaround. Of course, most homebrewers do not filter, and with enough time medium flocculators will settle out on their own; they just take longer than highly flocculent yeast. Medium flocculators, and their tendency toward clean fermentation characteristics, make them well suited to highly hopped beers like many American-style ales. Their clean flavors allow the hop aroma and flavor to come through.

Brewers rarely use low flocculators, because they do not settle out, creating haze and filtering problems. However, some beer styles should have yeast in suspension. For example, the German *hefeweizen* and Belgian *witbier* styles both require low flocculating yeast strains to create the desired cloudy appearance. Some breweries will filter their *hefeweizen* and then add back lager yeast at packaging time. Because lager strains are less flocculent and tend to stay in suspension longer, they are better able to clean up a beer during an extended fermentation and lagering process. There are some very dusty lager strains, which work well for providing that cloudy yeast appearance.

One important factor in flocculation is calcium. The yeast require certain minimal levels of calcium present for flocculation to occur. Wort usually has enough calcium, and the brewer does not need to add more. If you are working with very soft water, keep in mind the calcium requirement. In most cases, 50 ppm of calcium is enough to meet the yeast's needs.

Enzymes

Yeast is not the only beer ingredient that brewers fail to appreciate fully—enzymes are a close second. Consider this: without enzymes, there would be no beer. There are enzymes involved in all phases of the brewing process: malting, mashing, and fermentation. At its core, brewing is an enzymatic process. The more a brewer knows about enzymes, the more he can troubleshoot problems.

Enzymes are a special class of proteins that speed up chemical reactions. They are essential to life and are present in all living things. An enzyme is a protein created by living organisms (or synthetically) that acts as a catalyst in chemical reactions, initiating or speeding up the rate at which a reaction proceeds without altering itself in the process.

In the middle of the nineteenth century, chemists studying the process of fermentation proved the existence of enzymes. In 1897 Eduard Buchner was the first to prepare a cell extract that still exhibited catalytic activity. He showed that the filtered, cell-free liquor from crushed yeast cells could convert sugar to carbon dioxide. Buchner earned the 1907 Nobel Prize in Chemistry for his work. Enzymes were for many years called "ferments," a term derived from the Latin word for yeast. In 1878 researchers introduced the name "enzyme," from the Greek words meaning "in yeast."

Louis Pasteur made the most famous discoveries related to brewing. While not credited with discovering the role of enzymes, he proved that yeast were responsible for the conversion of wort sugar to alcohol. Chemists at the time adamantly stated that the living organism yeast had no role in sugar transformation. They insisted that the process was strictly chemical, not biological. They assumed it was something in the wort, such as oxygen, that catalyzed the transformation. The chemists were partially correct, as yeast contain enzymes for fermentation, which act as the catalyst for many parts of the conversion of sugar to alcohol. From a fermentation standpoint, yeast cells are just bags of enzymes.

Enzymes are proteins, and proteins are made of amino acids, one of the main biological components in living systems. Hundreds of amino acids make up a single protein molecule. Proteins are about ten times the size of sugar molecules, and about 1,000 times smaller than yeast cells. Not all enzymes are the same size; they can vary from about fifty amino acids to 500,000 and are often larger than the substrates they act upon. The part of the enzyme that is most important is the active site within the enzyme. The active site is a region of the enzyme with amino acids in the correct orientation to facilitate a given chemical reaction on a substrate—very similar to a key and lock. Each enzyme can catalyze one unique chemical reaction, but they can catalyze the reaction in both directions. The direction depends on the conditions and the available substrate. Let us look at the enzyme alcohol dehydrogenase and the reaction of acetaldehyde to ethanol.

acetaldehyde + NADH → ethanol + NAD+

We usually think of the reaction of acetaldehyde to ethanol, but the same enzyme catalyses the reverse reaction. As an example of the reverse reaction, humans have alcohol dehydrogenase, which our bodies use to break down ethanol into acetaldehyde.

Without the enzyme alcohol dehydrogenase, the above reaction would still theoretically take place, but it would take days instead of picoseconds. Life is so dependent on enzymes (each human cell has more than 3,000 of them) that before the 1950s, chemists were convinced enzymes contained the genetic code and DNA was just a structural component.

Brewing yeast do not possess all of the enzymes needed to make beer from barley. For example, yeast cells do not produce amylase enzymes, which convert starch to sugar. This is why a brewer must first utilize the barley enzymes in the mash, in order to convert the starch to sugar.

How Do Enzymes Work?

To catalyze a particular reaction, an enzyme binds to a substrate. These bonds are tight, but the completion of the reaction changes the substrate and changes the nature of the bond, releasing the enzyme to be attracted to a new substrate. An analysis of the mechanisms and kinetics of enzyme action is beyond the scope of this book, but a simple formula is:

enzyme + substrate → enzyme-substrate complex → enzyme + product

Enzyme activity (measured by product formation) depends on several factors: pH, temperature, ionic strength of the solution, and substrate concentration. Brewers can control most of these factors, so it is important to understand what the enzymes need, and thereby control the activity and products. Controlling temperature is perhaps the most important factor. Enzymes are made of amino acids, and each enzyme folds a specific way to make the active site available. If the enzyme denatures, it loses its activity and does not recover. Heat is the main cause of enzyme unfolding. Boiling will denature most enzymes, but even slight temperature increases will denature many. For example, mash temperatures near the maximum for amylase enzymes will denature many proteases.

pH is also very important because it affects the binding of the enzyme to its substrate. Binding involves the interaction of individual amino acids, and that interaction is usually dependent on the electrostatic charge on those amino acids. Without the correct charge, binding does not take place. The charge varies with pH, depending on the amino acid, and each enzyme has its own optimal pH. Just like temperature, a pH that is too low or too high can permanently denature (deactivate) the enzyme. When adding enzymes, you should note the temperature and pH activity profiles the manufacturer recommends.

Enzymes in Malting

Most brewers are familiar with the conversion of starch to sugar via enzymatic reactions during the mashing process, but enzymes also play a big role during the malting process. Starch breakdown during malting is critical to producing high-quality malt. The barley embryo (grain) needs sugar to grow. Enzymes in the growing embryo break down starch and proteins into smaller, soluble fractions in preparation for the embryo to grow. Three types of enzymes are responsible for this action:

cytase group	degrade the cell wall of the endosperm
amylases	degrade starch to sugar
proteolytic enzymes	degrade large proteins into smaller proteins

The cytase group and proteases break down cell wall structures to make starch available. The proteases (enzymes that degrade proteins) then degrade the matrix proteins. Next, protease action creates free amino acids groups, which the growing embryo uses to manufacture proteins.

The continuation of the malting process activates α-amylase and β-amylase. These enzymes break down starches into sugars; α-amylase is an endoenzyme and β-amylase is an exoenzyme. Endoenzymes remove pieces from the interior of a large molecule, and exoenzymes remove pieces from the end of large molecules. The amylase enzymes convert starch to sugar, which the embryo would use for growth. However, in the case of base malts or "brewer's" malts the maltster stops the process by drying the malt to a point where activity stops. If the maltster allowed enzyme activity to continue, the remaining starch would convert to sugar. This is part of the process of making crystal malts, but if the maltster made all malts that way, we would no longer conduct the mash. The maltster would have already determined the sugar fermentability for us, and we would only steep these grains to extract the sugars.

Enzymes in Mashing

It is not just α-amylase and β-amylase that can affect fermentation; the brewer's mash includes several other types of active enzymes, including beta-glucanases, proteases, and esterases. For example, performing a ferulic acid rest around 110° F (43° C) can increase the level of ferulic acid in the wort, which some yeast strains can convert to 4-vinyl guaiacol, a characteristic flavor and aroma component of German *weizen.*

Protein rests can have an impact on fermentation, too, because they can increase the amino acid levels in the wort. This is not necessary when using well-modified malt, but undermodified or six-row malts may require a protein rest.

The one thing that most brewers understand is that controlling the mash temperature to effect the enzyme activity affects the balance of simpler sugars versus more complex sugars. Wort with a higher percentage of complex sugars (dextrins) is less fermentable. While some strains may have more success with maltotriose, the effect is relative. As a general rule, the higher the mash temperature, the less fermentable the wort.

When a brewer boils wort, the heat denatures most enzymes present, and many precipitate out of solution as part of both the hot and cold break.

Enzymes in Fermentation

Now the money part begins. There would not be a large market for beer if yeast did not create alcohol during fermentation. The conversion of sugar to alcohol can be simply stated as:

$$C_6H_{12}O_6 \rightarrow 2\ CH_3CH_2OH + 2\ CO_2$$

glucose → ethanol + carbon dioxide

However, the conversion of sugar to alcohol is not as simple as the formula might depict. In fact, it happens in many more steps, and requires many enzymes, with different enzymes catalyzing each step. Yeast use the energy created from the oxidation of sugar to ethanol to strengthen themselves and to reproduce. As far as yeast cells are concerned, the alcohol they produce is a by-product. Each chemical reaction also has the potential of producing by-products. Each step can lead to the production of those flavor and aroma compounds you desire, or those you do not.

Even though brewers rarely add enzymes to fermentation, there are some cases where they can be beneficial. Even though it is very rare, a stuck fermentation can be due to inefficient starch conversion or too many long-chain, unfermentable sugars. In such a case, the brewer could add α-amylase directly to the fermentor to catalyze further breakdown of the sugars, which may result in increased attenuation. Of course, there are drawbacks to this method. The manufacturers propagate these enzyme preparations from a microbial source, so they may contain a small quantity of bacteria. Adding these enzymes to the beer, without the benefit of the boil, has the potential to spoil the beer. From a food and safety perspective, the quantities of bacteria are small and harmless, but from a brewer's perspective, it is unacceptable. The allowable levels of bacteria in these enzyme products often range in the area of 1,000 to 5,000 colony forming units (CFU), and that is just not acceptable in beer (Briggs, et al., 1981; Mathewson, 1998; Walker, 1998).

Esters, Alcohols, and More

Brewer's yeast can produce five hundred different flavor and aroma compounds (Mussche and Mussche, 2008). After pitching, yeast undergo a lag phase, which is then followed by a very rapid exponential growth phase. During both the lag and exponential phase, yeast build amino acids, proteins, and other cell components. Most of these components do not affect the flavor of the beer, but the pathways involved in their production also create many other compounds that do leak out of the cell and impact beer flavor. The compounds with the largest flavor impact are esters, fusel alcohols, sulfur-containing compounds, and carbonyl compounds like aldehydes and ketones (including diacetyl). Although many of these compounds play a role in the characteristic flavor and aroma of beer, it is a beer flaw when some of these compounds reach higher, easily detectable levels.

Esters

Esters play a big role in the character of beer, especially in ales. An ester is a volatile compound formed from an organic acid and an alcohol, and it is esters that provide the fruity aromas and flavors that you find in beer. Even the "cleanest-tasting" beers contain esters, with some beers having as many as fifty (Meilgaard, 1975). Without esters, a beer would seem quite bland. We can measure esters by gas chromatography, and ester profiles are a good way to differentiate beers. Ester production varies by yeast strain and fermentation conditions. Examples of common esters are ethyl acetate (solvent), ethyl caproate (apple), and isoamyl acetate (banana).

The process of combining an acid and an alcohol to form an ester takes some time, since the yeast need to create the alcohols first. Esters have more of a flavor impact than acids and alcohol independently (Bamforth, Beer flavours: esters, 2001). The alcohol acetyltransferase enzymes AATase I and II catalyze ester formation. These enzymes combine an alcohol with an activated acid. In beer, the most abundant activated acid is acetyl-CoA. Pre-fermentation, when the brewer adds oxygen, the yeast produce sterols in preparation for budding new cells. This sterol production takes away acetyl-CoA from ester production, which results in lower ester levels in the beer (Bamforth, Beer flavours: esters). This is one explanation of the oxygen effect, where higher aeration levels result in lower ester levels. Another explanation might be that oxygen directly represses the expression of the AATase encoding genes (Fugii, 1997). Many other factors affect ester production, but factors that increase yeast growth and take away acetyl-CoA will often minimize ester synthesis. Three main factors control ester production: the concentration of acetyl-CoA, the concentration of fusel alcohol, and the total activity of certain enzymes.

Fusel Alcohols

We can use gas chromatography to measure fusel alcohols at the same time we measure esters. Beer can contain any combination of approximately forty fusel alcohols (Meilgaard, 1975). Fusel alcohols such as n-propanol, isoamyl alcohol, and isobutanol taste similar to ethanol, although they can add warming, hot, or solvent flavors to beer depending on type and concentration. There are no beer styles where hot and solventy are desired traits. However, many good-tasting beers do contain fusel alcohols in quantities at or a little above their flavor thresholds, so they are important yeast-derived flavor components of beer. Of the fusel alcohols, beer contains primarily amyl alcohols, such as isoamyl alcohol. In wine, isoamyl alcohol can account for more than 50 percent of all fusel alcohols (Zoecklein, et al., 1999). People generally attribute headaches to the fusel alcohols in alcoholic beverages. High levels of hot fusel alcohols in an average-strength beer are a true flaw. Even in bigger beers, they should be, at most, a background note. There is no excuse for brewing beer that tastes like paint thinner.

During the lag phase of fermentation, yeast begin to form fusel alcohols either from pyruvate and acetyl-CoA during amino acid synthesis or from uptake of amino acids (nitrogen). The formation of fusel alcohols involves the reoxidation of NADH to NAD+ in the final step, and some scientists believe that yeast produce fusel alcohols to make NAD+ available again for glycolysis (Kruger, 1998).

Yeast strains vary in fusel alcohol production, with ale strains generally producing higher fusel alcohol concentrations than lager strains. Researchers often attribute this to the higher fermentation temperature of ales. It is true that fusel alcohol concentrations increase with fermentation temperature; however, other fermentation conditions have an effect on fusel alcohol production as well. For example, wort with either too little or too much nitrogen can also result in the production of higher alcohols. In general, fermentation conditions that promote cell growth, such as temperature, aeration, and nitrogen, result in higher levels of fusel alcohols. When there is more fusel alcohol substrate, there is a greater opportunity for ester formation with any acetyl-CoA present. Brewing a lower-ester beer is a balancing act of controlling the factors that help prevent ester formation but also increase fusel alcohol production.

Diacetyl

Even though many classic beer styles allow for low levels of diacetyl, and some consumers find it pleasant, many brewers consider diacetyl a flaw in any quantity. Diacetyl, even at low levels, can contribute slickness or slipperiness to a beer's mouthfeel. In higher quantities, diacetyl gives beer a buttery or butterscotchlike aroma and flavor. Diacetyl is a small organic compound that belongs to the ketone chemical group. Another ketone commonly found in beer is 2,3-pentanedione. It is so similar to diacetyl that when a lab measures a beer's diacetyl level it reports a vicinal diketone level (VDK) instead, which includes both diacetyl and 2,3-pentanedione. The flavor threshold of diacetyl is 0.1 ppm in "light" beer. Homebrewed and craft-brewed beer can often have levels from 0.5 to greater than 1.0 ppm.

One reason many brewers do not like the presence of diacetyl in their beer is because it is an indicator of a possible fermentation or contamination problem. However, there are exceptions where diacetyl is an intended characteristic of the beer. This is most likely because of the yeast strain and the fermentation profile the brewery practices. Some yeast strains, particularly highly flocculent English ale strains, are heavy diacetyl producers. Crashing the fermentation temperature early, which keeps the yeast from reducing diacetyl, is another way beer ends up with a detectable level of diacetyl. Just remember, the longer the yeast stay in suspension, the more time they have to reduce many intermediary fermentation compounds. Fortunately, yeast will reabsorb diacetyl and reduce it to acetoin in order to regenerate NAD.

The pathway for diacetyl in beer is relatively simple. Valine is one of the amino acids yeast produce during the lag and exponential phase. An intermediate compound in valine production is acetolactate. Not all of the acetolactate yeast produce becomes valine, as some leaks out of the cell and into the beer. The acetolactate that leaks from the cell into the beer chemically oxidizes into diacetyl. While this is true for all yeast strains, different strains will produce different levels of diacetyl under the same conditions.

Organic Acids

During fermentation, yeast also produce varying levels of organic acids such as acetic, lactic, butyric, and caproic. In most fermentations, the concentrations produced are below the flavor threshold, which is usually a good thing. These acids have flavors and aromas of vinegar, vomit, and barnyard animals. However, these acids are necessary, as they play a key role in ester formation.

Sulfur Compounds

Who farted? Many first-time lager brewers may ask that question. Lager brewing produces more sulfur compounds than ale brewing. The lower temperature of lager brewing is a key factor in higher sulfur levels (Bamforth, Beer flavour: sulphur substances, 2001). Yeast produce sulfur compounds in large quantities during fermentation, but these compounds generally are volatile enough that strong fermentation activity drives them from solution along with the CO_2, greatly reducing sulfur levels by the time you (or a customer) drink the beer. The lower temperatures of lager fermentation generally result in a less vigorous fermentation (less physical movement of the wort) and less evolution of gases due to higher gas solubility at those temperatures. Therefore, lager beers tend to retain detectable amounts of sulfur aroma and flavor, while it is unusual to find sulfur in most ales.

The sulfur compounds typically found in beer are dimethyl sulfide (DMS), sulfur dioxide, hydrogen sulfide, and mercaptans. Some of these sulfur compounds come from malt, while others come from yeast or a combination of both. For example, dimethyl sulphoxide (DMSO) is present in wort at varying levels, depending on the source malt. The level of this oxidized DMS compound is not affected by the boil like DMS and its precursor S-methylmethionine (SMM). Unfortunately, yeast has the ability to reduce DMSO back to DMS during fermentation, increasing the level of those canned corn and cooked cabbage types of aromas and flavors in the beer.

Yeast produce sulfur dioxide, which not only flavors the beer but gives it antioxidant properties. People often describe the aroma of sulfur dioxide as similar to a burnt match. Sulfur dioxide easily reduces to another sulfur compound, hydrogen sulfide, which is the compound with a rotten egg smell. Fortunately, the CO_2 released from fermentation carries most of the hydrogen sulfide out of the beer. The key to reducing these sulfur compounds in beer is to have an active, healthy fermentation.

Phenolic Compounds

Phenolic compounds, which are hydroxylated aromatic carbon rings, can come from ingredients and from fermentation. Phenol-based antiseptics contain them, which is why people often describe phenolic compounds as medicinal tasting. Phenolic compounds are also described as plastic, Band-Aid, smoky, and spicy. Phenolic compounds are less volatile than fusel alcohols, which means they stay in the beer throughout aging. Once phenolic compounds are present at a detectable level, you will probably always taste them.

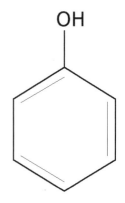

In most beer styles, phenolic flavors are a flaw, although there are some obvious exceptions. Bavarian *hefeweizen* must have clove, *rauchbier* must have smoke, and some Belgian beers have other phenolic characters, but when phenols turn up unintentionally, it can be a disaster.

Figure 2.9: Phenol, a hydroxylated aromatic ring.

The major phenolic compound most yeast produce is 4-vinyl guaiacol (4 VG). Malt and hops supply ferulic acid, and yeast produce 4 VG from the decarboxylation of the ferulic acid by the enzyme ferulic acid decarboxylase. (Decarboxylation is the chemical reduction of a compound by the evolution of CO_2.) Those yeast that produce phenols have an intact phenolic off-flavor (POF) gene, which is required for coding ferulic acid decarboxylase.

Most brewer's yeast strains have a natural mutation in the POF gene preventing them from producing 4 VG. In fact, the unintentional production of a phenolic character is a good indication that wild yeast has con-

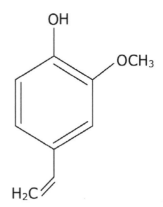

Figure 2.10: 4-vinyl guaiacol.

taminated the beer. In rare circumstances, it is possible for a mutation in brewer's yeast to cause the yeast to produce a phenolic character again.

You might ask, what about the yeast strains for making Bavarian-style *hefeweizen*? These are good examples of once wild yeast strains that brewers purified and cultured over time, without selecting against phenolic compounds. The POF gene remains intact in these strains, and they produce the characteristic phenols for the style.

Brettanomyces is another genus of yeast that many brewers and winemakers consider a contaminant, while some see it as a unique genus capable of producing flavors and aromas not possible with the average brewer's yeast. *Brettanomyces* is naturally abundant in the environment, often found living on fruit skins. It does not mind fermentation conditions, and it is alcohol tolerant. It can produce flavors and aromas reminiscent of a barnyard, horse blanket, sweat, and a wide array of other flavor compounds, including 4 VG. Its presence in beer is easily detected and even desired in some beer styles such as Belgian *lambic,* Flanders red, and many newer craft beer creations.

Fermentation is not the only source of phenolic compounds. Sometimes a brewer adds them intentionally, by using smoked malts, for example. In wine, phenolic character comes from the yeast, but it can also come from oak contact and from the fruit used. Whiskey also gets phenols from ingredients, yeast, and barrel aging. Beer produced with certain fruits and wood aging can pick up phenolic compounds, as well.

3

How to Choose the Right Yeast

When faced with an opportunity to craft a new beer, many brewers stick with what they know. A yeast strain that they have used for countless batches is what they will use for this new creation as well. In many cases, using the house strain is their only option. That is understandable, but when a brewer has the option to choose any strain he or she wants, it is a shame to stick with just one. Often it is not that these brewers lack creativity or an interest in exploring new strains, but rather that they are unsure how to select the best candidates to produce the desired character.

Selection Criteria

When trying to select a new strain for fermentation, it pays to know your priorities. It is like building a house; you know you need fasteners, but the type of fastener depends on the type of house you are building. Townhouse, dollhouse, outhouse, they all have similar but different fastener requirements. What is it you are trying to build? It is important to start with a concept of the beer you are trying to craft. Is it dry and hoppy? Sweet and malty? Clean or estery? High in alcohol or low? Once you have a feel for what you are creating, then you can begin finding strains that might work. Certainly, it is possible and even likely that you will not find a single strain that meets all your requirements, but do not forget that it is also possible to use multiple strains in one beer. At a minimum, always consider the following criteria when selecting a new yeast strain:

- Attenuation
- Flavor profile
- Flocculation
- Reliability of supply
- Working temperature range

Interestingly, a brewer can affect most of these attributes to some extent by manipulating the recipe, the process, or the fermentation parameters, but there is a limit to how much you can affect each attribute. In most cases, manipulating one fermentation attribute causes a shift in another. For example, pushing the working temperature of a yeast strain higher to fit the needs of your brewhouse will most likely produce more flavor compounds than you intended. Fermenting at a cooler temperature to minimize ester production can reduce the level of attenuation. All of the yeast attributes are interrelated, and you cannot manipulate one without affecting another.

How do you make a choice? How do you decide which yeast is best for your brown ale? You can review company literature, talk to other brewers, or search the web, but the best way is to do some experiments. Make enough of your brown ale wort to divide it into several different fermentors, and pitch a different strain into each fermentor. It is necessary to keep the same conditions, especially pitching rate and temperature, so you can compare the effect each strain has on the beer. Once you zero in on a strain, then you can repeat the experiment using that strain at different temperatures, oxygen levels, or pitching rates. If you practice yeast re-use, you might also want to repeat the experiment on a small scale five or more times to see how the character changes over generations.

Beer Styles and Yeast Selection

Some brewers might ask why there is a need to discuss beer style in a book on yeast. After all, isn't beer style determined by the grains and hops used? Yes and no. With wine, the main ingredient, grapes, often determines the style. The wine world uses the grape varietal, or sometimes the production region, to classify the wine.

For beer, we determined the style mostly by a combination of grains, hops, and yeast, but not necessarily where the ingredients were grown or the beer brewed. When brewing, you can use malt and hops from different regions interchangeably. Yes, citrusy American hops are a signature trait in some styles. Biscuity British pale ale malt and grainy continental Pilsener malt provide a key component of some other styles, but the main differentiators of beer styles are process, recipe, and yeast selection. In fact, yeast play such a big role in the character of a beer that in some cases the yeast strain is the key difference between two styles. Compare the grist of a typical California common and a Düsseldorf *altbier* recipe: even though they are very similar, the beers are significantly different because of the yeast selection.

The average beer consumer will often divide beer into ale and lager categories, but that is the broadest of divisions. Although ale and lager are technically valid style categorizations, there are yeast strains and beer styles that defy those boundaries. There are hybrid styles of beer that fall in between ale and lager. These are beers fermented with lager yeast at ale temperatures or ale yeasts fermented at colder than normal ale temperatures.

As of this publication, the Beer Judge Certification Program (BJCP) recognizes eighty distinct beer styles in twenty-three categories. The BJCP groups many of the styles by ale, lager, or hybrid and by geographic origin and strength. Because mass-market lager beers are so popular, you might think they count for a disproportionate number of styles, but they do not. Lagers compose less than one-quarter of the styles, which makes sense because lagers are relatively new to the brewing world. Many of these styles are the result of brewers tailoring their beer to local preferences. Unknowingly or not, those brewers were selecting for preferred characteristics by harvesting and reusing only the yeast that produced beer that they and their customers wanted. This selective pressure is what resulted in the beer styles and yeast strains we use today.

You will find that most yeast suppliers identify their yeast as ale or lager first, then further identify the strains by geographic location (country, region, city) or by style name. If you are purchasing yeast from one of these suppliers, it is easy to identify potential choices based on these broad categories and the yeast description. Want to brew a Belgian-style beer? Identify the strains with "Belgian" in the description, and make your selection from one of those. If you want to brew a German-style lager or

English-style ale, that is just as easy. Of course, this just gets you in the ballpark, and you will want to take into account all your selection criteria to determine exactly which strains best fit your needs.

Yeast Strains

The late George Fix devised a unique system for categorizing brewing yeast that you might find useful. Fix divided yeast strains into five categories in an attempt at organizing them in terms of flavor characteristics. He divided ale yeasts into Clean/Neutral, Maltier/Ester Producing, and Specialty. He divided lager yeasts into Dry/Crisp and Full/Malty (Fix and Fix, 1997). The interesting and very useful core of Fix's concept is that it does not focus on region and style for grouping, but rather on fermentation character. This makes it easier to think outside the box. Approaching yeast strains in this way frees the brewer to do something different, like using European ale yeast in an American pale ale instead of the same old American strains almost everyone else uses. Yeast strains do not know style boundaries, and the brewer who recognizes this has a much wider choice of strains to fuel his or her other creativity.

We like Fix's approach and we will group strains by character for our discussion:

Ale

- Clean
- Fruity
- Hybrid
- Phenolic
- Eccentric

Lager

- Dry
- Full

Ale Strain Overview

Ale yeast is *Saccharomyces cerevisiae*, a large group that includes bread yeast, distiller's yeast, and many laboratory yeast strains. Brewers distinguish brewing ale yeast by their behavior and flavor production. Ale yeast do what a brewer wants: they ferment quickly, consume the correct profile of sugars, tolerate moderate alcohol levels, and survive the anaerobic conditions of fermentation.

Ale strains are also known as top-fermenting yeast, as the foamy head that appears on many ale fermentations usually contains a lot of yeast. During fermentation, the hydrophobic surface of the ale yeast causes the yeast flocculants to adhere to carbon dioxide and rise to the surface of the beer (Boulton and Quain, 2001). This allows brewers to collect yeast from the top of the fermentor, known as "top cropping." The advantage of top cropping is that you get a great crop of yeast. This yeast is very healthy and has little trub mixed in with it. The disadvantage lies in exposing the beer and yeast to the environment and contamination. Although few commercial breweries outside the United Kingdom top crop today, the process is gaining a small but growing following among homebrewers, because under the right conditions, it can be a very successful and effective yeast management technique. See the "Yeast Collection" section (pp. 148-156) of this book for details on top cropping techniques.

There are many varieties of ale yeasts, everything from very clean "Chico-type" strains to phenolic Belgian strains. Ale yeasts include strains that hardly flocculate at all and strains that fall like a ton of bricks. Compare one ale strain against another and you will find that they can flocculate differently, attenuate differently, and produce different flavor profiles.

Even though ale strains are diverse, they have similarities. Most ale strains have an ideal fermentation temperature range that hovers around 68° F (20° C). Also, most ale yeast can tolerate warm conditions up to 95° F (35° C), but produce the best fermentation flavor around the mid- to upper 60s (18 to 21° C). When in doubt, use 68° F (20° C) as a starting point when working with an unfamiliar ale yeast strain. All ale yeasts produce a variety of compounds that we recognize as characteristic ale flavors and aromas. If a strain produces a small quantity of these compounds, brewers think of it as a "clean-fermenting" strain. When a strain produces more of these compounds (especially esters and fusel alcohols), brewers refer to it as a "fruity" or "estery" strain.

Clean Ale Strains

Clean-fermenting ale strains are very popular in the United States, because even at ale temperatures and fermentation times, they can produce almost lagerlike ales with very low fruitiness and fusel alcohols. These clean fermenters showcase a brewer's recipe formulation more than other strains. The brewer controls the bulk of the flavor and aroma characteristics by his choice of malt, hops, brewing temperatures, and fermentation temperatures. Clean strains usually ferment more slowly than fruitier strains and flocculate at a medium rate, remaining in suspension long enough to condition the beer properly. These yeasts can produce trace amounts of sulfur under stressful conditions, such as high pressure, nutrient deficiencies, large temperature swings, or a too-cold fermentation temperature. Examples of yeast strains in this category are California/American, Scottish, and European ale.

Fruity Ale Strains

Fruity ale strains are traditional in England, and they are increasing in popularity in the United States as consumer education improves. While some brewers consider fruity ale strains a little less versatile than clean ale strains, others would argue that fruity strains are capable of creating beers that are far more interesting. Ale strains that produce more fermentation character can add a lot of character to your beer. They are as big a factor in the beer's character as are the other ingredients. While they ferment at the same temperature as the clean ale strains, these yeast strains produce and leak more of the unique and interesting flavors and aromas from the yeast cell at the same temperature. Fruitier ale strains usually ferment and flocculate very quickly, allowing the brewer to produce finished beer in less time than when using a clean ale strain. These strains tend to form large clumps of yeast during flocculation, resulting in bright, clear beer in short order. A common drawback with such rapid fermentation and flocculation is that the yeast tends to leave more by-products, such as diacetyl, behind. These beers can have hints of honey, plum, citrus, and tartness, depending on the strain. Examples of this category are those identified as British, Irish, Australian, and some Belgian ale strains.

Hybrid Ale Strains

Biologically, there are no hybrid ale strains. Lager yeast strains appear to have evolved through the rare hybridization of S. *cerevisiae* and S. *bayanus* (Casey, 1990), but that is not what most brewers mean when they say "hybrid." They are referring to ale strains that brewers commonly ferment at temperatures cooler than the average ale fermentation; these yeast strains produce a clean, almost lagerlike beer. Traditionally, brewers would use these strains for styles such as *altbier* and *Kölsch*. Even when fermented at warmer temperatures, the fruitiness is restrained. In recent times these yeasts have found popularity outside those limited beer styles, with brewers using them in everything from American wheat beer to barley wine. These clean strains usually ferment more slowly than the fruitier strains, and flocculate at a medium rate, remaining in suspension long enough to attenuate and condition the beer. They also produce trace amounts of sulfur, but not as much as lager yeast strains.

Brewers often refer to California common yeast as a hybrid strain. It is a lager strain, and the results are similar to an estery lager. Using lager strains at ale temperatures is an area open for experimentation, but keep in mind the results can vary substantially from strain to strain.

Phenolic Ale Strains

Phenolic strains are traditional in Belgian-type ales and German *weizen* beers. Increased phenolic production is the characteristic that most brewers equate with Belgian yeast strains. A phenol is a hydroxylated aromatic ring, a compound with a six-membered carbon ring bonded directly to a hydroxyl group (-OH). These are the same class of compounds used in some antiseptics, and some consumers describe their flavor and aroma as medicinal.

In many of these phenolic strains, attenuation tends to be high and flocculation tends to be low. Yet there are plenty of exceptions. For example, in the past some Belgian farmhouse ales had low starting gravities (6 to 8 °P), and the brewers seem to have favored reusing yeast from batches with low attenuation, perhaps to try to keep the beer from being too thin and dry. The result of that selective pressure today is that these strains only attenuate about 50 percent. Historically, the yeast pitches for many of those farmhouse ales were not pure. On the farm there was no lab to maintain a pure culture, and the pitch would have been a combination of strains and perhaps even some trace bacteria. This combination would have attenuated the beer further and perhaps added more character to it.

The German wheat beer strains produce a phenolic and ester character that is traditional in German *weizen* beers. Without this spicy clove and fruity banana character, it would not be a German *weizen*. A brewer using a clean ale strain with the same recipe and process ends up instead with a good example of an American wheat beer, which has none of those phenols or esters. If a beer contains these flavors unintentionally, when not using a phenolic strain, we would suspect wild yeast as a likely culprit. Yet used intentionally, in the hands of a skilled brewer, these yeasts can produce a pleasing balance of flavors that blend well with the other ingredients.

There are only a few commercially available German wheat beer strains. They differ slightly and are mainly distinguished by flavor profile. For example, one yeast strain will have a dominant banana ester that increases or decreases with fermentation temperature, while another will not produce much banana ester regardless of fermentation temperature.

These phenolic wheat beer strains rarely produce detectable diacetyl levels, although some will produce sulfur. It is important to ensure vigorous fermentation and let fermentation go to completion before capping the fermentor. Some brewers like to cap the fermentor near the end of fermentation to carbonate the beer by trapping the remaining CO_2. By doing this, the brewer also traps any remaining sulfur in the beer, which will not go away without extraordinary efforts. This applies to lager brewing as well.

Like wild yeast, most phenolic beer strains do not flocculate well. This is a desired trait in many traditional German wheat beers, helping to add some cloudiness. You still want the yeast to flocculate and settle to some degree; otherwise, the beer would be as milky as a yeast culture and would taste like one, too.

Typical phenolic strains are German *hefeweizen*, Belgian ale, and Belgian Trappist/abbey ale.

Eccentric Ale Strains

Brewers often consider ale strains that do not fall into the previous categories to be eccentric. They use more of them in brewing Belgian-type ales than in other beer styles. These include strains that produce unusual flavor compounds that some might consider interesting, such as earthy, barnyard, or sour, and strains that exhibit unusual behavior, such as super-high-gravity yeasts.

There is some overlap between this category and the phenolic strains, but there is so much diversity in Belgian-type ales that the strains almost defy classification. However, all of these Belgian beer styles share a common characteristic: the significance of yeast character to the style. Some beers may have a more restrained yeast character, others are more forward, but they all rely on fermentation compounds particular to the yeast strain, if they are a good example of the style. Of the strains most brewers prefer for Belgian-style beers, most tend to attenuate well, do not flocculate well, and have interesting flavor profiles, many of which include phenols. However, there is still a lot that distinguishes one Belgian-type strain from another. You cannot just take any "Belgian-style" yeast and make a Belgian-style *witbier*. While some consumers might say it has a "Belgian character," it will not have the same aroma and flavor as a traditional Belgian *witbier* unless you ferment with an authentic Belgian *witbier* strain. In fact, many Belgian-style yeast strains do much more than produce phenols. Although there are some strains that are relatively clean, many produce a lot of esters, fusel alcohols, and earthy and even sour flavors. They do not flocculate well, which is not necessarily a desired trait, except that this is part of what makes these yeast strains attenuate a beer to a greater degree than more flocculent strains.

Today, for most Belgian brewers, yeast is everything. While many Belgian brewers will freely share information about the rest of their brewing process, their yeast is sacred and something to be protected. Belgian brewers believe that the yeast they use for their beer is so important that many of the larger Belgian breweries, and even some of the smaller ones, have some of the most sophisticated lab equipment, processes, and quality control in the industry.

The Chimay brewery is a good example. Father Theodore isolated Chimay yeast in 1948 by the use of pure culture techniques. Chimay has brewed its beers with a single strain ever since. Chimay fermentation and yeast practices include a significant amount of laboratory testing. The brewers use new yeast cultures for every batch, and they centrifuge their beer three times to remove the yeast after fermentation and add back yeast for bottle conditioning. All of this is a testament to how important they believe yeast health is to the quality of the beer.

Similarly, other Belgian breweries have closely managed and guarded their yeast strains, creating selective pressure for unique flavors and aromas. Because of the importance of beer in Belgian culture, a great number of ale yeasts, each with different sets of characteristics, are available today to experiment with for making traditional Belgian-style beers or for new interpretations on the traditional styles.

Lager Strains

Besides the ability to ferment melibiose (pp. 254-256), what are the differences between ale and lager yeast? Brewers sometimes refer to lager yeast as "bottom fermenting," because during fermentation most lager strains do not rise to the top or rise only minimally. Of course, there are always exceptions, and a few true lager strains do rise to the top like ale yeast. Even though most lager strains are bottom fermenters, they are not high flocculators. Many brewers often mistakenly think of flocculation as the process of yeast dropping to the bottom of the fermentor, and a strain that does not rise to the top during fermentation must be a highly flocculent strain. As mentioned earlier, flocculation is the aggregation of yeast into clumps of yeast, not the process of dropping to the bottom. The more flocculent a strain, the more it tends to rise on CO_2 bubbles during fermentation. Because most lager strains are not very flocculent, they tend not to rise to the top. Instead, they stay in suspension for longer periods than most ale strains, allowing them to reduce more of the by-products formed during fermentation.

Lager yeast work more slowly and produce fewer esters and fusel alcohols at cooler fermentation temperatures, usually 50 to 55° F (10 to 13° C), but the slower fermentation and cool temperatures also keep more sulfur in solution and make it harder for the yeast to reabsorb diacetyl. While all strains generally produce fewer esters at lower temperatures, some brewers may wonder why most lager strains produce fewer esters than most ale strains at the same temperature. One reason is that the excretion of esters depends on the cell membrane, and most lager strains will retain more esters inside the cell (Mussche, 2008).

Lager strains fall into two basic groups: those that produce a drier, cleaner, crisp, refreshing quality and those that, while still clean and lager-like, produce a maltier, rounded, and complex flavor. Select one of the crisp, dry strains when brewing most American, Scandinavian, and some German-style lagers. By comparison, use the maltier strains for styles from Munich *helles* to Munich *dunkel* and all the other malty lager styles. Besides an increased malty character, these strains often produce a beer with more sulfur and a slight fruitiness. Manufacturers often label these yeasts as German lager or Munich lager, and the description emphasizes the malty character.

Multiple Strains in Your Brewery

"I'll have a taster set please." We have all walked into a brewpub, sat down to a taster set, sampled each one, and decided, "These beers all taste the same." How can this be, when the brewer used different grains and hops in each beer? Often the reason is that the brewery uses a single yeast strain throughout its product line. Some brewers stick with only one strain because they are concerned that using more than one may cross-contaminate other batches, adding an unintended flavor to a beer. For others, the key concern is the effort required to keep more than one strain alive and healthy between brews.

Fortunately, more brewers are beginning to explore the benefits of multiple yeast strains. A chef is not restricted to cooking everything with just one seasoning at just one temperature; should a brewer settle for less? A brewer cannot be expected to express his creativity fully without access to different yeast strains. So why not emphasize variety and creativity by trying a different yeast strain?

We discussed seven yeast categories earlier, each with many strains capable of producing great-tasting beer. This gives a brewer many strains to choose from, resulting in many opportunities to create a unique beer flavor profile. There are hundreds of different strains out there, and most brewers have ready access to fifty or more. How does a brewer determine which strains to use? Figure 3.1 is just one example of the choices available when using multiple strains within one particular brewpub.

With this example of ten beers continuously made in the brewpub, five strains provide the most variety. Without some of these strains the brewer cannot brew an authentic example of some beer styles. Different strains allow the brewer to highlight different flavors, aromas, and beer characteristics. For example, switching from California ale yeast to English ale yeast in a brown ale increases the malt sweetness and fruity esters, along with other subtle yeast characteristics.

The concern about keeping multiple strains healthy is a valid one. How does a brewer determine how many strains will be workable in the

Typical Beer Menu	Using 1 Strain	Using 2 Strains	Using 3 Strains	Using 4 Strains	Using 5 Strains
Blonde Ale	California/American	California/American	California/American	California/American	California/American
Pale Ale	California/American	California/American	California/American	California/American	California/American
Red/Amber Ale	California/American	California/American	California/American	English	English
IPA	California/American	California/American	California/American	English	English
Pilsener	California/American	California/American	German Lager	German Lager	German Lager
Hefeweizen	California/American	German Hefeweizen	German Hefeweizen	German Hefeweizen	German Hefeweizen
Dunkelweizen	California/American	German Hefeweizen	German Hefeweizen	German Hefeweizen	German Hefeweizen
English Brown Ale	California/American	California/American	California/American	English	English
Dry Stout	California/American	California/American	California/American	English	Irish
Bock	California/American	California/American	German Lager	German Lager	German Lager

Figure 3.1: A brewery enjoys more variety and flexibility when employing multiple strains.

brewery? Use the following equation to get a general idea of how many different strains you might be able to keep alive in your brewery.

of different strains = # of brew days per month / 3

For example, twelve brews per month would equal four possible strains. This gives the brewer nine to ten days from the beginning of fermentation to when he or she needs yeast for repitching. Usually ale fermentations are complete in five days, with four to five days for yeast to settle, the beer to mature, and the brewer to collect the yeast. Highly flocculent strains, such as English ale, will be ready more quickly, while lager strains will take longer. View this number of strains as an upper limit, and only experienced brewers should attempt to keep track of four strains while brewing three days per week. You will not use all strains equally, because your more popular beers, like pale ale or amber, will sell faster.

Cost may be another concern for some brewers who are considering using more than one strain, but it is not much different than using a single strain, since you can reuse each for five to ten generations, just as in using a single strain. This way the brewery is getting the benefits of increased pitching rates and spreads the cost of yeast out over many batches. Consider also that having a greater variety of unique beers might result in capturing more customers and more sales across your product line. If that is the result, multiple strains would be well worth the cost and effort.

Cross contamination is another common concern of brewers who have never used multiple strains. There is some truth to this concern, because the concentration of these "other" strains is high in brewery usage. The higher the concentration of an organism in your brewery, the greater the chance of cross contamination. However, as with anything relating to fermentation, attention to cleanliness and sanitary practices determines much of your success. With good cleaning practice, brewers experience no problems with cross contamination from multiple strains. Brewers who do use multiple strains often feel that if current procedures do not result in contamination, adding more strains will not be a problem. Keep the following in mind when working with several strains at the same time:

- Be consistent. Always try to collect your yeast at the optimal stage for that strain and pitch a consistent cell count or wet cell weight. Consistency helps identify problems before they become significant.

- Use "yeast only" storage containers. Use a different container for each strain and label them clearly. When storing yeast, remember to store it cold, keep air out, and keep CO_2 pressure low.

- Store the yeast containers in their own clean, refrigerated area. Avoid using the food walk-in or other multi-use areas.

- Fresh is best. Keep storage time to a minimum. Yeast stored at 33 to 36° F (1 to 2° C) and used within seven days of collection is the goal. Consider 14 days the maximum storage time.

- Monitor the pH of the yeast slurry while in storage. A pH rise of more than 1.0 indicates significant cell death, and you should discard the slurry.

- Document everything and keep good records. You should pay particular attention to fermentation temperatures, times, flocculation patterns, and attenuation from beer to beer. Do not forget to record data such as sensory qualities of the beer, source of the yeast, number of generations, storage temperatures, storage time, etc.

- Learn the needs and behaviors of each strain in your brewery. Each strain is a little different.

- Use a taste panel, and conduct weekly sessions. Having a few trusted people tasting each beer every week gives you a consistent measuring stick to identify problems early. Make sure to taste beer from the fermentors to head off a potential problem prior to reusing the yeast.

- As always, clean and sanitize thoroughly, including fittings, whenever making a connection. Regularly monitor common trouble spots such as the heat exchanger and fermentor surfaces. Change soft goods, such as rubber gaskets, before troubles arise.

Multiple Strains in One Beer

Brewers today typically use a single, pure yeast strain for fermentation. This has been the practice since Emil Christian Hansen's development of pure culture techniques. Before then, a brewer most likely was pitching several different strains in his wort to either the detriment or possibly the benefit of his beer. Nowadays the majority of brewers consider a single strain to be part of their beer's signature flavor profile. For example, we have heard that Anheuser-Busch still ferments with its original lager yeast strain, in use since the late nineteenth century. Even many smaller craft breweries use a single strain for most of their beers. Even if a brewery uses different strains for different beers, the usual practice is to use only one strain per beer.

Would there be a benefit to using multiple yeast strains in a single fermentation? In some beers, yes:

- A brewer could dry out an otherwise too sweet beer by adding a higher-attenuating, neutral strain to the batch. This way he keeps the flavor profile of the more complex but low-attenuating strain while gaining the attenuation power of the neutral strain.
- A brewer could blend two strains with different but complementary flavor profiles to derive a more complex flavor.
- A brewery could craft a unique signature flavor profile for its beers that would be hard for other brewers to duplicate.
- A brewer could use an alcohol-tolerant strain in conjunction with the house strain, to cope with seasonal high-gravity beers.

Goal	Strains	Timing
Higher Attenuation or Achieving Higher ABV while Maintaining House Flavor	One yeast for flavor + one yeast for attenuation	Add flavor yeast initially, then add attenuation yeast during last third of fermentation
Increase Complexity or Unique Flavor Profile	Two or more strains	All yeast at beginning of fermentation

Figure 3.2: Multistrain fermentation to achieve specific goals.

One thing to keep in mind is that yeast cells produce most of their fermentation flavor compounds in the first 72 hours. Therefore, if a brewer wants to blend flavors from different yeast strains, he or she needs to add all of the strains at the beginning of fermentation.

This is different from adding a strain for greater attenuation or alcohol tolerance. In this case, the brewer adds the alcohol-tolerant or high-attenuating strain towards the end of fermentation, and it adds little in terms of flavor compounds, although it will work through the remaining sugars to achieve the desired attenuation. The disadvantage to this method is that you cannot repitch the yeast without the second strain having a greater flavor impact on subsequent batches.

There are some tricks to adding yeast to an already ongoing fermentation. Since the fermentation is devoid of oxygen and alcohol is present, the yeast needs to be in a very active state. They should be going through an active fermentation, either from a starter, propagation, or from a one- to two-day active fermentation when pitched into the beer.

Many brewers eschew using multiple-strain fermentation, concerned that the strains will compete against each other and one will win out. Interestingly, most brewer's yeast strains grow at a similar rate in beer fermentation, so competition is rarely a factor when mixing two or more strains. Many yeast strains in the wild do compete against each other, and some even have kill factors, but brewer's yeast does not. Perhaps this is due to generations of brewers protecting their house yeast from competing strains. Brewers concerned about one strain outgrowing another can do a simple experiment to compare the growth rate of each strain separately and mixed to determine if the yeast strains grow well together.

The most relevant concern about mixed-culture fermentations is the difference in flocculation. Even though poorly flocculating strains will co-flocculate with a higher flocculating strain, improving their flocculation, there will still be some differences in overall flocculation. Harvesting and repitching from a mixed-strain fermentation requires some attention to those differences, otherwise it can affect the percentage of each yeast strain harvested. For example, if the mixed-culture consists of a highly flocculent strain and a low-flocculating strain, collecting the yeast from the bottom of the fermentor increases the percentage of the highly flocculent strain. In real-world brewery use, we have seen the percentage change in as few as five generations. In this case, the mix went from an equal distribution to one strain making up 90 percent of the pitch. Interestingly, the brewer was still seeing the benefit of both yeast strains and was surprised to learn of the magnitude of the drift.

You should not be too concerned about the possibility of drift as it is relatively easy to monitor a pitch for strain drift. This book includes several techniques for monitoring yeast in "Your Own Yeast Lab Made Easy." The easiest method of checking for drift is similar to techniques used to determine purity of a yeast strain. Simply plating the yeast on Wallerstein Nutrient (WLN) plates makes the amount of each strain in a mixed culture visible without the use of a microscope or genetic analysis.

In the interest of exploring the efficacy of mixed strains in real-world brewery use, White Labs provided mixed cultures to a number of breweries. The responses from brewers were positive.

Beer Type	Goal	Strains Used	Brewer Comments
German *Hefeweizen*	Improved Flavor	WLP300 (50%) WLP380 (50%) both added at start	Balanced and more complex than previous batches with just WLP300
Weizenbock	Improved Flavor	WLP380 (70%) WLP830 (30%) both added at start	Good *weizen* flavor
Saison	Improved Attenuation	WLP566 (at start) WLP029 (at 1.022) OG 1.048 FG 1.009	Achieved *saison* flavors with WLP566 and dryness with house yeast strain (WLP029)
Barley wine	Improved Attenuation	WLP002 (at start) WLP001 (at 1.030) OG 1.094 FG 1.014	House yeast strain (WLP002) flavor dominant while achieving dryness from WLP001
Very Strong Beer	Improved Attenuation	WLP001 (at start) WLP715 (when feeding with sugar) WLP099 (at third feed) OG 1.095 + sugar FG 1.008 ABV 15.3%	Complex flavors. Attenuation reached with WLP099. Flavor profile was dominated by WLP001

Figure 3.3: Brewery multistrain test results.

While mixed culture fermentation is not a panacea for all flavor or attenuation issues, it is easy to see how using multiple strains from one or more suppliers can be a useful tool in the creative brewer's arsenal.

Brettanomyces

Most experienced brewers know that *Brettanomyces* is yeast, although new brewers often think of it as a bacterium. Like ale and lager strains, *Brettanomyces* strains are a non-spore-forming yeast. Brewers often refer to it as "Brett," and for some it is a curse, while others love it.

In 1904, N. Hjelte Claussen, director of the New Carlsberg Brewery in Copenhagen, Denmark, isolated and introduced *Brettanomyces* to the world. He showed that strong English stock beer underwent a slow secondary fermentation of *Brettanomyces,* and this secondary fermentation produced flavors characteristic of high-gravity British beers. In fact, the name Brettanomyces comes from the Greek for "British fungus." He was able to duplicate this flavor by inoculating beer with a pure culture of this newly named *Brettanomyces.*

Before the work of Hansen and his development of pure culture technique, *Brettanomyces* was present in many beers. The beginning of the pure brewery culture was the beginning of the dark ages for *Brettanomyces,* which brewers eliminated at every turn. While the majority of wineries and breweries today still shun *Brettanomyces,* some embrace it, and a new day is dawning for this much-maligned yeast. The descriptors for *Brettanomyces* fermentation compounds read like Old MacDonald's Farm: horse blanket, barnyard, sweaty horse, Band-Aid, leather, wet wool, enteric, burnt beans, burnt plastic, peppery, mousey, and more. It is easy to see why many brewers view it as a negative influence rather than a positive one. However, it is a critical component of *lambic* and some other Belgian-type ales. Today many breweries are embracing *Brettanomyces.* Bold craft brewers and homebrewers are also experimenting with it, some with tremendous success. It is considered an integral part of the flavor production of such beers as *Rodenbach Grand Cru, Orval, Cuvée de Tomme, lambic,* and a host of others from breweries such as Lost Abbey Brewing Company of San Marcos, California, and Russian River Brewing Company of Santa Rosa, California.

Why do these breweries use this odd yeast if the flavors sound so nasty? It is because these flavors are like adding the spices of an Indian grocer to your local supermarket (unless you live in India, of course). All of a sudden, you have many new flavors and aromas to use when crafting that next great beer. With the right skill and the right balance, these flavors create a beer that is both complex and delicious.

Contamination Concerns

The one thing that stops many brewers from experimenting with *Brettanomyces* is the worry about cross contamination. If you are not careful, you could quickly find *Brettanomyces* character developing in all your beers. *Brettanomyces* spreads easily, like other organisms, through airborne dust, wood, fruit flies, transfer lines, and other equipment. The trait that makes *Brettanomyces* a bit more troublesome is that it can form a biofilm, which requires proper cleaning before you can sanitize the surface. However, attention to proper cleaning and sanitizing procedures goes a long way to preventing problems. If you also keep separate soft goods, one set for *Brettanomyces* and one for all other beers, you should never have a problem.

Brettanomyces Strains

Brettanomyces is a non-spore-forming genus of yeast in the family *Saccharomycetaceae*. The spore-forming types constitute the genus *Dekkera*. The *Brettanomyces* group grew as researchers added many new strains over the past century. Researchers have identified five species, based on ribosomal DNA sequence homology:

- *B. bruxellensis*, which includes *B. intermedia, B. lambicus*, and *B. custersii*
- *B. anomalus*, which includes *B. claussenii*
- *B. custersianus*
- *B. naardenesis*
- *B. nanus*

There are only three *Brett* strains brewers regularly use for brewing:

- *B. bruxellensis* is a great strain for secondary fermentation. Orval uses this strain to produce secondary flavor in its Trappist ale. New Belgium, Southampton, and Mackenzies have also used this strain in production beers.
- *B. lambicus* is most often found in *lambic*-style and Flanders red and brown beers. Russian River is using this strain in several beers, most notably *Sanctification*.

- *B. anomalus* is not as well known as the other two, but it is reputed to be a strain of *B. bruxellensis*. This is perhaps the strain isolated from the stouts of England and Ireland. Its flavor is much more subtle than that of the other strains, trending more toward fruitiness.

What Makes *Brettanomyces* Special?

Brettanomyces behaves differently than your typical brewing strains. Probably the most significant difference is the Custer effect. The Custer effect is the inhibition of alcoholic fermentation in the absence of oxygen. While our everyday strains produce alcohol in the absence of oxygen (anaerobic fermentation), *Brettanomyces* produces alcohol at a higher rate in the presence of oxygen (aerobic fermentation). With oxygen present, *Brettanomyces* turns glucose into ethanol and acetic acid.

One of the reasons many wineries worry about *Brettanomyces* is that it can consume the wood sugars present in oak barrels. *Brettanomyces* produces the enzyme ß-glucosidase, which allows it to grow in wood sugars called cellobiose. The firing process for new oak barrels creates cellobiose. New barrels also contain higher amounts of cellobiose than used barrels, and therefore have the potential to support higher *Brettanomyces* populations. The ß-glucosidase breaks down the cellobiose and produces glucose, which the cells use for energy. It is possible that this glucosidase activity generates some fruitlike flavors. While many wineries destroy any barrels that develop a *Brett* population, some brewers treasure it. If you want to favor ß-glucosidase, be aware that high levels of ethanol inhibit its activity, and its optimal pH range is 5 to 6.

Brettanomyces produces four key by-products: volatile organic acids, esterases, tetrahydropyridines, and volatile phenols. One common acid they produce is acetic acid, and we usually find that *Brettanomyces* beers with high levels of acetic acid also have high levels of the solventlike ethyl acetate. Other flavor-active, fatty acid-derived compounds common to *Brettanomyces* are isovaleric, isobutyric, and 2-methylbutyric.

Tetrahydropyridines are responsible for mousy flavors. *Brett* fermentation forms volatile phenols such as 4-ethylphenol (Band-Aid) and 4-ethylguaiacol (burnt wood). Volatile phenols also produce spicy cinnamon, peppery, barnyard, horsey, and other classic *Brettanomyces* flavor compounds. In fact, the presence of 4-ethylphenol is a strong indicator of *Brettanomyces*.

Inoculation Rates and Other Factors

As many brewers know, if you are trying to avoid *Brettanomyces,* it only takes a few cells for a *Brettanomyces* character to appear in your beer. Even if you are purposely trying for *Brettanomyces* fermentation, too many cells can be bad. We find a pitching rate of 200,000 cells per milliliter is effective, far less than what you might pitch for ale or lager strains. When working with wood barrels, Tomme Arthur of Lost Abbey recommends inoculating at twice that rate for new barrels, so the strain can get established in the barrel. Vinnie Cilurzo of Russian River starts with half that rate but tops up his fermentations with another pitch of *Brettanomyces* once a month. Like any fermentation, you need to experiment with the pitching rate to find the right amount to get the results you desire.

Brettanomyces grows slowly and lives for a long time. While some strains take five months to get to peak growth and develop the proper flavor profiles, the average strain can reach that point in about five weeks with the proper conditions.

Oxygen plays a big role in the growth of *Brett* and the production of compounds like acetic acid and ethanol. Moderate aeration of *Brett* stimulates growth. Researchers found the optimal oxygen supply for *B. bruxellensis* growth was 4 mg $O_2 l^{-1} h^{-1}$, which is an air flow rate of 60 l h^{-1} (0.1 volume of air per volume of medium per minute, or vvm), which is about four times higher than the recommended oxygen level for ales. Higher or lower rates reduced cell growth. Ethanol and acetic acid production also depends on the level of aeration—increased oxygen results in more acetic acid and less ethanol (Aguilar Uscanga, et al., 2003). If your goal is to grow *Brettanomyces* or to get a lot of vinegar character in your beer, then lots of oxygen is the ticket.

The specific gravity of the beer can also affect the flavor development of secondary *Brettanomyces* fermentation. Back when Claussen was working with *Brettanomyces,* he showed that inoculation of a beer with a specific gravity of 1.055 would achieve the "English" character. J. L. Shimwell later confirmed that certain conditions were necessary to achieve a "vinous" (winelike) flavor. A beer under 1.050 (12.4 °P) would be unpalatable and turbid, with insipid flavor and aroma, while a beer with a starting gravity of 1.060 (14.7 °P) would develop a vinous quality. Shimwell said *Brettanomyces* could behave "as a desirable organism in one beer and an undesirable one at one and the same brewery" (Shimwell, 1947).

Capturing Wild Yeast

Most of us have done it. There we are enjoying a superbly made Belgian *lambic,* and we begin to wonder about spontaneous fermentation in our own backyard. What if we set out a bucket of wort overnight? What if we dipped an apple from our tree in the wort? While most breweries try to avoid exposure to these influences, a number of bold souls encourage the inclusion of naturally occurring organisms in their fermentation process. When this topic comes up, many immediately think of the breweries in the Senne Valley around Brussels. Yes, they have led the way over centuries of brewing, but more and more brewers are exploring this exciting area of their craft. Jolly Pumpkin Artisan Ales in Dexter, Michigan, is one of them. According to Ron Jeffries, owner/brewer, the design of the brewery's heating and cooling system pulls in unfiltered cool night air, giving local microorganisms an opportunity to settle into his open fermentors. Jolly Pumpkin primarily ferments its beers with a commercial strain, but the long-term re-use of the culture from batch to batch, and the influx of other organisms, has developed a unique and flavorful profile over time.

In spontaneous fermentation, we depend on microbes already present on the ingredients (grapes, apples, pears) or traveling on airborne dust or insects for inoculation. As you might guess, the results are often highly variable. While there might be yeast capable of the kind of fermentation you want, it is often side-by-side with other microbes, such as bacteria and mold.

There is some debate about whether you can even find yeast that produce alcohol on the surface of various fruits. The theory is that the yeast is already present on the equipment used for processing and fermentation. However, studies have found *S. cerevisiae* in spontaneously fermented apples (Prahl, 2009). It does not mean that *S. cerevisiae* is present on all fruit or other plants, but it seems likely that most fruit would support at least a small population.

Whether collecting organisms from fruit or allowing them to settle with the night air, the amount of yeast present is going to be quite small in comparison to the amount we would need for even the smallest batch of beer. Many brewers get around this by first inoculating with a pure culture at an appropriate pitching rate, and then allowing additional organisms to settle into the open beer. The timing of the exposure and the primary pitching rate can have a huge impact on the results of the process. There are no rules, and all you can do is experiment with the initial pitching rate, the amount of time you leave the fermentor open, and whether you expose the wort before, during, or after fermentation is complete. The pH, IBUs, amount of alcohol present, season of the year, and amount of residual sugar all have an effect on the response of the secondary organisms.

What if you want more control and want to avoid all the other bacteria and mold? Perhaps you want to create your own pure culture from what is in your backyard. You can perform some small fermentations either by exposing them overnight or by dipping some fruit into the wort. Keep the wort simple, just pale malt and a low level of hops. You can taste the results to see if any of the experiments has a character you want to keep, then harvest and plate the organisms present in that beer. From the colonies that grow on the plate, run more fermentation trials to see which ones contribute the flavors you enjoy.

One factor you can leverage to your advantage is that the blend of organisms will change after repeated fermentations to favor the attributes that allow them to survive in the environment you provide. Let us say that again: the environment you provide puts selective pressure on the organisms and favors some over others. Use this to your advantage. If you have an alcoholic fermentation—where the pH has dropped, nutrients are limited, oxygen is nonexistent, and the alcohol level has risen—some variant of *S. cerevisiae* is probably going to be the strongest swimmer in the pool. It should be able to outcompete most of the bacteria present.

Once you have a favorite from your trial batch, take that result and ferment another test batch at the same specific gravity, IBUs, and other factors of the target beer. This will favor some organisms and not others, weeding out those that cannot handle your environment. If your goal is to make a high-ethanol beer with the newfound yeast, you might want to start with a neutral ale yeast at the same time. This will ensure a higher level of alcohol and will help eliminate any organisms that cannot survive in that environment. Re-use will eventually favor organisms with a higher alcohol tolerance.

If you want to isolate an organism, use these steps in repetition to create your own pure culture:

1. Harvest the sediment from fermentation.
2. Dilute the sediment and plate out so that you can pick single, pure colonies.

3. Transfer separate colonies to small trial batches of wort.
4. Verify the results of the trial through taste, aroma, or other tests. If there is a failure, start again. If the results are what you want, move forward.
5. Take the result and propagate up in a larger volume.

While working with native yeasts can be interesting, the reality is that getting good results is not trivial. Depending on the medium used, it is also potentially dangerous. Media under aerobic conditions and with a high enough pH can support the growth of pathogens. Use caution when tasting any native fermentation, especially if it does not smell like beer. Even if it is not funky, it could be dangerous. You might want to avoid tasting any spontaneous fermentation, waiting until you have isolated the yeasts and grown up a pure culture from them.

Fermentation

Fermentation is where we make beer. The saying, "Brewers make wort, yeast make beer," is true, but as brewers, we have a lot of control over how yeast make our beer. While it may seem that a specific strain will fight our desires from time to time, learning what makes a strain tick, and taking advantage of that knowledge, gives us some measure of control over our yeast. A large part of what makes a great brewer is understanding and manipulating fermentation for the ideal result. While you cannot make a strain do something it is not physiologically capable of doing, you can make it respond to the best of its ability.

Fermentation Timeline

Once you pitch your yeast, what do the cells do? The common answer: They consume wort sugar and turn it into new yeast cells, ethanol, carbon dioxide, and flavor compounds.

$$\text{Sugar} + 2\ \text{ADP} + 2\ \text{phosphate} \rightarrow 2\ \text{ethanol} + 2\ CO_2 + 2\ \text{ATP}$$

In order for you to maximize the correct flavor compounds, it is helpful to know how yeast proceed through beer fermentation. Some experts divide fermentation into four or more phases: lag, growth, fermentation, and sedimentation. The truth is, much of the yeast activity does not follow distinct phases with firm starting and stopping points; instead, there is a lot of overlap. For example, at the beginning growth and fermentation are occurring at the same time. Saying that the cells are in one phase or another at any given time is not necessarily true, as individual cells will progress through fermentation at different rates.

Let us simplify and say fermentation in brewer's wort follows three phases: lag phase for zero to 15 hours, exponential growth phase for one to four days, and the stationary phase for three to ten days. The exact phases are not important; rather, the brewer should understand what the yeast gain from fermentation and what they do for the beer.

Lag Phase (Zero to 15 Hours After Pitching Yeast)

When you pitch yeast into wort, it begins acclimating to the environment. Although you do not see any activity, the cells begin the uptake of oxygen, minerals, and amino acids (nitrogen) from the wort and build proteins from the amino acids. If the yeast cannot get the amino acids they need from the wort, they produce them.

All-malt wort is an excellent source of nitrogen, minerals, and vitamins. Wort supplies most of the vitamins yeast need for proper fermentation. Some examples of necessary vitamins are riboflavin, inositol, and biotin. Important minerals are phosphorus, sulfur, copper, iron, zinc, potassium, and sodium. As the yeast take up minerals and vitamins from the wort, they start to manufacture the enzymes necessary for growth. You can supplement the wort with additional minerals and vitamins using commercially available yeast nutrients to improve the health and performance of yeast. Zinc is one compound that is often in short supply.

The one nutrient that yeast need, which is not present in wort due to boiling, is oxygen. During the lag phase, yeast cells rapidly absorb available oxygen from the wort. The cells need oxygen in order to produce important compounds, most significantly sterols, which are critical in yeast membrane permeability. It is important that you provide enough oxygen to the yeast at the beginning of fermentation. Generally, you do not want to add oxygen later, as it can disturb the delicate balance of flavor and aroma compound creation. One exception is when brewing very high-gravity, high-alcohol beers. In those cases, where the yeast need large reserves to ferment the beer to completion, a second addition of oxygen between 12 and 18 hours after pitching can make a tremendous difference in attenuating the beer to the desired level.

Temperature directly affects yeast growth. Warmer temperatures result in more cells. A common technique when working with a slightly undersized pitch of yeast is to carry out the lag phase under warmer conditions. While it may not create off-flavors directly, it can increase some precursors, like alpha acetolactate, which is the precursor for di-acetyl. If you are going to pitch the yeast warm, be prepared to warm the beer back up to the same temperature or higher near the end of fermentation. This will help the yeast utilize some of these fermentation compounds and will result in a cleaner beer. Other than these precursors, yeast produce minimal flavor compounds during the lag phase. The yeast produce minimal ethanol at this stage, so ester formation is not a concern. Yeast do not create esters until they first make an appreciable amount of alcohols. However, the rapidity of growth during this time will affect flavors later in fermentation. Some brewers begin the lag phase for ales at 72 to 75° F (22 to 24° C), and complete the fermentation at 68° F (20° C). This can be done with success for lagers, too, by starting the lag phase at 72 to 75° F (22 to 24° C) and lowering the fermentation temperature to 50 to 55° F (10 to 13° C). This is an acceptable way to cope with a smaller but still appropriate-sized yeast pitch for a given-sized batch of beer. However, it is not a panacea for a grossly undersized pitch. When the brewer has an appropriate pitch of healthy yeast available, and has the ability to chill the wort down to fermentation temperatures within a reasonable amount of time, the better course for beer quality is often pitching at or slightly below fermentation temperature. The brewer allows the fermentation temperature to rise over the first 12 to 36 hours, until it reaches the desired temperature. The benefit of this process is controlled yeast growth, which often results in better overall yeast health, less leakage through the cell membrane, and thus a cleaner beer profile.

You will not see any visible activity during the lag phase (hence its name) but this phase is a very important step in building new healthy cells for fermentation. Pitching rate also plays a significant role in the quality of the lag phase. Overpitching can decrease the lag phase, but each individual cell will not be as healthy at the end of fermentation. Although a brewer may find it reassuring to see fermentation activity within one hour, it is not the optimal condition for the yeast. The same is true for underpitching and trying to compensate with temperature and nutrients. Too much cell growth often leaves the cells in less than optimal shape for the remainder of that fermentation and for the next fermentation as well.

Exponential Growth Phase (Four Hours to Four Days)

As the yeast come out of the lag phase, they start to consume the sugars in solution and produce CO_2, among other things. This is the beginning of the exponential, or logarithmic, phase of yeast growth. During this phase, the cell count increases rapidly, and the yeast produce ethanol and flavor compounds. The yeast start producing large volumes of CO_2 and create a layer of foam on the surface of the beer. For most neutral ale yeast, the aroma of fermentation during this phase has an "olive" smell.

The exponential phase occurs with the yeast rapidly consuming sugar, and they do this in a certain order. Yeast utilize the simple sugars first: glucose, then fructose and sucrose. The yeast can shuttle these simple sugars inside the cell and into metabolism very quickly. While glucose makes up roughly 14 percent of wort sugars, maltose is the centerpiece. Maltose makes up about 59 percent of the sugars in the average wort, and its fermentation is part of what enables yeast to create some of the characteristic beer flavors. In response to the presence of maltose, the yeast use maltase enzymes to hydrolyze (hydrolysis is the decomposition of a chemical compound by reaction with water) the maltose into glucose units by maltase enzymes. The yeast can then utilize the glucose through the normal metabolism cycle.

Yeast ferment the more complex sugars like maltotriose last. This is a tricky sugar for yeast to digest, and some strains ferment maltotriose better than others. Some strains cannot ferment maltotriose at all. The more flocculent a strain, the less maltotriose it tends to be able to ferment. The ability to ferment maltotriose is what determines each strain's characteristic attenuation range.

We call the height of yeast activity "high kraeusen." The head of foam on top of the fermentation turns color ranging from yellow to brown. The colors stem primarily from precipitated malt and hop components, with the brown spots or "brown yeast" (*braun hefe*) from oxidized hop resins.

Stationary Phase (Three to Ten Days)

At this point, yeast growth slows down, and the yeast enter into a stationary phase. The yeast have already produced most of the flavor and aroma compounds, which include fusel alcohols, esters, and sulfur compounds. We call this "green beer," because at this point there are still many compounds present that we associate with young beer that has not yet reached a proper balance of flavors.

Beer matures in the stationary phase, also known as the conditioning phase. Yeast reabsorb much of the diacetyl and acetaldehyde produced during fermentation, and hydrogen sulfide continues to escape from the top of the fermentor as a gas. The kraeusen falls, and yeast flocs start to settle out. When working with a new strain, it is important to check the degree of attenuation at this point to confirm that the yeast has indeed completed fermentation. Some strains flocculate and settle out before the beer fully attenuates, and the brewer needs to take corrective action that may include rousing the yeast, raising the temperature, or repitching.

At this point many professional breweries cool the contents of the fermentor gradually to 35 to 40° F (2 to 4° C), which forces most of the yeast to flocculate and settle. Commercial brewers do this to produce beer as quickly and efficiently as possible. While homebrewers could do this by moving the fermentor to a refrigerated space or adjusting the temperature controller colder, we recommend against this approach. One of the things you do not want to do is force the yeast into dormancy before they have had every opportunity to clean up after themselves. One commercial brewery we know of had a high level of diacetyl in its ales, because it was rushing the process. Once it provided a little extra warmth and time, the beer went from buttery to fantastic. Our recommendation, especially for homebrewers, is to wait for the yeast to finish their tasks and clean up fermentation by-products as much as possible. The traditional homebrew advice to "wait seven days and then transfer" is not the best advice. Different beers and different yeast have different requirements. Wait until the yeast show no more activity, let the fermentor clear naturally, and then package the beer.

In summary, it is important that you can recognize these major phases, as you will be better able to identify potential trouble areas. When it comes to fermentation, focus on beer quality instead of speed for key factors such as temperature, time, and pitching rate.

Wort Composition

Wort composition is very important to fermentation, from the nutrients to the percentages of sugars. Without adequate nutrition and the right balance of sugars, the fermentation will not end as the brewer expects, and the beer will suffer.

Sugars

Most brewers know there is a correlation between mash temperature and the types of sugars created in the mash. Higher temperatures favor the enzymes that make more complex, less readily fermentable sugars, and the result is that the beer attenuates less than one with fewer complex sugars. Mash thickness also plays a very small role in the resulting fermentability of the wort, but the brewer can easily overcome its effect with a slight adjustment in mash temperature.

Time and temperature are the main parameters that the brewer should use to adjust wort fermentability. While conversion may occur rapidly, further enzyme activity can yet affect the fermentability of the wort.

Running a forced wort fermentability test is cheap, easy, and gives you valuable information on what you can expect from your fermentation. Having this piece of data makes it that much easier to determine if your fermentation problem is cold side or hot side related. Get in the habit of performing a wort fermentability test every time you brew a new beer and test periodically for those beers already in production. You can find more about this test in "Your Own Yeast Lab Made Easy."

One thing many brewers have been led to believe is that higher mash temperatures result in "maltier" beers. By this they mean that the beer has more malt sweetness. Higher mash temperatures do not develop more malt character or flavor, nor does it really result in much sweetness. The long-chain dextrins created at high mash temperatures are at most only very slightly sweet. It is possible to brew two beers, one with a higher mash temperature and a high finishing gravity, and another with a lower mash temperature and a lower finishing gravity, yet the beer with the higher finishing gravity tastes drier (less sweet) than the second beer. There are many examples of very low finishing gravity Belgian-style beers that still have a sweet character upfront. There are many factors in the relative sweetness of a beer beyond fermentation, including alcohols, bittering compounds, tannins, carbonation, and sugars the yeast did not consume.

Enzymes

Homebrewers are known for their desire to make extreme beers, pushing the limits at every turn. Those brewing giant beers sometimes turn to over-the-counter enzyme products that break down starches. The fundamental problem with adding enzymes to fermentation (besides the risk of bacterial contamination) is that without the boil, the enzymes retain their full activity. They will continue to break down starches and dextrins, completely drying out a beer and degrading the quality of the beer flavor. The only reasonable way for a brewer to stop enzyme activity is to pasteurize the beer at a temperature and duration capable of denaturing the enzyme. Few craft brewers and even fewer homebrewers pasteurize their beer, so this is not an option in many breweries.

High-gravity beers, especially all-malt ones, start with a high percentage of nonfermentable sugar. The problem is that fermentation often stops short of the brewer's goal. Adding α-amylase enzymes to a stalled high-gravity fermentation often restarts fermentation. As expected, the enzymes continue to work, but the high alcohol concentration prevents the yeast from working, even when the enzymes make new fermentable sugar available. Some brewers have reported success with this method, although the results might be less beerlike than desired. As the popularity of high-alcohol beers continues to increase, more brewers are sure to experiment with enzymes.

Nutritional deficiencies can also cause fermentation to proceed slowly. When using wort containing a large portion of nonmalt sugars or utilizing undermodified malts, it is important to ensure that there is adequate nitrogen in the wort for proper cell development and fermentation. Undermodified malts should undergo a protein rest to ensure the wort contains enough amino acids, and wort utilizing a high percentage of nonmalt sugar may require supplemental nitrogen. Sometimes the reason for a lackluster fermentation is a mineral deficiency. To work, or work efficiently, many enzymes need certain minerals as co-factors. For example, brewer's wort is often zinc limited. Zinc is a co-factor for the enzyme alcohol dehydrogenase, the enzyme responsible for alcohol production in yeast. The enzyme cannot utilize other metal ions in place of zinc.

Enzymes can come from many sources, including plant-based sources such as malt. Most commercial manufacturers produce their enzyme products from microorganisms. It is economically efficient to grow large quantities of microorganisms (either bacteria or fungi) in high cell density fermentations. The organisms usually excrete the enzyme of interest, so they just need to remove the cells and concentrate the surrounding media, which contain the enzyme. Each product's specification and intended use determines if it continues with further purification. The products do not purify most enzymes completely, as this would be too expensive. Therefore, each preparation usually contains a number of different enzymes. Manufacturers can also produce enzymes from recombinant DNA sources (genetically modified organisms, or GMO), but their use in brewing today is still very rare. Brewers are conservative and aware of potentially adverse customer reaction to adding GMO products to beer. One GMO product, Maturex, from Novo Nordisk, has gained Federal Drug Administration approval for use in beer. It is an acetolactate decarboxylase, which converts acetolactate directly to acetoin without producing diacetyl, eliminating the need for a diacetyl rest. However, Maturex cannot remove diacetyl that is present as result of either yeast metabolism or *Pediococcus*. The bottom line is that using this enzyme may eliminate waiting for a diacetyl rest, but shortening the beer maturation time may have other consequences for beer flavor.

When you purchase these enzyme products, do not be surprised at how little you get. Since catalyzing a reaction does not consume the enzyme, you only need a very small quantity. Exact usage rates vary, but typically, they are near 1 gram per U.S. barrel. The product you buy is most likely packaged in liquid or powder form. If you purchase enzymes in powder form, it is best to use "dustless" preparations to help prevent inadvertent contact with skin, eyes, or lungs. The proteases present in the mixtures, and the high concentration of the enzymes, can cause skin irritation. You can extend enzymes' shelf life by keeping them cold. The shelf life for most preparations is one year when stored at 40° F (4° C).

Yeast Nutrition

Yeast need an adequate supply of sugar, nitrogen, vitamins, phosphorus, and trace metals. Exact nutrient requirements vary between ale (*Saccharomyces cerevisiae*) and lager (*Saccharomyces uvarum*) yeast cells, and for each strain within the species. Nutrient requirements can also vary between breweries, even when they are using the same yeast strain.

An all-malt wort contains all the nutrients yeast need for fermentation except oxygen and zinc. Adjuncts such as corn, rice, or sugar syrups do not contain many essential nutrients, such as nitrogen, minerals, and vitamins. Even with all-malt worts, brewers may find advantage in adding nutrients to improve and fine tune fermentation performance. Several yeast nutrient products available provide a balanced source of nitrogen, minerals, and vitamins. Brewers can also add specific nutrients individually, but keep in mind that excessive amounts of nutrients can also cause problems. Your goal is to find the optimal balance for your fermentation conditions.

Nitrogen makes up about 10 percent of the dry weight of yeast cells. The nitrogen in brewer's wort is mostly in the form of amino acids. There are twenty different types of amino acids, and yeast can either make the amino acids they need or assimilate them from the wort. Both wort amino acids and inorganic nitrogen supplements affect flavor, which may be good or bad depending on your goals.

Similar to how yeast approach different sugars, yeast assimilate and utilize wort amino acids as rapidly and efficiently as possible. Yeast take up and utilize some wort amino acids (Group A) within the first day, while others (Group B) are taken up gradually throughout fermentation. Yeast do not take up some others (Group C) until after a substantial lag. And yeast do not utilize the most abundant amino acid in wort, proline (Group D), at all. The specificity of permeases that transport amino acids across the plasma membrane control the utilization rates. The fastest way for yeast to utilize nitrogen is through transamination. In this process, a donor amino acid gives up its alpha-amino nitrogen to the keto acid to form the desired amino acid. Therefore, for the most part, wort amino acids are converted to alpha-keto acids. This is why yeast do not utilize proline, because it is the one amino acid where the alpha-amino group is a secondary amine (bound to two carbons) and cannot be transaminated.

This process has profound implications for flavor. The alpha-keto acids formed are decarboxylated to form an aldehyde, which is subsequently reduced to alcohol, and this is the source of fusel alcohols. This is why amino acid supplements can affect the quantity and type of fusel alcohol formed. In addition, changes in the fusel alcohol profile affect the ester profile. This is one reason why amino acid supplements are not necessarily superior to inorganic nitrogen.

Common inorganic nitrogen sources are ammonium sulfate and diaminophosphate (DAP). DAP has become by far the most preferred nitrogen source in the wine industry, as it also provides phosphate. Phosphorus is an essential component of deoxyribonucleic acid (DNA), as well as phospholipids within cell membranes. Phosphorus makes up 3 to 5 percent of the dry cell weight, most of which the yeast store in vacuoles. If the yeast lack phosphate, fermentation troubles can arise due to problems with DNA replication, and this also can result in stuck and incomplete fermentations. In fermentations where phosphate is limiting, such as adjunct beers or non-barley-based worts, the addition of phosphate may prove beneficial.

Vitamins are essential in many enzymatic reactions, yet yeast cannot synthesize many of the essential vitamins. Typical vitamin requirements include biotin, nicotinic acid, and pantothenic acid. Biotin is the most important vitamin for yeast. It is involved in almost all enzyme reactions that create critical yeast compounds: proteins, DNA, carbohydrates, and fatty acids. Biotin deficiency results in slow yeast growth and stuck fermentations.

Necessary minerals include calcium, potassium, magnesium, zinc, and many more trace metal ions. Enzymatic reactions use minerals as co-factors. Minerals facilitate the cell uptake of materials, and yeast use minerals in cell structural material. Calcium is important for yeast flocculation and metabolism, but researchers do not think it is normally a limiting factor for yeast growth and fermentation in malt-based wort. Brewers sometimes add calcium salts to fermentations to adjust pH and improve flocculation. Manganese, which can stimulate yeast growth, is often added to many yeast nutrient formulations. Potassium has many functions within the cell and represents up to 2 percent of the dry weight of a yeast cell, which is very high for a mineral (most are under 0.1 percent). Magnesium is important in ATP synthesis, which is the form of energy used within cells. In fact, yeast cannot grow in the absence of magnesium. With limited magnesium, yeast cells must try to produce compounds that can compensate for some of its functions. Researchers have shown that magnesium improves a cell's ability to withstand stress and plays a role in preventing cell death when ethanol builds up within the cell (Walker, 2000).

As we mentioned earlier, wort is often zinc limited. Zinc is important in the cell cycle (reproduction) and is a co-factor for alcohol dehydrogenase, the enzyme responsible for alcohol production. Even though other metal ions might be present, there is no substitute for zinc. The ideal range for fermentation is 0.1 to 0.15 milligrams per liter. You can use either food grade (FCC) or pharmaceutical grade (UPS) zinc sulfate or zinc chloride. One thing to be aware of when determining dosage and cost is that the FCC or USP grade of zinc sulfate is invariably zinc heptahydrate salt ($ZnSO_4 \cdot 7H_2O$), which is only 23 percent zinc by weight. On the other hand, zinc chloride is 48 percent zinc by weight. Also, keep in mind that some of the zinc is absorbed by the hot break, and you will need to add more than the target amount for fermentation. Adding approximately 0.2 to 0.3 mg/L of zinc near the end of the boil should result in a high enough zinc level in the fermentor.

Interestingly, brewer's yeast also has very high levels of chromium, when compared to other yeast. We do not yet know what role chromium has in fermentation, but the chromium levels are so high that brewer's yeast is often included in many nutritional and cosmetic products solely for its chromium contribution.

Even when wort has a technically sufficient mineral composition, it does not guarantee the minerals are bio-available to the yeast cells. Metal ions tend to chelate, meaning they bind to proteins or other compounds, making them unavailable to yeast. Even when metals successfully enter yeast cells, they can chelate within the cytoplasm. This is actually a natural defense mechanism for yeast, and it helps keep toxic metals from hurting fermentations. For example, cesium, lithium, and lead all inhibit yeast growth.

One unique supplement that may address this issue is Servomyces, which White Labs represents in North America. The manufacturer uses a patented process, by which it grows brewer's yeast in the presence of metal ions, including zinc and magnesium. Fluorescent tests show that the manufacturing process binds most of the minerals within the cell wall, which may prevent them from chelation when added to wort. When a brewer adds Servomyces, it provides necessary zinc and magnesium along with the other nutrient value of the dead yeast cells. Accordingly, the effect of adding Servomyces is greater than only adding the same quantity of nutrient salts (Mclaren, et al., 2001).

Aerating for Fermentation

Yeast are not strictly anaerobic; they need oxygen for reproduction. Brewers typically pump oxygen into the wort before adding yeast, before anaerobic fermentation begins. Even though brewers are terrified of oxidizing their final product, they know that yeast require oxygen to have a healthy and consistent fermentation.

Proper oxygen levels during the early stages of wort fermentation are necessary, as oxygen plays an integral role in lipid synthesis for cell wall production (Fix and Fix, 1997). There is a strong correlation between oxygen supplied to wort, the quantity of sterols synthesized, and fermentation performance (Boulton, et al., 1991, Boulton and Quain, 1987). Without an adequate supply of sterols, yeast cells characteristically display low viability and poor performance in fermentation.

When Sierra Nevada Brewing Company of Chico, Calif., first started brewing commercially in the early 1980s, the brewers tried for three months to make acceptable pale ale. For some unknown reason, the flavor was not what they wanted. One clue: the fermentations were sluggish. They discovered that the problem was slight underaeration. The fix was simple but profound. To improve aeration, they modified the equipment so it would spray the wort into the fermentor (Grossman, 2009).

The Need for Oxygen

When yeast reproduce, they need to make new lipid membranes for their progeny. In order to do this they need two types of compounds: sterols and unsaturated fatty acids. Sterols keep the structure of lipid cell membranes fluid and regulate permeability. Yeast can acquire sterols from the wort or can manufacture them. However, there are not always enough sterols (and not all the right types) in brewer's wort for adequate fermentations, so yeast need to make them. Interestingly, even if all the right sterols were available in the wort, yeast has a hard time importing sterols in the presence of oxygen (Shinabarger, et al., 1989).

Sterol syntheses and regulation is complex. In brief, yeast utilize glycogen to derive acetyl-CoA, which they use to create squalene. Then, in a series of steps using oxygen, they convert squalene to 2,3-epoxysqualene, which they then cyclize to form lanosterol, the first sterol in the synthetic pathway. They then create other sterols, including ergosterol, in various reactions, some of them involving more oxygen. There are ten enzymatic reactions from acetyl-CoA to squalene, and another ten to twelve to form ergosterol. Most of the free sterol goes to the plasma membrane, some to various membrane-bound organelles inside the cell.

The other important components of lipid membranes are unsaturated fatty acids (UFAs), such as palmitoleic acid and oleic acid. As with sterols, synthesis begins with acetyl-CoA. For example, conversion of acetyl-CoA into the fatty acid palmitic acid requires ten steps. Oxygen then desaturates palmitic acid into palmitoleic acid.

Many commercial brewers worry that adding oxygen to wort may increase the rate of staling later in the beer's life, so they are interested in finding new ways to supply yeast with the sterols needed for fermentation. New Belgium Brewing Company in Fort Collins, Colorado, experimented with adding UFAs into yeast cultures as a way to eliminate wort aeration. It chose olive oil as a rich source of oleic acid. The highest concentration of olive oil the brewery added, 1 milligram per 25 billion cells 5 hours before pitching, resulted in a fermentation time most similar to the aerated control, which was 94 hours for the oil versus 83 hours for the control. Because fermentation reached terminal gravity, it was assumed that the olive oil addition had a positive effect on UFA levels. The resulting beer, an amber ale, did have the expected higher levels of esters and lower levels of fusel alcohols (from no aeration), but the taste panels could not detect the differences (Hull, 2008). New Belgium did not implement the technique permanently, but the experiment has sparked interest in many brewers. Here are some thoughts to consider:

- What are the positive and negative effects of no wort aeration?
- What are the effects of no oxygen additions over generations of yeast?
- Would adding olive oil in conjunction with yeast or wort aeration improve fermentation?
- Would the addition of ergosterol or ergosterol and olive oil improve fermentation?

Can yeast have too many sterols? No, since yeast carefully regulates its metabolism, too much oxygen does not result in excess sterols. Instead, the yeast use the oxygen for making more flavor compounds.

How Much Oxygen Is Needed?

Using proper levels of dissolved oxygen is just as important as using proper pitching rates. Lack of dissolved oxygen causes many fermentation problems. Stuck fermentations, long fermentation times, underattenuated beers, yeast stress, and off-flavors are often the result of too little oxygen. In addition, underaerating can result in lower viability with each generation of reused yeast.

For the average wort and yeast pitching rates, the proper amount of dissolved oxygen is 8 to 10 parts per million (Takacs, et al., 2007). When it comes to high-gravity wort, brewers often wonder whether they should oxygenate based on gravity or the amount of yeast pitched. Your goal is to supply the optimal amount of oxygen for the number of yeast cells present and the amount they need to grow. Of course, with higher-gravity wort you should pitch more yeast, so the oxygen requirement will be higher. In some cases, brewers try to make up for a lack of cells by adding more oxygen to drive more growth, and excessive growth is rarely optimal for beer flavor. The wort splashing devices employed by many homebrewers will result in approximately 4 ppm, less than half the required amount. Commercial brewers using similar methods will find they get comparable results. With plenty of headspace, a strong back, and lots of vigorous shaking, a home-brewer can get levels as high as 8 ppm into the wort. This is about the maximum using air. Using an aquarium pump with a sintered stone will not result in more than 8 ppm, even with extended times. In fact, extended aeration can be detrimental to the head formation and retention. The only way to reach the recommended 10 ppm minimum is with the addition of oxygen. Filling the headspace of the fermentor and shaking vigorously can result in dissolved oxygen levels past 10 ppm, but once you have bottled oxygen, it is much easier to use a sintered stone. With bottled oxygen or an oxygen generator and a sintered stone, it is possible to reach high levels of dissolved oxygen. There are a number of commercially available systems for both the professional and homebrewer that can reach the necessary levels.

Too much oxygen is rarely a problem. However, it seems that urging brewers to use lots of oxygen has resulted in some instances in which they have reached oxygen levels detrimental to beer flavor. Even though most yeast strains are able to cope with high levels of dissolved oxygen, it is possible to provide so much that it becomes a beer flavor problem. Excessive usage of pure oxygen results in high levels of fusel alcohols, increased acetaldehyde, and other flavor problems. Most small brewers do not measure the actual amount of dissolved oxygen but instead rely on a procedure (see p. 82). This can easily fool a brewer if there is a subtle problem with the equipment, temperature, or other variable, resulting in high, or more often low, dissolved oxygen levels. The equipment to measure the dissolved oxygen level of wort is not too expensive for most commercial breweries, around $1,000.

What is the homebrewer to do? While some homebrewers are willing to buy testing equipment in pursuit of the perfect beer, the average home-brewer cannot make the investment. Yet, it is important to strive for some sort of control over your process. If you can consistently deliver the same amount of oxygen flow from your equipment, you can control the total dissolved oxygen level by varying the duration of delivery. Many home-brewers want to know how much oxygen they get from their method. The exact number is not important, unless you are willing to buy the test equip-ment. Lacking that, what you can do is try different amounts of oxygen and evaluate the resulting beer quality. If one minute of oxygen at your consistent flow rate does not deliver the results you desire, try increasing delivery to a minute and a half or decreasing it to just thirty seconds. If the beer improves, then stick with the new duration. You will find that using this method, you can find the sweet spot for the strain you are using in a given beer. The hard part is ensuring you have the same flow rate every time. Regulators that provide a consistent flow are available and are a good solution if the budget allows. Otherwise, you will need to try to ensure the same flow rate visually each time you add oxygen.

To help homebrewers with the question of how much oxygen to add to a batch of beer, White Labs ran an experiment injecting pure oxygen into 5.3 gallons (20 L) of 1.077 (18.7 °P) wort using a 0.5 micron stainless steel sin-tered stone at a flow rate of 1 liter per minute. The results show that to reach the desired 8 to 10 ppm, you would need to inject oxygen for one minute:

Method of Aeration	Observed O_2 PPM
Shaking, 5 minutes	2.71 ppm
30 seconds, pure O_2	5.12 ppm
60 seconds, pure O_2	9.20 ppm
120 seconds, pure O_2	14.08 ppm

Figure 4.1: Dissolved oxygen levels with various aeration times in 20 liters of wort. 18.7 °P wort at 75° F (24° C). Pure oxygen injection at 1 liter per minute using a 0.5 micron sintered stone.

To demonstrate the effect of varying dissolved oxygen levels on fermentation, White Labs then pitched White Labs WLP001 at a rate of 12 million cells per milliliter into the worts from the dissolved oxygen tests. Figure 4.2 shows that wort samples around 3 and 5 ppm of oxygen did not attenuate as fully as the other samples, which attenuated a full degree Plato over the shaken sample. Increasing the oxygen level past 9 ppm did increase the pace of fermentation slightly for the first three days, but both beers ended up at the same terminal gravity.

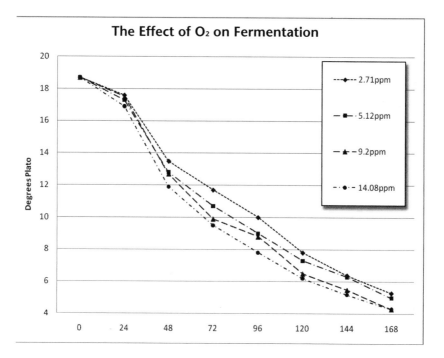

Figure 4.2: Comparison of how oxygen levels (ppm) affect fermentation progress over time (hours). 18.7 °P wort starting at 75° F (24° C).

Homebrewers are not the only brewers struggling to figure out how much oxygen to add to their wort. White Labs research has shown that many small breweries still overaerate or underaerate (Parker, 2008). White Labs checked wort aeration practices at a dozen commercial breweries and found the following dissolved oxygen levels:

Wort Volume (bbl)	O₂ Flow Rate (L/min)	O₂ Duration (minutes)	Wort Gravity (°P)	Dissolved Oxygen (ppm)
40	6	40	12.5	5.00
15	6	45	13.2	5.42
15	12	75-80	25.5	5.50
10	6	35	12.3	5.85
40	7	40	12.3	6.20
15	7	40	12.7	6.54
10	7	35	12.5	7.20
10	6	30	14.4	8.10
10	7	30-40	12.0	8.25
20	7	20	12.8	9.00
15	5	90	12.7	24.40
10	6	25-30	12.8	35.80

Figure 4.3: Sample of craft brewery dissolved oxygen levels (Parker, 2008).

Clearly very few brewers are achieving the recommended 8 to 10 ppm. None of these breweries measured the actual dissolved oxygen in their wort. Most were using a flow meter, introducing pure oxygen inline, and then estimating the dissolved oxygen level based on the wort fill time.

Further testing showed that by enhancing the oxygen levels to bring them into the recommended range, the number of cells grown increased significantly improved fermentation speed, in some cases finishing 24 to 48 hours earlier (Figure 4.4).

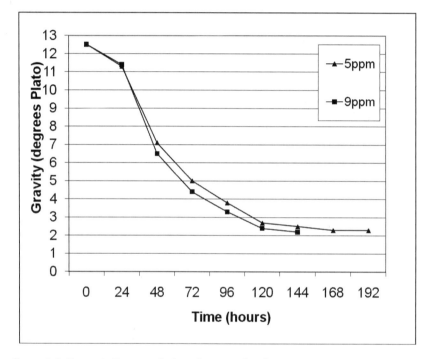

Figure 4.4: Fermentation speed of one brewery showing current versus oxygen-enhanced wort. The higher-oxygen wort reached terminal gravity 24 to 48 hours sooner than the lower-oxygen wort (Parker, 2008).

White Labs also investigated the results of chronic underoxygenation. Figure 4.5 compares the fermentation performance for yeast that had undergone multiple generation fermentations at a dissolved oxygen level of 5 ppm. By the fifth generation, the fermentation displayed a significant increase in lag time, an increase in the time to complete fermentation, and a higher terminal gravity than the earlier-generation fermentations.

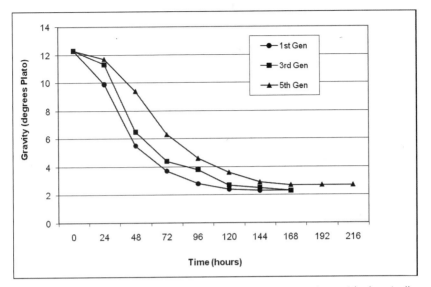

Figure 4.5: Fermentation performance of various yeast generations with chronically depleted oxygen resources (Parker, 2008).

The takeaway from this study is not only that proper oxygen levels are required for good fermentation, but that underaeration has an impact on yeast for re-use. Not only does a lack of oxygen result in less yeast, it results in yeast that do not perform as well in the next fermentation. Without access to ample resources to build up cell walls, fewer cells have the glycogen reserves and cell membranes that can withstand the stress of fermentation and the alcoholic, low pH environment of beer (Priest and Campbell, 2003).

High-Gravity Beers

As mentioned earlier, the specific gravity of the wort affects the yeast and changes fermentation character in various ways. One way brewers try to cope with higher-gravity wort is through higher cell counts and wort aeration prior to fermentation. If it is a very high-gravity wort, more than 1.092 (22 °P), you must aerate with pure oxygen, as air will not provide a high enough level of dissolved oxygen.

Unfortunately, that still might not be enough for beers higher than 1.083 (20 °P). For high-gravity beers, adding a second dose of oxygen between 12 and 18 hours can help fermentation speed and attenuation (O'Conner-Cox and Ingledew, 1990). The yeast quickly takes up this oxygen and uses it for cell membrane maintenance and the production of some needed intermediary compounds. Research also indicates the addition of oxygen (some say more than 7 ppm, some say more than 12 ppm), at 12 hours increases fermentation speed by 33 percent and decreases flavor compounds such as diacetyl and acetaldehyde (Jones, et al., 2007). Why wait until 12 hours? You are waiting for the yeast to complete at least one cell division. There is little or no benefit from additional aeration before the yeast has had a chance to divide at least once.

You might also consider adjusting your pitching rate and temperature. For a 1.106 (25 °P) wort, the optimal pitching rate is 35 million cells per milliliter or a rate of 1.4 million/ml/°P (D'Amore, 1991). At 48 hours into fermentation, after yeast growth is complete, raise the temperature to 77° F (25° C) for ale or 68° F (20° C) for lager. The rise in temperature keeps the yeast working at their maximum.

Fermentation Systems

We can ferment beer in any container, as long as it can hold liquid, right? You can use all sorts of vessels, in all different volumes and in all different dimensions, but not all fermentors are created equal. Today the common fermentation vessels in use span the range from plastic buckets to high-tech commercial-sized cylindroconical fermentors.

Why does it make a difference which type of fermentation system you use? Ferment the same beer in two different types of fermentors, and more often than not, you will get two different beers. The fluid mechanics of fermentation are unique to each type of fermentor. A brewery using two different types of fermentors will find it gets two different fermentation results. The results in some cases differ more widely than in others. Most of the time, if the fermentors are of the same general shape and size, the results are close enough that the brewer can blend the two beers into one commercially acceptable product.

Can a brewer tweak the fermentations to make the beers turn out the same? That is possible, but it usually takes alterations in fermentation procedure, and sometimes it even requires adjustments in wort production. Let us look at two drastically different-sized batches to illustrate a point. If you ferment a 10-hectoliter batch at 70° F (21° C), you might need to ferment a 20-liter version at 66° F (19° C) to get the same ester profile. Fermentor characteristics such as hydrostatic pressure, the saturation point of certain gasses, temperature gradients, and dead spots all make it necessary to use a lower temperature in a plastic bucket versus a large conical fermentor. You might think this does not apply at your brewery—since most commercial breweries never ferment in plastic buckets—but differences in fermentor design can impact fermentation. Often when a brewery adds new fermentors, it needs to experiment with different fermentation conditions until the beers produced are identical. Sierra Nevada head brewer Steve Dressler said that when the company opened its newest brewery in 1997, it took a month of testing to match the flavor in the new fermentors. The brewery found that the fermentor size was a greater variable than anticipated. It also investigated fermenting with top pressure, different aeration schemes, and pitching rates before it could get the desired fermentation character. Often brewers do not anticipate the variations between different fermentors. We recommend running test batches with any new fermentors.

Homebrewing Fermentors

The vast majority of homebrewers make beer in approximately 20-liter batches using plastic buckets or glass carboys. Many homebrewers start with plastic buckets but eventually migrate to glass carboys because they are easier to keep free of contamination. Unfortunately, glass carboys are heavy and are dangerous when wet. Glass carboys have seriously injured more than a few homebrewers when broken. Plastic buckets are more prone to contamination because the plastic is quite soft and easily scratched. Scratches in the plastic can harbor and hide contamination from cleaning and sanitizing regimes. As long as the brewer regularly replaces his buckets, they work fine. A recent addition to the homebrew scene is a carboy made from plastic called the Better-Bottle. Made from PET, this fermentor is less susceptible to scratching than a plastic bucket, is lighter-weight than glass, and is essentially unbreakable. It is a good compromise between two popular old favorites.

Homebrewers also ferment in all sorts of other vessels, from food-grade barrels to trash cans to right in the boiling kettle. A number of homebrewers are even experimenting with open fermentations by taking the lids off their plastic buckets. Homebrewers are creative and many are tremendously passionate about their hobby. Some use small versions of professional conical fermentors. Some models come with high-tech heating and cooling, racking ports, sanitary fittings, and more.

Figure 4.6: Typical homebrew fermentors: Better Bottle, plastic bucket, glass carboy. Photos courtesy of MoreBeer.com.

Figure 4.7: Homebrew-sized, high-tech, cylindroconical fermentors with thermoelectric cooling/heating and other options. Photos courtesy of MoreBeer.com.

Homebrewers often use stainless Cornelius kegs, once used by soft drink producers, to serve their homebrew. Some even choose to ferment in these vessels. The benefits are durability and the ability to make closed transfers. The drawback is the size and dimensions of the vessel. Its tall narrow shape results in fermentation characteristics different from those of most other homebrew-sized fermentors. The 5-gallon size also makes it impossible to produce a full five gallons of finished beer without diluting with water, because there is insufficient headspace. Still, brewers that use them for fermentation seem to like it. If you try it, make sure to figure out some way to relieve the buildup of CO_2 pressure during fermentation. While the vessel is quite strong, a high enough pressure can kill the yeast. Even if the pressure does not reach fatal levels, elevated CO_2 pressure may decrease yeast growth, lower ester production, and increase diacetyl and acetaldehyde production.

Commercial Fermentors

Breweries historically used open wooden fermentors, open stone fermentors, and open copper fermentors. Eventually they started using stainless steel tanks that were still open to the atmosphere. These tanks were much easier to keep clean and sanitize than wood or other materials. In open fermentors, yeast act quickly, and brewers can easily harvest yeast from the top. (See "Top Cropping" in the "Yeast Handling" section, pp. 149-152)

It is still somewhat rare in the United States, but there are a growing number of craft breweries using open fermentation. Sierra Nevada maintains some of its original open fermentors and uses them for specialty beers. It produces the famous Bigfoot Barleywine-Style Ale in 100-barrel open fermentors. These are almost ten times smaller than its largest fermentors, but Sierra Nevada believes the fermentations in the smaller, open fermentors give more character and uniqueness to the beer. The same is true for Jolly Pumpkin Artisan Ales, where owner Ron Jeffries strives to create beers of unique character. Anchor Brewery in San Francisco says open fermentation is critical to the character of Anchor Steam Beer.

The shallow depth of open fermentors, the ready access to atmospheric oxygen, and even the square corners of some open fermentors have

Figure 4.8: Open fermentation at Magic Hat Brewery, South Burlington, Vermont. Photo courtesy of Teri Fahrendorf.

an effect on the character of the beer. Without a doubt, the same wort fermented in a cylindroconical fermentor would not taste the same.

Today, most professional breweries use cylindroconical tanks (Figure 4.9). These are much taller than they are wide, are made of stainless steel, and have a conical bottom and an enclosed top. It is easy to see why the business of brewing moved to cylindroconical fermentors, because they have many advantages.

- They require less floor space, which is important when you pay rent by the square foot.
- You can use clean-in-place systems (CIP), which are lot easier than humans with scrub brushes.
- Cylindroconical fermentors offer good hygiene, since they are sealed from the environment.
- The conical bottom and vertical nature take advantage of fluid dynamics to ensure good mixing and rapid fermentation.
- To collect yeast, just wait, and then open a valve on the bottom.
- They are usually jacketed, so controlling temperature is just a button away.

Figure 4.9: Cylindroconical fermentors at Goose Island Beer Company. Photo courtesy of Peter Symons.

One of the early selling points of cylindroconical tanks was that a brewer could use them for both fermentation and conditioning once the yeast had dropped. We rarely see that today, as most small breweries use separate conditioning tanks, but this is one of the selling points now associated with the homebrew versions of cylindroconical tanks.

The most interesting aspect of these fermentors is their geometry. The more vertical the fermentor, the faster the fermentation. The fluid dynamics of the cone create CO_2 bubble movement from the bottom of the cone up through the center of the tank. The taller the tank, the larger the bubble formed as it reaches for the surface. The movement of CO_2 helps carry the beer to the top, where it migrates downward again along the sides of the fermentor. The position of the cooling jackets can even enhance this effect and can affect the fermentation rate.

Fuller's Brewery in London now use cylindroconical fermentors, but it and many other British breweries used to use tanks with a "dropping system" (Figure 4.10). The brewer would transfer the wort to an open tank, then after 24 hours would "drop" the wort to another tank below. This helped remove cold break and picked up oxygen for the early stages of fermentation. The tank was shallow, and a "Griffin slide" would direct the yeast from the top of the tank into collection vessels.

Figure 4.10: Looking down into a dropping vessel at Fuller's Brewery. Photo courtesy of Peter Symons.

During the mid-nineteenth century, brewing was booming in Burton upon Trent, England. The Bass Brewery was in Burton, and it developed a method of fermentation and yeast collection called the Burton Union system. The brewers placed a series of wooden barrels in line, with each containing a swan neck coming out the top of the barrel. The swan neck emptied into a trough. The beer fermented in the barrels, and the CO_2 from fermentation pushed the excess yeast crop up through the swan neck, where it collected in the trough and allowed the beer to return to the barrel. Back then, this was thought to be a great way to "cleanse" the beer.

Figure 4.11: Marston's Burton Union system. Photo courtesy of Matthew Brynildson.

Unfortunately, this was an expensive system, since brewing commercial beer volumes required many small wooden casks and employing a cooper to service them. Bass used this system until the 1980s and it is almost extinct now. Marston's in Burton still uses it to ferment about 10 percent of Marston's Pedigree (Figure 4.11). This collects enough yeast to pitch all the wort made in the brew house and keeps tradition and flavor alive. Even this modest amount of production in Burton Unions required millions of dollars in investment and ongoing maintenance.

Firestone Walker Brewery of Paso Robles, California, uses a modified version of the Burton Union, which it calls Firestone Union (Figures 4.12-4.14). Instead of the complex swan neck and trough, it uses flexible tubing running to buckets. There is still the expense of the barrels, but it

Figure 4.12: Firestone Union system. Photo courtesy of Arie Litman.

Figure 4.13: Filling the Firestone Union system. Photo courtesy of Matthew Brynildson.

Figure 4.14: The Firestone Union system pushes brown yeast out of the barrels, resulting in cleaner beer. Photo courtesy of Matthew Brynildson.

is far less expensive than a Burton Union. Brewer Matt Brynildson says that the brewery experiences better attenuation, faster diacetyl reduction, and excellent flavor development in the barrels. The beers start fermentation in stainless cylindroconical fermentors under controlled temperatures for proper flavor development. After 24 hours, the brewers transfer the actively fermenting beer to the unions, which are not temperature controlled. Although the fermentation may reach high temperatures, the first 24 hours under temperature control ensure any warm fermentation in the barrels does not result in typical warm fermentation characteristics. Fermentation in the unions pushes a considerable amount of brown yeast from the barrels, leaving a cleaner beer. The beer finishes fermentation and diacetyl reduction (maturation) in the barrels, before it is transferred to a temperature-controlled stainless tank for cold stabilization and further yeast removal.

The Yorkshire square fermentation system was once popular in Northern England, although we rarely see it used today. Traditionally

Figure 4.15: The Black Sheep Brewery in Masham, North Yorkshire, uses a modern, round Yorkshire square made of stainless steel. Photos courtesy of Black Sheep Brewery.

the vessels were square or rectangular and made of slate, with a collection deck above the wort level. During fermentation, yeast rises up through holes on the deck where the brewer can harvest it. Very few breweries still use this system, as it is expensive to build and maintain. The Black Sheep Brewery in Masham, North Yorkshire, pioneered the use of a round version made of stainless steel, which it believes provides a distinctive bitterness and a silky mouthfeel to the beers (Figure 4.15).

What is the future of fermentation systems? Large stainless steel tanks are expensive and require dangerous chemicals to keep clean, so we might see more inexpensive, disposable fermentation systems in the future. The biopharmaceutical industry has embraced sterile bags for fermentation. They are used for many reasons, such as to rely less on cleaning and sanitation procedures. Bag-lined beer serving tanks already exist, and you-brew stores in North America use disposable bag-lined fermentation systems. Perhaps these liners could even be made biodegradable?

Another innovation may be stirred fermentations. Stirred fermentors are popular in the biopharmaceutical industry for their faster fermentation, but the beer industry has shied away from them because of the fear of oxygen pickup and ester formation. More breweries have been looking at these recently, and there is a rising interest in stirred fermentors for improved fermentation speed, but at what cost to beer flavor?

Use of Antifoam

Fermentation generates a lot of CO_2 and that creates a lot of foam. This is a particular problem when a brewer is trying to make the most of his fermentor capacity, leaving very little headspace. Ensuring that you have enough headspace can be expensive, since some fermentors would need more than 25 percent extra capacity to accommodate the foaming, so the option most breweries look at is adding antifoam.

Brewers usually add antifoam near the end of the boil. This sanitizes it and mixes it into the wort. Most of these products are silicone-based, and you would add about 5 milliliters per U.S. barrel or 1 milliliter per 20 liters. Besides allowing a more complete fermentor fill and preventing blowoff (which will also improve hop utilization), antifoam products can actually improve head retention by preventing foam-positive proteins from denaturing in the foam. At the end of fermentation and before packaging, the brewer either filters out the antifoam or allows it to settle out via gravity.

Given these positive attributes, why do many breweries avoid anti-foam? Many brewers do not want to add anything to their beer other than malt, hops, water, and yeast. For these brewers, antifoam is not an option. Some brewers also worry about the effect of antifoam on yeast health, although it appears that antifoam products currently on the market have little or no impact on yeast health or performance.

Fermentation Temperatures

When yeast ferment beer, they create heat from the energy of metabolism. The heat of fermentation will raise the wort temperature, and if the temperature is not contained, yeast can:

- Die from extreme heat
- Create off-flavors
- Mutate

One of the brewer's main jobs is to control the temperature of fermentation. In a small brewery or home brewery, this can be quite easy. In large fermentation systems, this takes more complicated engineering.

What temperature is best for fermentation? It depends on the type of yeast strain, the type of beer, and the flavors the brewer is looking for. Traditionally, brewers ferment ales around 68° F (20° C), and lagers around 50° F (10° C). However, these are not the temperatures the yeast prefer. Ale strains grow fastest at 90° F (32° C) and lager strains at 80° F (27° C), so why do we ferment our beers at lower temperatures? At higher fermentation temperatures the yeast ferment too fast and grow too much, and can create flavors we do not want in our beer, such as fusel alcohols. Over the course of brewing history, brewers and yeast have settled on a temperature range that is not too low for the yeast, but low enough that it moderates cell growth rate and improves beer flavor.

Temperature Differences for Lager and Ale Strains

Lager strains cannot tolerate the same high temperatures as ale strains. In fact, lager strains die at much lower temperatures than ale strains, so it is important to keep lager strains cooler during handling, shipping, and storage. One laboratory method for differentiating ale and lager yeast takes advantage of this fact by incubating yeast cells above 90° F (32° C). If the cells grow, they are ale yeast.

Let us talk about ale yeast in more detail. From a flavor perspective, it is important to keep fermentation at the correct temperatures, usually around 68° F (20° C). This is not a cool temperature to humans; most people would have difficulty telling the difference between a beer at 68° F and one at 72° F (20° C and 22° C). However, for a yeast strain submerged in beer, that is a big difference. Remember that yeast are single cells. A small difference in temperature is something they readily notice. If the temperature rises up from 68° F (20° C), the cells will speed up their metabolism until it reaches the cell's maximum. If the temperature continues to rise, the cells begin to express heat shock proteins to protect their cell membranes. The same happens with a significant temperature drop from 68° F (20° C). The cells switch from metabolism to expressing heat shock proteins to protect their cell membrane. Do not let the name fool you, yeast express heat shock proteins in response to stress, and that stress can come from a number of environmental factors. These proteins help keep other proteins from unfolding under the stressful condition. Unfortunately, expressing heat shock proteins takes away from the cell's ability to express other proteins needed for cell division, fermentation, or other cell functions.

From a brewer's perspective, the lower the fermentation temperature, the slower the yeast activity. Excessively low temperatures result in slow, sluggish, and possibly stalled fermentations. Higher temperatures result in increased yeast activity—up to a point. Excessively high temperatures, above 95° F (35° C) for ale yeast, will halt fermentation. Keep in mind that higher fermentation temperatures also increase production of secondary metabolites and flavor active compounds.

White Labs used gas chromatography to compare two beers from the same wort, both fermented with WLP001 California Ale Yeast. The lab maintained one fermentation at 66° F (19° C) and the other at 75° F (24° C), a temperature commonly found in many breweries.

Compound	Perception Threshold	66° F (19° C)	75° F (24° C)
Ethanol	1.4% ABV	4.74% ABV	5.04% ABV
1-Propanol	600 ppm	23.78 ppm	22.76 ppm
Ethyl acetate	30 ppm	22.51 ppm	33.45 ppm
Isoamyl alcohol	70 ppm	108.43 ppm	114.92 ppm
Total diacetyl	150 ppb	7.46 ppb	8.23 ppb
Total 2,3-pentanedione	900 ppb	5.09 ppb	3.17 ppb
Acetaldehyde	10 ppm	7.98 ppm	152.19 ppm

Figure 4.16: Gas chromatography comparison of two beers from the same wort and yeast, fermented at different temperatures.

The warmer fermentation shows a small increase in production of ethanol, fusel alcohols, and esters, but in sensory analysis, the beers tasted very different. The main flavor difference was a substantial increase in acetaldehyde, 10.5 times higher than the perception threshold.

Yeast make most flavor compounds in the first 72 hours of fermentation, so this is the most critical time for temperature control. If the temperature is too low, your fermentation may take a long time to get started. If it's too high, the yeast will produce lots of flavor compounds. First-generation yeast are particularly susceptible to pitching temperature.

Near the end of fermentation, temperature control is still very important. If you are cooling your fermentors at a steady rate (such as a homebrewer relying on a refrigerator or a cold ambient temperature) and not taking into account changes in yeast heat production, fermentation can stop early. Yeast slow down and produce less heat towards the end of fermentation. If your cooling does not adjust for this decrease, the yeast can sense this temperature drop, causing them to slow or stop fermenting. This can result in a higher than anticipated final gravity, along with the yeast failing to clean up some of the intermediary compounds of fermentation. This tends to be more of a problem with lager brewing, where temperatures are already low and cooling equipment capacities are higher. However, brewers fermenting ales at an aggressively low temperature, with the aim of a cleaner beer, can easily run into this issue as well.

When working with a proper pitch of healthy yeast, the optimal starting temperature for the majority of fermentations is just a couple degrees (1 to 3° F/1 to 2° C) below your target fermentation temperature. Pitch the yeast and slowly raise or allow the temperature to rise to your target fermentation temperature over the course of 18 to 36 hours. Once it reaches fermentation temperature, hold the temperature steady until at least the last one-third to one-fourth of fermentation. At that time raise the temperature several degrees or more (4 to 10° F/2 to 5° C) over the course of a day or two. The yeast have already produced most of the flavor compounds, so there is little risk of increased flavors. The benefit is that the higher temperature near the end of fermentation aids yeast activity. The yeast are more likely to attenuate fully and reduce intermediary compounds produced earlier in fermentation. The rise in activity will also aid in driving off some volatile compounds, such as sulfur. This is an especially good trick in lager brewing, where the cold, slower fermentations tend to retain more of the volatile aromatic compounds.

Of course, if your fermentation temperature is already quite high—as in an extreme Belgian-style beer fermentation—you will want to watch out that you do not heat stress the yeast.

Fermentation Temperature Control

Most commercial breweries now use cylindroconical fermentors and control their temperature with cooling jackets filled with glycol or another fluid. They monitor fermentation temperature at one or more points in the fermentor, and they regulate the flow of coolant to maintain the desired temperature. Tanks can have multiple jackets, providing more capacity and the ability to control different portions of the fermentor at will. It is particularly important to have the cone jacketed, as the yeast will spend time in the cone when settling.

The ability to control the jackets at different temperatures can be advantageous. For example, with a separate temperature setting for the cone, the brewer can cool the cone before dropping the fermentation temperature of the tank. This encourages flocculation and ensures the cone is cold enough to keep the yeast from building up too much heat as it sits in the cone until harvested.

It is important for the brewer to know where the fermentor jackets begin and end, and to sample the beer temperature regularly. Not only can a gauge be wrong, but stratification and dead spots can cause temperatures to vary across points in a fermentor. This next story illustrates the problem. A brewer in Texas called to talk about off-flavors in his beer. He used multiple yeast strains at his brewery and was getting a peculiar, "earthy" off-flavor with just one strain. His assumption was that there must be something wrong with the strain. However, it was not a normal characteristic of the yeast, and other breweries were not experiencing the same off-flavor. Since it was the middle of a hot summer in Texas, our suspicion was that it had something to do with the heat. The brewer soon found the problem. When the fermentors were full, the top of the fermenting beer was above the last cooling jacket. The yeast strain in question is an excellent top cropper, and it was determined to stay on top of the beer. Unfortunately, during the hot Texas summer, without cooling, the top of the beer was too hot. The yeast would rise to the surface of the beer, get cooked to death, and then drop back down, adding autolysis flavors. The other yeast strains in use behaved differently. They were falling to the bottom quickly, never staying long at the top, so the same flavors did not develop. The brewer solved the problem by making slightly smaller batches of the beer during the summer to keep the yeast within the jacketed cooling zone.

Temperature Control for the Homebrewer

Homebrewers use a variety of temperature control methods, ranging from high-tech thermoelectric cooling to a "do nothing and pray" method. It is a shame that most rely on the luck of the ambient temperature to control fermentation. One of the greatest things a brewer can do to improve his beer is manage the fermentation temperature. This is far more important than using fancy fermentors or even all-grain brewing. The experienced extract brewer with temperature control and an excellent grasp of fermentation will almost always outshine the all-grain brewer relying on luck for temperature control. Lack of proper temperature control makes it harder for the yeast to do what you want them to do. If you make it easy on them, the yeast will reward you with the flavors you desire.

The next step up from only brewing when the weather report indicates it will not be too hot or too cold for the next week or two is to utilize natural cooling. First, try to pick a location for your fermentor that is as close to your desired fermentation temperature as possible. Interior walls, closets, and basements tend to have more stable temperatures, as they are farther from the exterior changes in the weather. Keep an eye out for heating/cooling ducts or radiators as well. Blowing hot air on a fermentor by day and turning it off at night can ruin a fermentation, because yeast do not cope well with big swings in temperature.

To deal with hot ambient temperatures, many homebrewers put their fermentor in a water bath and then add ice as necessary to keep the temperature down. Sometimes this is in a plastic bucket or even the family bathtub. The benefit of this method is that it is cheap and there are no moving parts to break. The big drawback is that it requires a great deal of attention and lots of practice to keep the temperatures where you want them, especially near the end of fermentation when the yeast are no longer generating as much heat. However, if time is abundant and you enjoy fiddling with your fermentor as much as possible, this method can work.

Another nice thing about the water bath method is that it also works for heating. All you need is a nominal investment in an aquarium heater. When using a heater, keep a few things in mind. The combination of water and electricity is deadly. Always use a ground-fault circuit inter-rupter (GFCI) outlet for your heater and leave a loop in the cord lower than the outlet, to keep water from running into it. When purchasing a heater for the water bath, you will want to get one that is completely submersible or come up with some other way of mixing the heated water. Placing a submersible heater near the bottom develops convection cur-rents, which mix the water. Sizing the heater is simple. It takes 0.1018 watts over 24 hours to provide 8.34 BTU, which is the amount of energy required to heat one gallon of water by 1° F (0.5° C). If you believe your setup requires about 15° F (8° C) of heat input over 24 hours, and the total volume of your fermentor plus the water bath is 20 gallons (76 liters), you will need a heater of at least 30.54 watts.

24-hour heat input x total liquid volume x 0.1018 = wattage required

15 x 20 x 0.1018 = 30.54 W

However, the reality is that you will need a larger heater than that. These heaters are not 100 percent efficient at converting electricity into heat, and the heater rating may not realistically represent its actual output. You have a fair amount of leeway in selecting a proper wattage heater, and it is difficult to get too big a heater. However, if you get a lot more heater than you need and the internal controller should stick, you could end up killing your yeast with temperatures exceeding their upper limit.

Evaporative cooling is another popular method of countering heat in homebrew-sized fermentors. In this method the brewer sets the fer-mentor in a tray of water and drapes a cloth covering over the fermentor, with the end hanging into the water. The wicking effect carries water up the fabric, where it evaporates. The conversion of the liquid water to a gaseous state takes considerable energy, which helps cool the fermentor. Some cloth materials work much better than others. Our advice is to avoid manmade fabrics and go with cotton. Highly textured fabrics, such as terrycloth, may work better or worse than low-nap fabrics. A small fan blowing on the cloth will help increase the speed of cooling, but this method is not very effective when the humidity is high. Again, the big drawback to this method is controlling temperatures precisely over the entire course of fermentation. It takes a lot of attention to keep the temperature from swinging by several degrees over the course of a day. That lack of precision is just not good enough if you want to make the best beer possible.

Both heating and cooling get significantly easier if you add a switching temperature controller. They come in all sizes and types, from analog to digital, with various settings and degrees of accuracy. The great thing about a controller is that it automatically adjusts the heating or cooling when the yeast generate more or less heat during different phases of fermentation. The drawback for the frugal homebrewer is cost, but most homebrewers, once they acquire one, believe they are well worth the investment.

With a controller, heating becomes much easier. Homebrew shops sell special heating wraps, or you can even use a heating pad. You do not want to use any device that concentrates heat in one small area, because as the heater cycles, it can potentially crack a glass carboy.

Homebrewers can easily cool their fermentors using a spare refrigerator or freezer and a temperature controller. Many homebrewers quickly realize the value of having a spare refrigerator in the garage. Some homebrewers prefer to use a freezer instead of a refrigerator. Freezers often have better insulation than refrigerators and come in configurations that might provide more usable space. Avoid the top-loading freezers, unless you have a very strong back. Loading fermentors into such a freezer can be challenging at best. The main drawback to freezers is that they are not designed to run at typical fermentation temperatures. Running freezers at ale temperatures, and even lager temperatures, usually results in a humidity problem. The freezer, with its high cooling capacity and good insulation, ends up not running frequently enough to deal with the humidity. Moisture builds up in the freezer and rust follows. Many homebrewers with freezers spend money and time dealing with the moisture problem. (DampRid or a spare computer fan to move the interior air around can help.) Another issue with excessive cooling capacity is the potential to make the fermentation temperature vacillate by applying too much cooling too quickly.

Many homebrewers initially think of using a freezer because they want to lager beer at near freezing temperatures—32° F (0° C). However, that is still warmer than a freezer normally runs, and it still is not the best option. Most refrigerators can get cold enough to lager a beer properly.

When running a refrigerator or freezer on a controller, it is important to avoid short cycling the compressor. Short cycling is running the refrigerator or freezer's cooling cycle, shutting it off, and then starting it up again before pressures have had a chance to equalize in the system. This can damage the compressor and will shorten its service life. Some controllers have an anti-short cycle setting, which delays restarting the compressor for a set amount of time. This is a great option for those buying a controller for a refrigerator or freezer. If you have a controller without this feature, you want to make sure you are not leaving the controller probe hanging in the air by itself. Use the mass of the fermenting beer to help avoid rapid cycling of the controller, either by attaching the probe to the outside of the fermentor or by using a thermowell.

There are a number of additional, very creative ways to cool or heat a fermentor. One of the more interesting methods is the use of solid-state thermoelectric cooling and heating on the homebrew-sized cylindro-conical fermentors from MoreBeer of Concord, California. The company has built both heating and cooling into a device that is attached to the outside of its fermentors. The homebrewer, much like his commercial counterpart, just needs to select the appropriate temperature on the controller. The main drawback to this method is the cost.

In all of these methods, it is critical that you measure the temperature of the beer. You want to control the beer temperature, not the air temperature. Many homebrewers make the mistake of seeing a recommended fermentation temperature and thinking that is the temperature of the room where they place the fermentor. The air temperature in a room can vary widely throughout the day. It can even change dramatically in just a few minutes, but that does not mean the beer is fermenting at the same temperature. The larger the batch of beer, the longer it takes the beer temperature to change from the surrounding air. Conversely, the fermentor may be warming up due to yeast activity, but the temperature of a batch of beer does little to change the temperature of a large room or refrigerator.

There are several ways to measure the temperature of the beer. The stick-on thermometer strips work quite well. They are fairly accurate, but they deteriorate over time and eventually need to be replaced. If you are using a temperature controller, a popular option is a thermowell. The thermowell is either built as part of the fermentor or is inserted through a stopper into the beer. You place the probe from the controller inside the thermowell, and it accurately measures the temperature of the beer. A less expensive and less invasive option is just taping the controller probe to the outside of the fermentor. If you do this, you must cover the probe with some sort of insulation. This can be anything from several layers of bubble wrap, to a folded-up cloth, to a block of Styrofoam. Styrofoam is an excellent option, as it is usually free and highly effective. With the exposed side of the probe covered, the reading will match the temperature of the beer inside the fermentor very closely. As long as there is any fermentation activity in the fermentor, the temperature will be the same throughout the beer.

Many temperature controllers have settings for differential, which is the difference between the set point of the controller and the point where it shuts off or turns on. For fermentation, you generally want to use as tight a setting as the control allows. A 1° F (0.5° C) differential setting is best, but only if you are measuring the temperature of the beer. With some controllers, a very small differential is possible. Using a setting of less than 1° F (0.5° C) can cause the controller to cycle rapidly. If your controller does not have protection against a short cycle, then increase the differential to avoid rapid cycling. Some controllers also allow you to control both heating and cooling from the same controller, which is a nice option, especially in areas with extreme summers and winters.

Optimizing Fermentation Flavor

Yeast contribute much of the aroma and flavor to beer. Esters, fusel alcohols, aldehydes, and other compounds blend together with ethanol, carbon dioxide, and even mouthfeel to make up the character of a beer, and all of these are properties of yeast fermentation. In fact, even with the exact same ingredients, different fermentations yield different results. This happens because so many enzymatic pathways are involved in yeast fermentation. Environmental factors not only affect which genes are active, but also how actively the yeast cells grow, the health of the cells, what sugars they consume, and many other things. Everything we do for yeast, from temperature to nutrition, has a big impact on yeast growth. It should come as no surprise that one way a brewer can optimize fermentation flavors is to understand and control yeast growth.

Fermentation Compound	Flavor or Aroma
Ethyl acetate	fruity, solvent
Higher alcohols	headache
Isoamyl acetate	banana, pear
Acetaldehyde	green apple (green beer)
Diacetyl	butter
Hydrogen sulfide	rotten egg
DMS or DMSO	vegetal, cooked corn
Phenols	spicy, pepper, clove, smoke, medicinal

Figure 4.17: Flavor contributions of fermentation compounds.

An important part of controlling yeast growth is knowing how much yeast you are adding to your fermentation. Different pitching rates will lead to different amounts of cell growth. The growth rate affects the quantity and makeup of flavor compounds. If you add 10 units of yeast, and at the end of fermentation you have 75 units of yeast, you will have a different quantity or set of flavor compounds. More cell growth usually results in more flavor compounds. This will come up again when we discuss pitching rates, because the pitching rate will also have an impact on how much the yeast grows.

Increasing	Ester	Fusel Alcohol
OG	⇑	⇑
FAN (high or low)	⇑	⇑
Lipids	⇓	⇑
pH	−	⇑
Aeration	⇓	⇑
Zinc	⇑	⇑
Temperature	⇑	⇑
Agitation/Stirring	⇑	⇑
Head Pressure	⇓	⇓
Multiple Fermentor Fills (non-aerated wort)	⇑	⇑
Multiple Fermentor Fills (aerated wort)	⇓	⇑
Pitching Rate	⇓	⇑

Figure 4.18: Increase of various fermentation factors and how they impact ester and fusel production in beer. (Laere, et al., 2008)

Flavor Compound	Flavor Threshold in Beer	Typical Level in Beer	Typical Level in Wine	Typical Level in Whiskey
Ethyl acetate	20-40 mg/L	10-50 mg/L	<150 mg/L desired	100-200 mg/L
Ethyl hexanoate	0.15-0.25 mg/L	0.07-0.5 mg/L	0.3-1.2 mg/L	
Isoamyl acetate	1-2 mg/L	0.5-5 mg/L	0.1-4 mg/L	2.5 mg/L
Caprylic acid	5-10 mg/L	2-8 mg/L		15 mg/L
2-phenyl ethanol	125 mg/L	25-40 mg/L		5-50 mg/L
n-Propanol	800 mg/L	10-100 mg/L	10-70 mg/L	
Amyl alcohol (2-Methyl-2-butanol)	50 mg/L	10-150 mg/L		100 mg/L
Isoamyl alcohol (3-Methyl-2-butanol)	70 mg/L	30-150 mg/L	6-490 mg/L	200 mg/L
4-vinyl guaiacol	0.3 mg/L	0.05-0.55 mg/L		
Glycerol	2500 mg/L	1400-3200 mg/L	2500-15000 mg/L	5000-15000 mg/L
Acetaldehyde	10-20 mg/L	2-20 mg/L	5-100 mg/L	2-3 mg/L
Diacetyl	0.07-0.15 mg/L	0.01-0.6 mg/L	0.02-0.6 mg/L	0.6 mg/L

Total SO₂	20 mg/L	10-100 mg/L		
H₂S	4 µg/l	1-200 µg/l	10-80 mg/L	
DMS	25-50 µg/l	20-150 µg/l	10-60 mg/L	
Acetic acid	60-120 mg/L	30-200 mg/L		30-50 mg/L
Ethanol (%)	1.5-2%	3-8%	5-15%	30-60%

Figure 4.19: Fermentation compounds and their flavor threshold in beer. Typical ranges in beer, wine, and whiskey (Meilgaard, 1975; Saison, et al., 2008; Reed, et al., 1991).

Yeast strain and condition also impact the hop character of a beer. For example, comparisons of White Labs California Ale (WLP001) and English Ale (WLP002) fermentation at the same pitching rate and temperature show the former results in a higher finished IBU level than the latter. Many factors determine the final IBUs of a beer, and yeast are a major player. Differences in the cell surface, cell size, pitching rates, growth rates, and flocculation characteristics all play a role in determining the amount of isomerized hop acids that make it through to the finished beer.

Fermentation Endgame

Attenuation

In brewing, attenuation is the measure of how completely the yeast fermented the wort, and it is usually expressed in a percentage. The more sugar the yeast break down during fermentation, the greater the attenuation.

To calculate attenuation, the brewer checks the specific gravity of the wort, with a hydrometer or other tool capable of measuring the density of the beer, before pitching the yeast and again post-fermentation. The specific gravity of pure water is 1.000 at 4° C, and wort has a higher density relative to water because of the sugars present. The more sugars dissolved in the wort, the higher the density of the solution. As the yeast consume the sugars, the density of the solution decreases. Brewers express the difference in the starting measurement and the ending measurement as a percentage of apparent attenuation. Most modern hydrometers have a specific gravity scale, but different industries have historically used other scales, such as Plato for brewing and Brix for winemaking. Any scale is acceptable, as long as the brewer uses the same scale for the measurements before and after fermentation.

You should always log the starting or original gravity (OG), the terminal or finishing gravity (FG), and any other specific gravity measurements, along with the dates and times of the measurements. A brewer can learn much about the progress and quality of fermentation by daily checks of the beer's specific gravity, although it is critical to ensure any sampling does not contaminate the beer. Once the gravity remains the same for three days in a row, fermentation is most likely complete. When measuring attenuation using specific gravity, you can calculate attenuation percentage using the following equation:

$$[(OG-FG)/(OG-1)] \times 100$$

For example, if the starting gravity is 1.060 and the finishing gravity is 1.012, then the apparent attenuation is 80 percent. We call this *apparent* attenuation, because alcohol is less dense than water and the presence of alcohol affects the reading post-fermentation. To obtain the real level of attenuation, the brewer must remove the alcohol and replace it with water. Usually it is only the larger breweries that go to such lengths to report the "actual" attenuation, while the attenuation most other brewers measure is "apparent" attenuation. In general, when a brewer mentions attenuation, the reference is to apparent attenuation, which is what we do in this book.

While it is possible for some fermentations to reach 100 percent or greater apparent attenuation, it is quite rare for a beer fermentation to consume all the sugars present and reach 100 percent real attenuation. Keep in mind that the presence of ethanol exaggerates the apparent attenuation due to ethanol having a specific gravity lower than water. A real attenuation of 100 percent is rare, because brewer's wort contains a complex mixture of carbohydrates, with many of them being unfermentable. Wort contains five fermentable sugars: glucose, fructose, sucrose, maltose, and maltotriose. Typically, the largest percentage is maltose, followed by maltotriose and glucose. Yeast cannot ferment dextrins, and yeast strains differ in their ability to ferment maltotriose. The attenuation range for brewer's yeast strains in beer is typically 65 to 85 percent. In contrast, wines often reach 100 percent attenuation, due to the simple sugars present. While complex carbohydrates result in a higher finishing gravity, they do not contribute to the residual sweetness of a beer. A well fermented beer with a lot of complex carbohydrates has a fuller mouthfeel but does not necessarily taste sweet. If there is an impression of sweetness in a completely attenuated beer, it is often the result of other factors, such as the presence of various alcohols and other flavor compounds.

Wort characteristics and fermentation conditions cause attenuation to vary; therefore, each yeast strain has a predicted attenuation range rather than a single attenuation number. Checking the current level of attenuation against the predicted range is one way to see if the yeast has completed, or is close to completing, fermentation. Being within the range is no guarantee that fermentation is 100 percent complete, but not being within the range (for the average wort) would be an indicator of a problem. Many brewers make the mistake of worrying about a beer before they even check attenuation. It is possible that the yeast strain will have already reached the expected attenuation level. The general rule is that the higher the starting gravity of a beer, the higher the final gravity. However, two worts of differing composition can reach different levels of attenuation, even with the same yeast and same starting gravity.

Checking attenuation is one simple step in creating consistent, high-quality beer. How will you know when fermentation has gone awry if you have not tracked the attenuation of successful batches? The level of attenuation is a key piece of knowledge when troubleshooting fermentation problems. All a brewer needs to do is a simple check of the specific gravity at the beginning and end of fermentation and perform some simple computations.

Flocculation

It is always possible that the yeast will refuse to drop or will flocculate too early. Some highly flocculent strains may drop prematurely, causing problems for the brewer. Why use a highly flocculent strain if it might result in underattenuated beer? Why use low flocculating yeast if it is a hassle to brew clear beer? In both cases, the answer is flavor. Some of the most difficult and temperamental strains can be the most interesting in terms of flavor.

In general, colder conditions favor flocculation, while higher levels of sugar, the presence of oxygen, and poor yeast health inhibit flocculation. In most cases, it is something the brewer, lab, or handler did over the life of the culture that caused a change in flocculation. Yeast do not decide on their own to change flocculation patterns. Any of the following can make a culture change flocculation patterns:

- Harvesting and storage techniques
- Mineral, nutrient, or oxygen deficiency
- Yeast mutation
- Wild yeast contamination
- Mycotoxin-contaminated malt

Regardless of a strain's flocculation level, lower beer temperatures result in a higher flocculation rate. More yeast drop out of solution at 40° F (4° C) as compared to 70° F (21° C), and more yeast drop out at 32° F (0° C) as compared to 40° F (4° C). Some yeast strains require two weeks or more at 40° F (4° C) to clear completely. The more flocculent a strain is, the warmer the temperature at which it is capable of floccula- tion. For example, a highly flocculent ale strain will flocculate well at 65° F (18° C). If a week or two at cold temperatures does not help, or you cannot wait that long for the beer to clear, your options include fining, filtering, centrifugation, or a combination of the three. Many brewing books describe filtering and centrifugation well, so we will not describe them in detail. The advantage to filtering is that it is fairly inexpensive, quick, and consistent, but it does expose the beer to potential contami- nation. Centrifugation allows you to control the process better, leaving behind more yeast if desired, but it tends to be expensive. Fining is cheap and effective, but the results can vary. Brewers must find the optimal fining dose for their beer. As finings rely on cross-linking, too little or too much fining agent can give poor results. Another common problem is adequately mixing the finings with the beer.

Your philosophy when adding finings should be to add only enough to accomplish your goal. If you plan to bottle-condition your beer, the concentration of yeast after fining can be quite low. Ales fined with isinglass typically contain fewer than 100,000 cells per milliliter, but you will want 1 million cells per milliliter of beer for proper and timely carbonation.

Isinglass is an effective yeast fining agent made from fish swim bladders. It is undernatured collagen with three collagen polypeptides associated in a triple helix structure. While gelatin is an alternative fining agent, it is not as effective as isinglass. Gelatin is denatured and is made up of single polypeptides.

There are many forms of isinglass on the market, including freeze-dried, paste, and liquid. Preparation and use of isinglass depends on the form of the product. You must properly hydrate isinglass for it to work. Pre-hydrolyzed isinglass is easy to use. At about 60° F (16° C) you blend it at high speed for a few minutes, let it sit for a half-hour, and it is ready to use. If you are using a product that is not pre-hydrolyzed, you need to make a properly acidified solution using sterile water and an organic acid. Adjust to about 2.5 pH and slowly stir in an appropriate amount of isinglass, usually about 0.5 percent by weight. Mix off and on for 30 minutes, then let sit for 24 hours at about 60° F (16° C). Once properly prepared, it should be a thick, translucent solution.

When you add the isinglass to beer, the higher pH of the beer causes the collagen to start to precipitate from solution. As it falls through the beer, the positively charged collagen electrostatically binds with the negatively charged yeast cells, pulling yeast to the bottom of the fermentor. Not all yeast will respond the same to fining, with some strains more or less affected. Ideally, you want to perform a test first to ensure you are using the right amount of fining agent and no more. Measure out equal samples of beer into 9-to-12-inch- (23- to 30-centimeter-) tall containers. Add measured amounts of finings to each. A good starting point is about one milliliter of isinglass per liter of beer. Once you have determined the most effective rate, you can scale up from there.

Diacetyl Rest

Yeast has the ability to reduce diacetyl enzymatically. During growth yeast produces acetolactate, the precursor for diacetyl. Later, during the stationary phase, yeast reabsorbs diacetyl and converts it to acetoin and subsequently to 2,3-butanediol. Both acetoin and 2,3-butanediol can escape the cell, but both have a high flavor threshold and contribute little in terms of flavor.

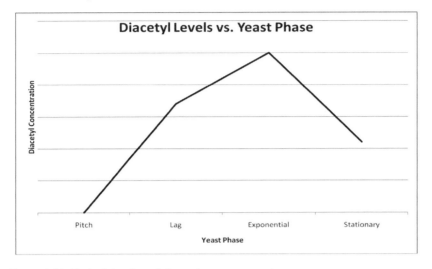

Figure 4.20: Typical timeline of diacetyl versus yeast phase.

Yeast health and yeast activity play a major role in diacetyl levels. Since temperature plays a major role in yeast activity, your control of temperature also affects diacetyl levels. As fermentation temperature increases, so does diacetyl production and reduction. Higher temperature results in faster yeast growth and more acetolactate. The higher the acetolactate peak, the higher the diacetyl peak, but this is not necessarily bad, since higher temperature also increases diacetyl reduction. A warm-fermented ale may have a higher diacetyl peak than a cold-fermented lager, but the reduction of diacetyl happens much faster at ale temperatures.

Most yeast strains, when healthy and active, will rapidly reduce diacetyl below flavor threshold given enough time and temperature. While lower yeast growth rates can reduce the amount of acetolactate produced, it can result in higher levels of diacetyl in the finished beer if the lower growth rate results in lackluster fermentation. It is often beers that ferment more slowly and produce less acetolactate that have diacetyl problems, since the yeast are still slowly producing acetolactate late into fermentation.

The key here, besides ensuring yeast health and vigorous fermentation, is to provide sufficient maturation time and temperature for diacetyl reduction in every beer. Do not separate the beer from the yeast before it has had an opportunity to reduce the intermediary compounds created during the bulk of fermentation. Separating the yeast from the beer too soon or cooling the beer early can leave a considerable amount of diacetyl and diacetyl precursors in the beer. Even though you might not taste diacetyl, the beer may still contain high levels of the diacetyl precursor acetolactate. Any oxygen pickup during transfers or packaging will most likely result in diacetyl, and once you remove the yeast, there is no simple way to get rid of diacetyl or its precursor. Before separating the yeast and beer or cooling the beer, conduct a force test for diacetyl (see "Your Own Yeast Lab Made Easy"). It is a simple and effective way to determine if your beer has excessive amounts of the precursor acetolactate.

Since diacetyl reduction is slower at colder temperatures, a cold-fermented lager may require a diacetyl rest. To perform a diacetyl rest on a lager fermentation, simply raise the temperature into the 65 to 68° F (18 to 20° C) range for a two-day period near the end of the fermentation. While it is possible to do a diacetyl rest once the fermentation reaches terminal gravity, the proper time for a diacetyl rest is two to five specific gravity points (0.5 to 1 °P) prior to reaching terminal gravity. Some lager brewers prefer a Narziss fermentation profile, which incorporates diacetyl reduction. The first two-thirds of fermentation happens at 46 to 50° F (8 to 10° C), then the temperature is increased to 68° F (20° C) for the final one-third of fermentation. Another technique practiced by some lager brewers is to add freshly fermenting wort (kraeusen), which will reduce diacetyl during carbonation and storage.

For ale production, fermentation is usually already at a warmer range, 65 to 70° F (18 to 21° C). Temperature modification is not absolutely necessary, but a two-day rest at fermentation temperature once the beer has reached terminal gravity can help reduce diacetyl. If the fermentation was sluggish, raising the temperature 5° F (3° C) above fermentation temperature will accelerate diacetyl reduction. What you do not want to do is allow the fermentation temperature to drop at the end of fermentation. This will greatly slow or stop diacetyl reduction. Many brewers make the mistake of lowering the beer temperature immediately upon reaching terminal gravity, because they assume fermentation is complete and the beer is ready.

Lagering

It seems that every beer improves with some period of cold conditioning. How long and how cold seems to vary depending on the beer. The conditioning time for ales tends to be shorter than the times for lagers.

Cold lager fermentation has many consequences for a beer. In a cool environment, usually 50 to 55° F (10 to 13° C), yeast work more slowly and produce fewer esters and fusel alcohols. However, the slower fermentation and cool temperature also keep more sulfur in solution and slow diacetyl reduction.

Jean De Clerck published a list of lagering objectives in 1957 that still hold true today:

- To allow yeast and turbid matter to settle out
- To carbonate the beer with artificial carbonation or secondary fermentation
- To improve flavor
- To precipitate chill haze, to prevent haze formation when the beer is chilled after filtration
- To avoid oxygen pickup in order to prevent oxidation (De Clerck, 1957).

Once fermentation is complete, including any steps such as a diacetyl rest, you need to lower the beer temperature. This encourages flocculation of any remaining yeast. You can cold condition both ales and lagers at near freezing temperatures. Many people ask if they can crash the beer temperature, or should they lower it slowly? The concern comes over sending the yeast into a dormant state, thereby preventing them from continuing the uptake of compounds during the long cold-conditioning period. The reality is that very little happens once you take the yeast below 40° F (4° C). If you want the yeast to be active and to carry on reduction of fermentation by-products, it happens much faster at higher temperatures. As far as yeast activity goes, crashing the temperature or lowering it slowly makes little flavor difference if you are dropping the beer below 40° F (4° C). However, very rapid reduction in temperature (less than 6 hours) at the end of fermentation can cause the yeast to excrete more ester compounds instead of retaining them. In addition, if you plan to use the yeast for repitching, you should avoid very rapid temperature changes (up or down), as they can cause the yeast to express heat shock proteins.

Traditional lager conditioning utilizes a slow temperature reduction. As fermentation slows and the yeast begin to flocculate, the brewer starts the process of slowly cooling the beer at a rate of 1 to 2° F (0.5 to 1° C) per day. They use this slow cooling rate to avoid sending the yeast into dormancy. After a few days the beer has reached a temperature close to 40° F (4° C) and there are still some fermentable sugars remaining, about 1 to 2 °P. At this point, the brewer transfers the beer into the lagering tanks. The tanks are closed, and the beer builds CO_2 pressure, controlled by a bleeder valve to avoid overcarbonation or damaging the yeast with excessive pressure. Although expensive in terms of storage capability, some breweries still lager their beer for months to get it into the proper condition. The thing to remember if you want to use this technique is that it depends on precise temperature control so that fermentation slowly continues throughout the lagering period. The yeast need to remain active for a long time if they are going to reduce any fermentation by-products.

Bottle Conditioning

We usually think of yeast for its role in fermentation, but it can also have a role after the fermentation when carbonating beer in the bottle. Brewers can carbonate the beer by two methods: through yeast or through forced carbonation. Most commercial breweries force carbonate their beer, but a surprising number go to the trouble of bottle conditioning. Brewers also refer to bottle conditioning as refermentation, bottle fermentation, secondary fermentation, or final fermentation.

You might have heard people claim that the carbonation from bottle conditioning is somehow different from the carbonation from force carbonation. Whether this is true or not, one thing is certain: the carbon dioxide is the same in both. Even though the carbon dioxide is the same, some large breweries collect CO_2 from fermentation and then inject it back into the beer at bottling time. There are a number of reasons for this practice, including environmental ones, but in the past, the German Reinheitsgebot forbade brewers from adding anything to the beer but water, malt, hops, and yeast. By collecting the

CO_2 from fermentation, they could later inject it back in, since it was part of the beer.

Traditionally, brewers carbonated all beer through a conditioning period with yeast. It remains the method for some homebrewers, small brewers, producers of cask beer, and numerous specialty and regional brewers, such as Coopers in Australia and Sierra Nevada. It is costlier, but the benefits can be substantial. Yeast in the bottle help scavenge oxygen, which is very damaging to beer flavor. Smaller breweries have a hard time keeping oxygen out of their bottles, so they often benefit more from bottle conditioning. The disadvantages are that the results can vary, consumers have a negative reaction to the appearance of yeast in the bottle, and the potential autolytic destruction of yeast cells, which can release unpleasant-tasting compounds into the beer.

The results of bottle conditioning may vary because you are relying on yeast to ferment a second time in an environment already full of alcohol, at a lower pH, and in the presence of little food. Higher-alcohol beers can present a problem for bottle conditioning, as alcohol becomes increasingly toxic with increased concentration. Brewers might also find beers that utilize bacteria, *Brettanomyces,* or wild yeast difficult to carbonate properly, as these microbes can utilize a variety of carbohydrates remaining in a beer attenuated by brewer's yeast, causing overcarbonation.

Use the smallest amount of yeast that will achieve carbonation. The greater the amount of yeast, the greater the eventual autolysis flavors. The same goes for yeast health. If you had a troublesome primary fermentation, or there is some reason to doubt the health of the yeast at the end of fermentation, then you will want to add fresh yeast at bottling time. A good rule of thumb is 1 million cells per milliliter of filtered beer, which is ten to twenty times less yeast than we use for fermentation. Usually breweries filter the beer first, then add 1 million cells per milliliter back to the beer. For unfiltered beer, besides yeast health, the brewer should take into account the existing yeast population. After the yeast has settled out in the bottle, it should look like no more than a dusting of yeast across the bottom. If there is a thick layer or mound of yeast on the bottom of the bottle, you used too much. Remember, you only need enough to carbonate the beer, and any excess serves no good purpose. High-gravity beers will require more yeast for carbonation, up to 5 million cells per milliliter, due to the high alcohol levels.

Homebrewed beer, if you do not filter it, usually has more than enough yeast left in suspension (1 million cells per milliliter can look clear) to carbonate the beer. If the beer sat for a month or more before bottling, or if the brewer added a lot of post-fermentation fining, it may warrant some additional yeast at bottling. However, in most cases, as long as the yeast health is good, simply adding some sugar at bottling time should be enough to carbonate the beer.

When adding yeast, it should be in the best possible health, free of contaminants, and harvested from an early generation (up to the third generation). In a commercial brewery, the lab should verify the yeast condition before its use in bottle conditioning.

Will the small refermentation in the bottle contribute flavor? Generally not, especially if you use the same strain that fermented the beer. We know of a brewer using a German *weizen* strain to carbonate a neutral pale ale without any wheat beerlike flavors. However, any time yeast ferment, they will produce some esters and fusel alcohols, so the amount of carbonation, the type of beer, and the strain used determines if the drinker will perceive those refermentation compounds or not. If you are a commercial brewer, you need to be aware if you have added flavor during bottle conditioning. That may be your goal, but you need to understand it. Do blind tasting of the beer before and after bottle conditioning using a statistically valid-sized taste panel. If you detect mouthfeel issues or flavors such as earthiness, cardboard, or other unwanted flavor compounds, you need to investigate. Use a different yeast strain, use different quantities of yeast, or alter your methods.

When you bottle condition your beer, there is always a chance that some or maybe all bottles will not develop carbonation. Live yeast do not always behave! As a commercial brewer, consider it mandatory that you hold on to the beer and confirm carbonation before release. This usually involves one to two weeks of storage time at the brewery. Holding the inventory until it is carbonated adds to the cost of bottle conditioning and is one of its drawbacks.

The way you store the beer also affects the degree of carbonation. If you store the bottles too cold, the yeast will not actively metabolize sugar and create CO_2. If you store the bottles too warm, the yeast can die before creating CO_2. Hold your beer at 65 to 69° F (18 to 21° C) for carbonation, and pay attention to how the bottles are stored.

Inconsistent results can occur when there is not enough air circulation around the bottles.

If you are bottle conditioning a new beer for your lineup, or using a new yeast strain, it is best to do a test run with ten to twenty bottles before bottling an entire batch. It is very difficult to open all the bottles from a run and redo the yeast and sugar additions!

Technically speaking, you can use almost any strain to bottle condition your beer. You can use the same yeast you used in the main fermentation, or you can filter and add a different yeast strain. Over the years, many breweries have claimed they filter their primary yeast strain out and bottle condition with a second strain, in order to protect the secrecy of their yeast, but in many cases, the story is just a myth.

The best choice is to use a strain with similar attenuation properties that forms a fine sediment. For example, WLP002 is a highly flocculent strain, and many people assume it would be great for bottle-conditioned beer. The problem is that it is so flocculent, it forms clumps. When you pour the beer, the clumps can stay together and plop out into your beer, which is not very pleasant for the drinker. Compare that to WLP001. While this strain does not flocculate as readily as WLP002, it flocculates well when it is cold and sticks to glass. More importantly, it forms a fine, even layer at the bottom of the bottle instead of clumps.

Unless you package the beer while it still has enough sugar left to carbonate, it will require additional sugar for carbonation. Brewers often debate the best sugar for bottle conditioning, and most homebrewers use corn sugar. Some swear by dry malt extract. Some breweries use fresh wort. One study found that the sugar used does have an impact on bottle conditioning. It found glucose, fructose, and sucrose ferment at equal rates, but maltose does not ferment completely. The researchers believed this was due to CO_2 pressure created in the bottles, which had a greater impact on maltose uptake than the other sugars (van Landschoot, et al., 2007). Residual sugar content also affects flocculation, so failure to consume all of the bottling sugar could potentially affect sedimentation. In most cases, you want to use simple sugars when bottle conditioning.

Cask Conditioning

Cask conditioning at the brewery level is a simple process. The brewer sets up the beer for carbonation and fining and then depends on the publican to handle the rest of the task. When discussing cask condition-ing, the term "conditioning" is not the same as "condition," which is the amount of CO_2 in the beer. Conditioning is actually part of the matura-tion process from brewery to glass. Great cask beer depends heavily on proper handling once the beer has left the brewery.

The brewer's role, other than brewing a great beer, is to rack the beer to the cleaned and sanitized casks once it reaches approximately 2 °P above its predicted finishing gravity. Although the yeast continue to consume the residual sugars and create alcohol and other by-products, the main purpose of the sugar is to carbonate the beer in the cask. If your beer has attenuated more than predicted, you can add priming sugar, as long as it will not result in excessive carbonation. The goal is a beer carbonated to a restrained 1 to 1.2 volumes of CO_2. Your beer should have a cell count around 1 million to 3 million per milliliter for cask conditioning. As most drinkers prefer a clear beer, you would add isinglass to speed up settling the yeast and other solids. You want to add the isinglass and any dry hops just before sealing up the cask for several days. Once sealed, roll the cask to mix the beer with the finings, then let it sit to carbonate and settle.

One important aspect of cask-conditioned beer is the temperature. It is not only important to the flavor and aroma when drinking the beer, but also to the effectiveness of the finings and carbonation. Even though the beer will carbonate faster at warmer temperatures, isinglass works best below 59° F (15° C). If the temperature gets too high, isinglass becomes less effective, and at a high enough temperature it denatures. When working with cask beer, one of the key benefits of isinglass over gelatin is that isinglass is good at resettling if disturbed. But isinglass loses this property if it has been denatured. The brewer needs to keep cask beer at the appropriate temperature, one that results in the right level of car-bonation in the right amount of time. This might range from 50 to 57° F (10 to 14° C). If this is your first time working with cask conditioning, try a temperature close to 54° F (12° C).

5

Yeast, Growth, Handling & Storage

Pitching Rates

Consistent, high-quality beer requires precise measurements. One of the most important measurements, especially in terms of fermentation, is pitching rate. Without consistent pitching rates, flavor can change significantly from batch to batch.

What are the consequences of overpitching or underpitching? In general, underpitching affects flavor more, while overpitching negatively affects yeast health more over generations. However, both can result in a less than ideal fermentation with high levels of diacetyl, acetaldehyde, and low attenuation. Too high a pitching rate can also result in low or unexpected esters, yeast autolysis flavors, and poor head retention. Too low a pitching rate can also result in slower fermentation and very long lag times, which allow competing bacteria and wild yeast to grow in the wort. If you have to choose between underpitching or overpitching, overpitching is a little more tolerant before fermentation defects are evident.

Many brewers worry about determining an exact cell count. While knowing the exact count helps, consistency is more important. Once you have determined the quantity (regardless of how you are measuring it) that works well for your beer, you want to use that same amount each time. The simplest method for determining yeast quantity is by measuring the volume or the weight of the slurry. Once you have a measure of the yeast slurry, you can use a microscope or spectrophotometer to count cells, and then determine how many cells you have in the entire slurry. The nice thing about using a microscope is that it is cheaper, and you can also use it to check the viability of the cells. (Refer to "Your Own Yeast Lab Made Easy" for more details.)

An often quoted pitching rate is 1 million cells per milliliter of wort per degree Plato.

Cells to pitch = (1 million) x (milliliters of wort) x (degrees Plato of the wort)

While many brewers stick with this formula, it is more of a guideline than a hard and fast rule. We prefer slightly lower rates for ales (0.75 million) and slightly higher for lagers (1.5 million). However, you should determine the ideal pitching rate for every beer in your lineup. Many ales will be ideal at 0.75 million and many lagers at 1.5 million. Some beers might require more or less before you feel your product is perfect. Pitching rates vary by yeast strain and beer style. You will find that lager beers require higher pitching rates, roughly double what you pitch for an ale. When you brew some British-style ales and German-style *weizen*, you might find that the ideal rate is a little lower, often around 0.5 to 0.75 million.

Keep in mind these suggested rates are for repitching harvested yeast, because that is what brewers are doing most of the time. When pitching a fresh, laboratory culture grown with aeration and good nutrition, a brewer can use up to a 50 percent lower pitching rate. For homebrewers who might be working with yeast cultures that have been on store shelves for some time, the need to revitalize the yeast or increase the pitching rate comes into play.

Let us run through an example of calculating the pitching rate for 12 °P ale wort. Since it is an ale wort, we will use a rate of 0.75. Multiply your pitching rate (0.75) by the specific gravity of the wort in Plato (12) to determine how many million cells you want per milliliter of wort. In this example you want 9 million cells per milliliter. Cells per milliliter (cells/ml) becomes your standard unit of measure. You then multiply that number (9 million cells/ml) by the volume of wort (in milliliters), to determine the total number of cells to pitch. If this is a 5.3-gallon (20 L) batch of homebrew:

(pitching rate) x (milliliters of wort) x (degrees Plato of the wort) = cells needed

(750,000) x (20,000) x (12) = 180,000,000,000

In this example, you would need 180 billion cells to pitch your homebrew batch at a rate of 0.75 million. What if it was a 10-hectoliter commercial batch instead?

(750,000) x (1,000,000) x (12) = 9,000,000,000,000

Now you need to measure out the appropriate amount of yeast. Typically, yeast slurries are in the range of 1 billion to 3 billion cells per milliliter, but it depends on how they were collected. If you have done a cell count, then you will have a good idea of the density; otherwise you will need to estimate.

Estimating Yeast Density

If you want to get an idea of what different slurry densities look like, get a vial of White Labs yeast and try this experiment. The entire volume of the vial is 47 milliliters, and each has an average fill level of 36 milliliters. That fill level is right around the bend near the top, where the vial becomes straight. After the vial has sat upright and steady for a good long time, the yeast packs down into the bottom portion of the vial, about 14 milliliters of space. Once that happens, the yeast (excluding the liquid above it) is at a very high density, somewhere around 8 billion cells/ml. If you shake the vial, so the yeast mixes evenly into the liquid, it will have a density of around 3 billion cells/ml. If you mix the vial contents with an additional 16 milliliters of water, you now have an idea of what a 2 billion cells/ml slurry looks like. Add 50 more milliliters of water and that is a 1 billion/milliliter slurry. Keep in mind that yeast harvested from fermentation often has more nonyeast material in it than lab-propagated yeast, so you will need to allow for that in your calculations.

There is another useful trick to estimate density without a microscope. In a standard 13-by-100 mm glass test tube, a yeast suspension of less than 1 million cells/ml is not visibly turbid. Above 1 million cells/ml it is visibly cloudy. You can adjust the cell density through serial dilution until the sample is just barely visible. By tracking the number of dilutions, you should be able to calculate original density and use serial dilutions to obtain other concentrations.

You will encounter a few other common densities during the brewing process. At the beginning of fermentation, cell density is around 5 million to 15 million per milliliter, and it is around 25 million to 60 million per milliliter at the end. Once you harvest the yeast from either the top or bottom, you will most likely have between 0.8 billion and 2 billion cells per milliliter.

If you are working with dry yeast, determining how much to pitch is relatively easy. Most dry yeast contains about 7 billion to 20 billion cells per gram, depending on the cell size and other nonyeast material, but that is not the number of viable cells per gram you will have once you rehydrate the yeast. That depends on a number of factors, such as storage and rehydration techniques. Find out from your supplier how many viable cells per gram you can expect (which might be as low as 5 billion), then simply divide the number of cells needed by the number of viable cells, and you will know the weight in grams of dry yeast needed. Of course, this assumes all the yeast is active and that you properly rehydrate it following the manufacturer's recommendations before pitching. Failure to rehydrate dry yeast properly will result in the death of approximately half the cells.

Once you know the density of your slurry, divide the total cells required by the cells/ml concentration in the holding tank or yeast storage container to determine how many milliliters of yeast slurry you need. For our homebrew-sized example, we need 180 billion cells. If we determine or assume that we have a slurry containing 2 billion cells per milliliter, then we would need 90 milliliters of slurry. If it is a 1 billion/ml slurry, then we would need twice as much.

Many commercial breweries pitch based on weight. For some volumes of yeast, that can sometimes be considerably easier to measure. Each yeast cell weighs around 8×10^{-11} grams (Haddad and Lindegren, 1953), so 100 billion cells only weigh about 8 grams without any liquid for the slurry. Depending on several factors, a density of 2 billion cells per milliliter weighs in the ballpark of 1.02 grams per milliliter (water weighs 1 g/ml and yeast 1.087 g/ml). For our homebrew example, if we wanted to measure our slurry by weight, we would need about 92 grams of slurry. For our commercial example, we would need 9 liters of slurry at a density of 1 billion cells per milliliter. By weight, that is about 20 pounds (9.1 kg).

You can see how small mistakes in estimating the slurry density could have a significant impact on your pitching rate. Ideally, you would first do an accurate cell count to figure out the density of the slurry. In fact, cell counting requires a measure of precision in working with small volumes of liquid and counting techniques. Any error gets multiplied many fold and can make for a substantial margin of error, making measurement by weight or volume not such a bad method. Therefore, if you cannot count the cell density with a microscope, do not despair. Remember that the name of the game is consistency. If you feel you may be pitching too little or too much, try raising or lowering the amount you measure out. In theory, as long as your slurry density remains the same and your measurement method remains consistent, you should be able to dial-in the ideal rate for your beer based on flavor. Regardless, it is much easier to remain consistent if you have the ability to measure accurately and inspect your yeast. One thing also bears repeating: It is important to use the same quantity and same rate of growth every time to ensure the same flavor production from batch to batch. The number of cells, the amount they grow, and the speed at which they grow all influence your beer.

When it comes time to pitch the yeast, handling a homebrew-sized pitch is easy. On a commercial scale, it can be difficult. The problem with lugging open buckets of slurry around is the potential for increased contamination.

Many commercial breweries using cylindroconical fermentors will use a "cone-to-cone" transfer to pitch yeast for the next batch. The brewer transfers yeast from the bottom of one conical fermentor into another via soft or hard piping. Many brewers like this method, because it avoids exposing the yeast to any airborne contaminants, and it does not require separate yeast storage. If you are going to transfer cone-to-cone, keep the following in mind:

- Set the racking arm to the best location in the cone to harvest yeast (above the trub and below nonflocculent cells) as determined by experience.
- Take a yeast sample before pumping cone-to-cone. Evaluate the sample physically (appearance, smell), and if in doubt, send a sample to the lab for viability and cell counts before you pump the yeast over.
- Use a variable frequency drive (VFD)-controlled positive displacement pump and calibrate it by pumping yeast at a standard power setting into a calibrated stainless container (use antifoam to kill the foam). Once you calibrate the pump, you will be able to pitch an accurate volume of yeast.
- If you cannot transfer the yeast to a new batch of wort within a day or two of settling, it is better to remove the yeast and store it cold.

One other common question about pitching rates involves larger fermentors that require multiple fills. Should you calculate your pitching rate based on the first fill or the total volume at the end? The rule of thumb is, if you are going to fill the tank in one brew day, then you should pitch the quantity of yeast for the full tank. If your filling stretches over two days, you should determine the pitch based on the amount of wort added during the first brew day. The wort and oxygen that you add during the first day cause the yeast to grow, often doubling the yeast within 24 hours. If you add additional wort and oxygen the second day, no additional yeast or a reduced pitch is all that is required.

Yeast Propagation

One of the great things about yeast is that with proper attention to sanitary practices and yeast health, almost anyone can grow yeast from small sizes into pitchable volumes.

When propagating yeast, the sanitation and oxygen needs are much higher than when brewing. The results of propagation can affect the flavor of the beer, but we do not care about the flavor of the propagation. Propagation is not just about growing yeast mass, but rather about growing the healthiest yeast possible. A smaller amount of very healthy yeast will make a much better beer than a very large number of unhealthy yeast.

As long as you can work in a sanitary fashion, propagation of yeast is straightforward, and it has even caught on in the homebrewers' community, where they refer to propagation as "starters."

Commercial Brewery Propagation

In large commercial breweries, propagation is a two-stage process. The lab handles the first stage of propagation, growing the yeast up from a pure culture off a slant or plate to a size where the brewery needs to take over. Small breweries may do both the lab and brewery steps, or they may purchase the lab step from a third party and grow it up to a pitchable size in their brewery. Some breweries do neither; they purchase a pitchable culture and eschew any propagation in-house.

It is critical that the lab focuses on the purity and health of the culture it provides to the brewery. The key to successful laboratory propagation includes:

- Aseptic technique. The laboratory staff needs to be competent in aseptic techniques, to ensure the purity of the culture.
- Sterile growth media. Brewery wort is not sterile. Growing low-contamination cultures requires sterile media. Every step in the process amplifies any contamination from the previous step.
- Never exceed appropriate increments in step-up volume. Appropriate inoculation rates ensure healthy growth and efficient use of media.
- Aeration
- Temperature. Slightly higher than in normal fermentation, 68 to 77° F (20 to 25° C), enhances growth rates.

In addition, it is critical that the lab space is clean and sanitary. Ideally, the lab should be a completely controlled and sterile environment. In reality, brewery labs are far from that standard, and in many breweries, the lab wort comes from the brewery boiled but not sterilized. Still the brewery can take many steps to ensure a successful lab, such as providing

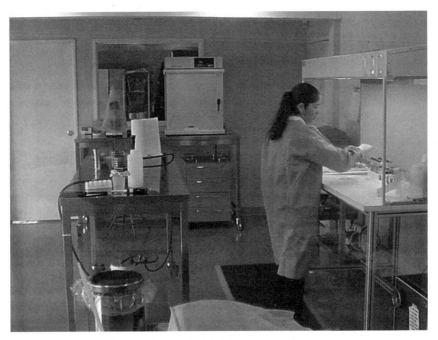

Figure 5.1: Propagation requires a suitable laboratory environment.

a means to clean and sanitize the room itself. The staff should be able to sanitize all room surfaces at regular intervals. A fully tiled room or other suitable surface allows the staff to clean and sanitize the walls, ceiling, and floor regularly. A dehumidifier keeps moisture levels low, helping prevent unwanted cultures from growing on surfaces.

Once the propagation lab is sanitary, other tools can help prevent contamination from being brought inside. Ultraviolet lights, footbaths, an airlock or double doors, and a positive pressure environment all help keep out unwanted organisms.

A lab might propagate ale yeast for its brewery using these steps:

Slope/Slant/Plate Culture
Strain selection/maintenance
↓
10 ml wort (8 °P)
25° C, 24 hours, aeration/shaking
↓

100 ml wort (8 °P)
25° C, 24 hours, aeration/stirred
↓
1000 ml wort (12-16 °P)
22° C, 24-48 hours, aeration/stirred
↓
10 L wort (12-16 °P)
22° C, 48 hours, aeration
↓
To the Brewery

Figure 5.2: Typical laboratory propagation for ale yeast.

Once the lab completes propagation in small stages, it transfers the culture to the brewery. The laboratory process is usually at least five days, although it may range up to two weeks or more. Even after the lab transfers the culture to the brewery, it should continue to monitor and test the yeast as it progresses through the brewery.

The brewery objective is similar to the laboratory's: to grow enough yeast biomass in good physiological condition to pitch into a production batch of beer. The yeast at this point have grown to such a size that they can now effectively outcompete other organisms, so most breweries do nothing more than boil the wort they use for propagation. A typical brewery scale-up might be:

	1 bbl →	10 bbl →	60 bbl →	300 bbl →	900 bbl
Ale	72° F	68° F	68° F	68° F	68° F
	(22° C)	(20° C)	(20° C)	(20° C)	(20° C)
Lager	64° F	64° F	61° F	57° F	54° F
	(18° C)	(18° C)	(16° C)	(14° C)	(12° C)

Figure 5.3: Typical brewery propagation steps and temperatures for ale and lager strains.

The lab usually propagates ale and lager strains at the same temperature, 68 to 77° F (20 to 25° C), but the brewery will often begin to lower the temperature of the lager yeast propagation in stages, so the yeast is ready for lager fermentation temperatures. Some breweries will continue to scale the propagation by a factor of 10, while others use increasingly smaller increments, as in Figure 5.3. This process can take another five to 15 days and will require the use of one to four vessels.

Most breweries like to target 100 million to 200 million cells per milliliter for propagation. This is two to four times as many cells per milliliter as a brewery fermentation. While they could propagate yeast to 300 million cells per milliliter or more, many brewers feel that growing yeast at too high a cell count often results in abnormal fermentations.

As mentioned earlier, Christian Hansen developed the first pure yeast culture method in 1883, and many current propagation systems still use this technology, called the Carlsberg flask. The volume is small, usually 6 to 13 gallons (25 to 50 L), and this is the first brewery step after the laboratory. The brewer heats the wort inside the vessel to sanitize it, which minimizes any potential contamination. Once the wort has cooled, the brewer inoculates it with pure yeast and adds air or oxygen.

Where Is the Yeast?

A brewery bought a yeast culture from White Labs to pitch into 10 barrels. The plan was to start in 10 barrels and then grow it up in stages to the 500-barrel final brew length. The brewery checked the cell count the following day and found it was only at 400,000 cells per milliliter. Where was the yeast? The brewery spent the next week scrambling to grow more yeast, but it turns out the yeast was already there—it was up in the foam. Later on, after mixing the contents of the tank, the cell count went from 6 million per milliliter to 35 million per milliliter.

This happens a lot with ale yeast strains. A brewer collects yeast from the bottom of a tank and does not find much yeast. If you cannot find the yeast at the bottom, check the top. You might have to transfer the beer to get at the yeast, and if the propagation is still ongoing, mix it back into the beer. It is always a good idea to check the gravity of the beer and use the decrease in gravity as one way to monitor the success of propagation.

A Danish company, Scandi Brew (now owned by Alfa Laval), still makes a vessel called a "Carlsberg Flask." Today it makes them from stainless steel, and the flasks have connections to make sanitary transfers into and out of the vessel. Carlsberg Flasks typically sell for $5,000 to $8,000.

Larger propagation systems usually consist of one to four vessels, with aeration. Alfa Laval Scandi Brew, Frings, and Esau & Hueber are three well known suppliers. Their systems begin at $100,000 to $150,000 for a 10-hectoliter-capacity system, which can pitch into 100- to 150-hectoliter fermentors. All three systems from these manufacturers produce high aeration and high cell counts. While the high aeration levels can cause foaming, you can use antifoam products to minimize the foam buildup or purchase a mechanical antifoamer.

These systems use a batch fermentation process. The brewer adds all the wort to the tank at once, and the yeast growth is limited to that volume of media. This is different from the fed-batch process, which manufacturers use to produce most dried yeast, baker's yeast, and yeast for pharmaceutical needs.

In the fed-batch process, the operator inoculates low-gravity media (typically 2 °P) with yeast. The yeast start to grow, and the glucose level is so low the yeast avoid the Crabtree effect (see p. 26). As the yeast run out of carbon (the sugar), the system introduces more at a slow rate. The system meters the input of carbon to maintain the growth phase. It is not as simple as pumping in sugar slowly; the process must monitor the dissolved oxygen or ethanol levels to ensure the yeast remain carbon limited. Otherwise, it becomes a normal Crabtree process. If the dissolved oxygen levels rise, then the yeast are not consuming all the oxygen available because their growth has slowed. If ethanol starts to increase, the yeast are no longer in aerobic growth. Either way, the system needs to restrict the influx of the carbon source.

Should brewers use a fed-batch process? These are expensive pieces of equipment, and systems need to be in place to make sure the yeast stays limited on carbon, otherwise the benefits are wasted. There is a definite advantage to producing more yeast per tank, but most brewers are concerned that the yeast will not behave the same in fermentation. Yeast from a fed-batch process are in a different metabolic state than yeast taken from a batch fermentation process. The brewer's concern is that this could lead to fermentation abnormalities and a different set of flavor compounds. Perhaps it would be possible to use a fed-batch process if the yeast went through an additional batch step at the end. Of course, then you would need to factor in additional equipment, expense, and time.

Many brewers have tried adopting the fed-batch process, but few employ it. David Quain, coauthor of *Brewing Yeast & Fermentation* and longtime Bass/Coors yeast guru, was once asked if they ever used a fed-batch process. His answer, "Fed batch has no place in brewing." (Personal conversation with Chris White.)

Homebrew Propagation

Homebrew propagation is somewhat easier, because you do not need as much yeast as a commercial brewery; it is essentially all lab scale. The greatest challenge for most homebrewers is meeting the sanitation requirements. The lab scale, starting from slants or plates, is the same as for commercial breweries. However, instead of propagating to 10 liters, you might stop at two, which you can use directly in your brew.

Most homebrewers do not go through the whole process of propagation from slants. Instead, they perform the final "brewery" propagation step, growing up a homebrew-sized culture. Homebrewers call this process "making a starter." Initially the domain of more advanced homebrewers, the starter has become a popular technique for many homebrewers over the past several years.

A starter is a small volume of wort that yeast use as an initial step to multiply and prepare themselves to ferment a batch of beer. The starter's purpose is to create enough clean, healthy yeast to ferment your batch under optimal conditions. The primary focus of a starter should always be yeast health first and increased cell growth second. Many brewers mistakenly focus on cell growth at the expense of yeast health. It is much better to have a smaller number of very healthy, young cells than it is to have a large number of weak cells. You should always make a starter if you suspect the viability or vitality of your yeast might be low. For example, if you have a package of liquid yeast that has been in transit during the heat of summer for many days, you should make a starter.

You should never make a starter if you cannot handle the steps in a sanitary way or you cannot provide proper nutrition for the yeast. If you can successfully brew a noncontaminated batch of beer, you should be able to successfully make a starter.

Also, even though you may find it easy to grow more yeast, do not get carried away. Overpitching can result in a less than ideal fermentation profile (e.g., low or unexpected esters, yeast autolysis flavors, and poor head retention) as compared to a proper pitching rate.

Another case where you normally do not want to make a starter is with dry yeast. Dry yeast is inexpensive, and it is usually cheaper, easier, and safer to buy more dry yeast than to make a large starter. Many experts suggest that placing dry yeast in a starter just depletes the cell reserves that the yeast manufacturer tries to build into their product. For dry yeast do a proper rehydration in tap water; do not make a starter.

Making a Starter

A starter is easy to make. It is like a mini-batch of beer, with the focus being on yeast growth and health, not drinkability. You will need a clean, sanitized container able to hold the starter plus some headspace, aluminum foil, light dried malt extract (DME), yeast nutrients, and water. When making starter wort, you want to balance yeast health, yeast growth, and convenience. Starters made at too low a gravity result in minimal growth. If you end up with multiple starter steps because of a lower-gravity wort, then the extra handling is less convenient and more likely to introduce contamination. You also do not want to make a high-gravity starter to grow yeast. The higher the gravity, the more pressure it puts on the yeast. Brewers should not believe the myth that yeast become acclimated to high-gravity fermentation from a high-gravity starter. In general, when dealing with reasonably healthy yeast, keep the starter wort gravity between 1.030 and 1.040 (7 to 10 °P). If you're trying to revive a stressed yeast, such as by culturing up yeast from a bottle-conditioned beer or from an old slant, use a lower-gravity starter wort, about 1.020 (5 °P). Lower-gravity starters are easier on the yeast but result in less growth. High-gravity starters result in more growth but are more stressful for the yeast.

The easiest way to make small batches of starter wort is with metric measurements, using a 10 to 1 ratio. Add 1 gram of DME for every 10 milliliters of final wort volume. For example, to make 2 liters of starter wort, add water to 200 grams of DME until you have 2 liters total volume. Add ⅛ teaspoon of yeast nutrient, boil 15 minutes, cool to room temperature, transfer to a sanitary vessel, and add yeast.

When using an Erlenmeyer flask made of borosilicate glass (such as Pyrex or Bomex) it is even easier. Put the DME and water in the Erlenmeyer flask, put a piece of aluminum foil over the top, drop in your nutrients, and put the flask directly on the stove burner. Boil gently for 15 minutes, let it cool, and then add your yeast. If you want to use sterile wort, you can use a stovetop pressure cooker or an autoclave to prepare the wort, instead of boiling.

Following this basic process results in the type of growth numbers shown in Figure 5.5 (p. 140). However, it is fairly simple to increase the amount of yeast growth through the addition of oxygen and agitation.

If you have pure oxygen handy, you can add a dose of oxygen to your starter at the beginning. You will get far healthier yeast and far more yeast growth if you provide a small, continuous source of oxygen throughout the process. Oxygen is critical to yeast growth, and not providing any oxygen to the yeast can have a long-term negative impact on yeast health. Yeast use oxygen to synthesize unsaturated fatty acids and sterols, which are critical to creating a healthy cell membrane and good cell growth. With oxygen present, yeast grow rapidly. With no oxygen, yeast grow far more slowly and reach a lower total mass of cells.

There are several ways to add oxygen: intermittent shaking, continuous shaking, a stir plate, pure oxygen, or an air pump with a sterile filter. If you have a stir plate, that is perhaps the most effective method. A stir plate provides good gas exchange, keeps the yeast in suspension and drives off carbon dioxide, all of which increase yeast growth (around two to three times as much yeast as a nonstirred starter) and improve yeast health. However, there are two things to be aware of when using a stir plate. The first is that some stir plates can generate enough heat to push the starter into a temperature range that is detrimental to the yeast, especially if used in a warm environment. One small stir plate we tested added 5° F (3° C) to the ambient temperature, so you will want to account for this bump in temperature when making a starter. The second thing to be aware of is that the stir plate's action of drawing air into the liquid can cause the temperature of the starter to mirror changes in the temperature

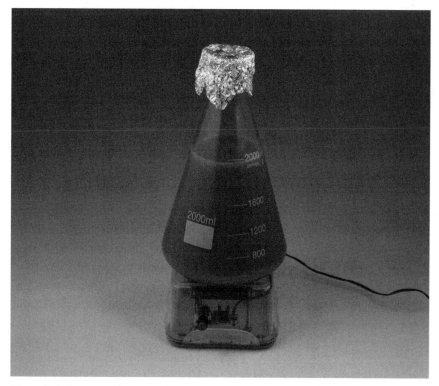

Figure 5.4: Starter on homemade stir plate. Photo courtesy of Samuel W. Scott.

of the surrounding air. Large temperature fluctuations in the room will result in large fluctuations in the starter temperature, and large swings in starter temperature cause less than stellar results. When using a stir plate, do not plug up the starter vessel with an airlock. A sanitized piece of aluminum foil, cotton plug, or a breathable foam stopper is all you need. Bacteria and wild yeast cannot crawl, and a loose-fitting cover will allow for better gas exchange. You can find information on making your own inexpensive stir plate on the internet, and most advanced homebrew shops sell reasonably priced models.

If you do not have a stir plate, shaking the starter as much as possible makes a big difference in the amount of yeast growth and health. For this reason, some homebrewers in Australia began using 2-liter plastic soda bottles for starters. The brewer can easily evacuate any built up carbon dioxide from the bottle by removing the cap and squeezing, then drawing fresh air back in as a replacement. (You will need to work in a dust-free environment to avoid pulling in dust along with its load of wild yeast and bacteria.) This is also a handy vessel for shaking the starter. Our tests showed that vigorously shaking a starter every hour results in approximately double the number of cells created when using a starter that is not shaken.

Continuous air from a pump and sterile filter can be quite effective, too. The major problems are being able to control the flow of air to prevent excessive foaming and evaporation of the starter. In this case, shaking is just about as effective as intermittent aeration with a pump. If you can set up your aeration to be sterile, not foam over, and to mix the full volume of the starter wort continuously, then it can be just as effective as a stir plate. The yeast do best when the starter setup continuously releases the carbon dioxide they create, keeps them in suspension and evenly distributed throughout the solution, and provides them with access to reasonable amounts of oxygen.

Every time you make a starter, keep in mind the four main factors that affect yeast growth and health: nutrients, temperature, sugars, and pH. Key nutrients include oxygen, zinc, amino acids, and nitrogen. Oxygen is one of the things many brewers ignore, yet it is critical to the survival and growth of yeast and tends to be the most limiting factor for most starters.

Almost everyone asks if they should add hops to starters. At a level of about 12 IBUs or higher, hops add some antimicrobial protection. The antimicrobial action is a result of trans-isohumulone, a component of isomerized alpha acids, which allows hop compounds to "invade" gram-positive bacteria and slow the cell's uptake of nutrients (Fernandez and Simpson, 1993). Even though lactic acid bacteria are gram positive, some strains are hop resistant, hence their contamination of beer. Even though adding hops confers some microbial activity, it is debatable how much it helps, since isomerized alpha acids also negatively affect yeast viability. Perhaps it is better to have less material floating around, with less expense and fewer steps to worry about. If you need to rely on hops to keep your propagation pure, then you should revisit your process.

Use all-malt wort for starters. The sugar in the starter needs to be maltose, not simple sugar. Yeast grown exclusively on simple sugars stop making the enzyme that enables them to break down maltose. Since brewing wort is mainly maltose, fermenting it with yeast grown on simple sugar results in a beer that will not attenuate properly.

The pH of a starter needs to be around 5, but if you cannot test it, do not worry. Typical wort ranges between 4 to 6 pH, so use a decent-quality DME, and as long as you do not have extreme water, the pH should be fine. If you do have a very high pH water source, you might consider using at least a portion of distilled or reverse osmosis water in your starters.

When adding yeast to the starter, work in a draft-free area and try to keep the containers open for as short a time as possible. The design of the White Labs packaging keeps the yeast out of contact with the outside surfaces of the vial. However, it is possible for dustborne wild yeast and bacteria to settle on the protruding lip near the top, so it is a good idea to sanitize the top of the vial to keep any settled dust from dropping into your starter. After you shake the vial to loosen the yeast inside, let it rest a few minutes, and slowly open the top to prevent excessive foaming.

The Wyeast packages do not require "smacking" the pack before making a starter, although it certainly does not hurt. The yeast is not in the little part that you pop, but instead it is in the main pack. However, we still recommend popping the pack inside. The liquid in the little pack is a high-quality nutrient and sugar source, and it helps rinse the yeast out from the main pack. Even though the chance of contamination while pouring is extremely low, you should sanitize the outside of the Wyeast pack before opening, as well as scissors if you use them to open the package.

Warmer starters (up to 98° F, 37° C) equal more rapid yeast growth, but there are practical limits as to how high you can go, and lager yeast tend to be especially sensitive to high temperatures. Using very high propagation temperatures negatively affects the viability and stability of the resulting yeast. Another problem with very rapid growth or excessive growth is that it can result in weaker cell membranes due to lower unsaturated fatty acid concentrations. Conversely, too cold a starter results in slower and often less growth, so we recommend against propagating yeast cold. A good rule of thumb is to keep starters between 65° F (18° C) and 75° F (24° C). Some brewers like to keep lager yeast starters a few degrees cooler and ale yeasts a few degrees warmer, but a temperature around the low 70s (72° F, 22° C) strikes a good balance of health and efficient propagation of both lager and ale yeasts.

Some brewers wait until the yeast consume all the starter wort sugars and settle out of solution before pitching. They decant the spent wort and pitch just the yeast into their batch of beer. This is particularly advantageous when using large starters subjected to continuous aeration or the stir plate. The starter liquid in this case often does not taste great, and you should avoid adding it to your beer. If the size of the starter is greater than 5 percent of the beer volume, let the yeast settle out first, then pitch only the yeast. If you use this method, make certain the yeast settle completely before decanting the spent wort. Storing the yeast in the same vessel for an additional eight to 12 hours after they reach terminal gravity allows them to build up their glycogen reserves. Separating the spent wort from the yeast too early selectively discards the less flocculent, higher-attenuating individuals in the yeast population. You may end up with a pitch of yeast that will not attenuate the beer fully. Allow the starter propagation to complete the fermentation cycle before decanting.

Other brewers like to pitch the starter as soon as the growth phase is mostly complete and the yeast are still at the height of activity. Some consider this the optimal time to utilize the yeast for the next step of a starter or for fermenting a batch of beer. The thought is that the yeast do not have to come up from the dormant stage again, thus ensuring quicker yeast activity in the beer. If you are going to pitch a starter at high kraeusen, it is best to keep the starter within 5 to 10° F (3 to 6° C) of the wort temperature of the main batch. Pitching a very warm, active starter into cold wort can stun the cells, and with lager strains this can possibly affect attenuation, flocculation, and increase hydrogen sulfide production. While you can slowly cool the starter over time, it will often defeat the whole purpose of pitching at high kraeusen. Any time yeast sense a big drop in temperature, they slow down and drop out, so if you want to pitch at the height of activity, it is better to keep the starter closer to fermentation temperatures from the beginning.

While there are benefits and drawbacks to both methods, the high kraeusen method is the only one to use if you are trying to restart a stalled fermentation or drive down the attenuation of a beer a few more points. The presence of alcohol and the low level of sugars prevents yeast from coming up from dormancy to ferment what is left. By pitching yeast already at high kraeusen, the cells will continue to consume the remaining sugars.

Most starters at this specific gravity, temperature, and inoculation rate reach their maximum cell density within 12 to 18 hours. Low inoculation rates and low temperatures can both extend that time out to 36 hours or more, but the bulk of growth should always be complete within 24 hours.

What Is the Best Starter Size?

The most important thing to know about starter size is that the inoculation rate affects the rate of growth. In other words, the "pitching rate" of your starter has a big effect on the amount of new yeast cells you will see from any propagation. It is not the volume of the starter that is important, but how many cells you add in relation to that volume. Too high an inoculation rate, and you get very little growth. If you use too low an inoculation rate, then you are not really making a starter, you are fermenting beer. Just as the pitching rate affects growth in a batch of beer, which is important to beer flavor, it also affects growth in a starter, although flavor does not matter.

Ideally, you want to grow your yeast in a large enough volume of wort to ensure optimal yeast health and to get a decent amount of growth for your trouble. Olau Nielsen introduced the concept of yield factor, which is a measure of the cell growth versus the amount of extract (sugars) consumed (Nielsen, 2005). It is a useful number to compare the effectiveness of propagation methods.

$$\text{Yield Factor} = (\text{millions/ml cells final} \rightarrow \text{millions/ml cells initial}) / \text{gravity decrease } °P$$

For example, if you inoculate a 1 liter starter with 100 billion cells, that is 100 million per milliliter. If that starter grows to 152 billion cells, you have 152 million per milliliter at the end. Beginning with 9 °P wort and ending with 2 °P of sugar after the starter is complete, means the yeast used up 7 °P of sugar.

$$\text{Yield Factor} = (152 - 100) / 7 = 7.4$$

The more efficiently the yeast grows, the higher the yield factor. A yield factor greater than twenty indicates aerobic growth, and a number less than that is typical of anaerobic fermentation. Most homebrewers making starters never attain that level of growth. It requires very precise control of sugars and oxygen throughout the cycle to achieve such high growth rates. Not to worry, on a homebrew or small brewery scale, it is not critical to get every bit of growth possible. Yeast health and keeping the culture pure is far more important. However, it is useful to understand at what point you are not growing much yeast, at what point you are maximizing your growth, and at what point you are really just making beer.

One factor that makes it difficult for homebrewers to get a good yield is that they are often making a starter from a large population of yeast. The average liquid yeast package for homebrewers has about 100 billion cells. With that sort of culture, you need a large starter to get substantial growth.

We ran experiments using 100 billion cells of White Labs WLP001 in different starter sizes. We used vessels of the same material and height-to-width ratio for each starter. We added no supplemental oxygen or agitation of the starter, and all were at the same temperature of 70° F (21° C) and a specific gravity of 1.036 (9 °P). The final gravity, after the starter was complete, was 1.008 (2 °P).

Starter Volume (liters)	Inoculation Rate (millions/ml)	New Cells Created (billions)	Total Cells at Finish (billions)	Number of Doublings	Yield Factor
0.5	200	12	112	0.1	3.4
0.8	125	38	138	0.4	6.9
1	100	52	152	0.5	7.4
1.5	67	81	181	0.8	7.7
2.0	50	105	205	1.1	7.6
4.0	25	176	276	1.8	6.3
8.0	13	300	400	3.0	5.3

Figure 5.5: Effect of inoculation rate on yield factor for typical propagation rates, starting with 100 billion cells.

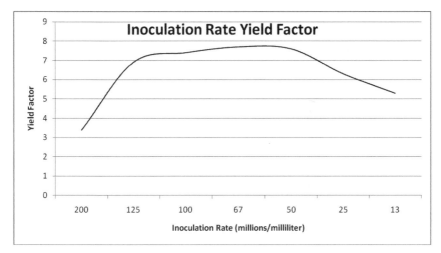

Figure 5.6: Yield factor curve across inoculation rates.

Notice the effect of the small starter. A high concentration of yeast in a small amount of wort results in very little growth. The 500-milliliter starter barely grew, only a fraction of a doubling. The fundamental fact is that yeast cannot grow unless they have enough sugar and nutrients for each cell to divide. While the cells do not multiply much when the inoculation rate is this high, it can still benefit the existing cells. The takeup of sugar, nutrients, oxygen, and the production of compounds such as sterols, improve cell health. Starters rarely have a negative side; even if there is little yeast growth, a starter helps to revive yeast for fermentation by activating metabolism, and therefore fermentation starts faster. If you wanted to achieve a higher yield factor with the 800-milliliter starter, you would need a smaller inoculation rate. As the inoculation rate drops, the yield factor climbs. In this example, once the inoculation rate drops to 67 million/ml (100 billion cells in 1.5 L of wort), significant growth occurs. The yield factor can show us how different propagation parameters affect our process. We could chart the yield for oxygen, specific gravity, zinc, agitation, or any number of other factors. If we chart the yield in this example against the inoculation rate, we see a curve indicating which inoculation rate is the most effective.

Eventually, as the starter volume increases, the yield factor declines. In fact, as the volumes approach beer-sized fermentations, the yield drops off significantly.

Starter Volume (liters)	Inoculation Rate (millions/ml)	New Cells Created (billions)	Total Cells at Finish (billions)	Number of Dou-blings	Yield Factor
20	5	500	600	5	3.6

Figure 5.7: Effect of inoculation rate on yield factor for typical beer fermentation rates, starting with 100 billion cells.

Pitching yeast at beer fermentation rates results in beerlike growth, doublings, and flavor development. Pitching at propagation-type rates results in growth and propagation-type flavors. That does not mean there is no additional growth for larger starter sizes and lower inoculation rates, but there is a limit to how much growth and how much doubling is possible for the cells. Eventually, as the inoculation rate reaches about 4 million/ml, the growth rate levels off. In fact, without additional efforts, the 100 billion cells are not going to grow into more than about 600 billion cells. Without aerobic fermentation you will reach the limit of the yeast's ability to double no matter how much more wort is present.

This does not mean you should always go for the most cost-effective inoculation rate when propagating yeast, especially as a homebrewer. If what you are planning requires multiple steps to grow your yeast and multiple transfers, realize that with each transfer there is the potential for introducing higher levels of contamination.

Do you recall our earlier homebrew pitching rate example? We wanted

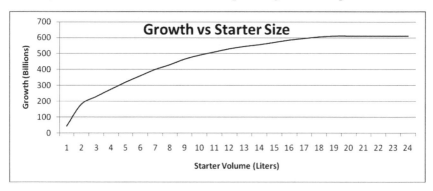

Figure 5.8: A similar experiment utilizing the same yeast strain, pitching rate, starter gravity, and temperature as in Figures 5.5 and 5.7. This shows the results of 100 billion cells into starters of increasing size, up to typical homebrew batch size. A curve shows how the possible number of doublings and growth becomes limited as the inoculation rate falls.

Starter Volume in Liters

Yeast Cells (billions)	1	2	3	4	5	6	7	8	9	10	11	12	13	14	15	16	17	18	19	20	25	28	32
100	1																						
150		1																					
200			1																				
250					1																		
300		2				1																	
350			2				1																
400				2					1														
450			3		2						1	1											
500				3			2								1	1				1			
550					3	3		2															
600				4			3			2													
650					4	4		3				2											
700							4			3				2									
750						5		4			3					2							
800							5		4				3						2				
850								5		4				3						2			
900									5		4										2	2	
950																3							
1000								6		5			4						3				2

Figure 5.9: Starter size needed to grow a given number of cells. The numbers in the grid represent the number of liquid yeast packages (~100 billion cells) to add to a starter. For example, to grow about 400 billion cells, you make a 4-liter starter using two packages or a 9-liter starter using one package.

180 billion cells total for our 20-liter batch of beer at 12 °P. If we were making a starter to the same specifications as in Figure 5.5, we would need one package of liquid yeast (100 billion cells) in a 1.5-liter starter. Of course, if you use different parameters, the results will vary, and the only way to know for certain how many cells you get from your propagation is to count them. However, it is possible to estimate with a reasonable degree of accuracy how many cells a specific inoculation rate, in a given propagation, will grow. Figure 5.9 shows how much yeast you can expect to grow using a simple starter and packages of liquid yeast.

If you are using a stir plate, shaking, or aeration, the yield will be higher. An easy way to determine the proper amount of yeast for your batch and how big a starter you need is the free Pitching Rate Calculator at www.mrmalty.com.

Stepped Starters

As we saw earlier, there is a limit to the amount of growth possible from a given propagation. You can go bigger, but you will not necessarily get more yeast. In order to grow large volumes of yeast, you need to move the results of propagation to another volume of wort. Either use a larger volume of wort for this next step, or harvest a portion of the yeast to grow again, setting aside the remainder in storage. The popular rule of thumb is that each step should be exactly ten times the volume of the previous step, but that is not a hard and fast rule. There is plenty of leeway in the size of the steps. Certainly, the size ratio of one step to the next can affect the health of the yeast and the amount of cell growth. Making the steps unnecessarily small will require more steps, more transfers, and increases the amount of work. Every transfer, every feeding, every bit of handling you do also increases the chance of contamination. Conversely, very large steps may not grow any additional yeast. Once the starter pitching rate drops below a certain level, the growth curve reaches a plateau (Figure 5.8, p. 142). This just wastes wort, unless the starter is actually a batch of beer. In general, you want to target an increase at each step of five to ten times the size of the prior step, but do not forget the practical considerations of handling, sanitation, and cell growth.

Here is a simple example of preparing a stepped starter. Assume you are trying to grow one package of liquid lager yeast to provide enough cells to pitch 5 gallons (19 L) of 1.048 (11.9 °P) lager wort. You start with about 100 billion cells, but you want to grow them up to 337 billion. Keep in mind that the inoculation rate affects how much growth is possible. In this case, you would need about 6 liters of starter wort to grow that much yeast. If you were limited to a smaller size for your propagation, you would use multiple steps to grow your yeast. Let us look at an example with a 2-liter maximum starter size:

1. Make a starter with 200 g DME, adding water to make 2 liters of finished volume.
2. Add the vial of yeast and grow for 24 to 48 hours.
3. You should now have a little more than 200 billion cells. You have created the equivalent of another vial of yeast. Refrigerate until all of the yeast settles and decant the spent wort.

If you were to add another 2 liters of starter wort, you would not double the yeast to 400 billion. Remember the effect of increasing the inoculation rate. If you added 2 liters more, you would only create about 100 billion additional cells. This gets you pretty close to the 337 billion desired. That is less than the 6 liters of wort you would have needed otherwise. That is because of the diminishing returns on low inoculation rates in large starters. You begin to make beer instead of yeast, but larger starters are safer because they require fewer transfers.

Now what if you had a vessel that only allowed you to make a 1-liter starter?

1. Make a starter with 100 grams DME, adding water to make 1 liter of finished volume.
2. Add the vial of yeast, and grow for 24 to 48 hours.
3. You should now have about 150 billion cells. You created 50 billion new cells.
4. Refrigerate until all of the yeast settles, and decant the spent wort.

Here is where people get confused. If you were to add another liter of starter wort, you would not create another 50 billion cells. Instead, you would create only 18 billion. Do you remember the effect of increasing the inoculation rate (Figure 5.5, p. 140)? You have reached an initial inoculation rate that yields less growth. If you were to harvest the yeast grown and then add 1 liter of wort, you would grow more yeast.

Working With Dry Yeast

While most commercial brewers rehydrate their dry yeast before pitching, many homebrewers just sprinkle the dry yeast on top of their wort. Perhaps they read it in a book, or their local expert told them rehydration was not necessary. Technically the beer will ferment if you pitch enough nonrehydrated yeast, but you are not giving the yeast an opportunity to make the best beer possible. Skipping rehydration kills about half the cells pitched. Besides having only half as much yeast as is needed, the dead cells immediately begin to break down and affect the beer flavor. Why would anyone recommend skipping rehydration? For the same reason you would avoid making a starter: Your process is either unsanitary or damaging to the yeast health. Even if you do rehydrate the yeast, you can easily kill it if you are lax in monitoring the water temperature. If your rehydration process introduces significant amounts of bacteria or wild yeast, perhaps you would be better off not employing these extra steps until you can master the process in a sanitary way. It is situations like this where an expert might advise skipping rehydration and just adding more yeast to make up for the loss of viable cells.

Every yeast strain has its own optimum rehydration process, but the basic process is as follows:

1. Warm the dry yeast to room temperature.
2. In a sanitized container, prepare an amount of sterile tap water at 105° F (41° C) equal to 10 times the weight of the yeast (10 ml/g of yeast).
3. Sprinkle the dry yeast on top of the water, trying to avoid setting up large, dry clumps. Let sit 15 minutes, then gently stir.
4. Once the yeast has reconstituted, gently stir once again to form a cream, and let sit another 5 minutes.

Figure 5.10: Rehydrating dry yeast. Photos courtesy of Samuel W. Scott.

5. Carefully and slowly, adjust the temperature of the yeast to within 15° F (8° C) of the wort temperature.
6. Pitch the resultant cream into the fermentation vessel, ideally as soon as possible.

Controlling temperature is the most important part of the process. Rehydration temperature generally ranges from 95 to 105° F (35 to 41° C) although some manufacturers may suggest a lower temperature range. The ideal temperature for each dry yeast product can vary, and you should strive to find out from the manufacturer what temperature is optimal for their product. Do not attempt to rehydrate yeast in cold water. Warmth is critical to the cell during the first moments of reconstituting its fragile cell membrane. Lower temperatures result in more cell material leaching out of the cell during rehydration, which permanently damages the cell. At the optimal rehydration temperature, it is possible to recover 100 percent of the cells. Too cold a temperature can result in the death of more than 50 percent of the population. You should measure the temperature of the water in the rehydration vessel just before adding the yeast. The temperature of the water can drop significantly if the vessel is colder than the water.

Most filtered tap water works well for rehydration. Ideally, the mineral content should range from 250 to 500 parts per million hardness. During the first moments of rehydration, the cell cannot regulate what passes through the membrane. High levels of sugars, nutrients, hop acids, or other compounds can enter freely and damage the cells. This is why adding dry yeast directly to wort results in such a high percentage of dead and damaged cells. Some sources recommend adding malt extract or sugar to the water, but we recommend adding a product such as Lallemand's GO-FERM or GO-FERM PROTECT, instead. Lallemand designed these products for dry yeast rehydration. They provide a selection of bioavailable micronutrients at a time when the yeast act like sponges. The result is healthier yeast that are better prepared for fermentation at the end of rehydration.

When the yeast has reached a creamy consistency, adjust its temperature to within 15° F (8° C) or less of the wort temperature. Avoid large temperature differentials that may cause yeast to produce petite mutants (p. 229). You can make the adjustment in steps of 5° F (3° C) or so using small additions of the main wort to the yeast, allowing a few minutes between each adjustment for the yeast to adjust. You might also gently stir with each addition to ensure a consistent temperature throughout the yeast. Once the yeast is ready, add it to the wort as soon as possible. At warm temperatures, the yeast cells quickly use up their energy reserves.

Yeast Handling

The fact that brewers can take a by-product of beer production, save it, and reuse it in successive fermentations is unique. We can do this because yeast is still alive and healthy after most beer fermentations. In wine, the level of alcohol after fermentation is so high that the yeast is not reusable. In most beer production, the level of alcohol present after fermentation is relatively low and the yeast does not die off, as it does in wine production. In fact commercial brewers ferment the majority of their batches with harvested yeast. The problem for most commercial brewers is not whether to reuse yeast, but how to store it and keep it healthy for future brewing sessions. Many homebrewers have never even considered reusing yeast as a possibility, but it is actually not as difficult as some may believe.

Yeast handling refers to the best practices when working with yeast. The most important aspect of working with yeast is maintaining a pure culture. A good brewer:

- Avoids drafts
- Uses either a sterile environment or an open flame during transfers
- Minimizes pouring from one container to another
- Uses foil or other sanitary covers
- Uses 70% alcohol spray or other appropriate sanitizer
- Practices general cleanliness at every opportunity

Yeast Collection

As we discussed, it is common practice in commercial brewing to harvest yeast for re-use. Brewers generally harvest the yeast once fermentation is complete, but that is not the only time a brewer can harvest it. In some cases, the brewer may harvest the early flocculating yeast prior to fermentation being 100 percent complete, in order to separate the beer from the yeast that may break down via autolysis. Early flocculating yeast contain more dead cells and more trub. When harvesting early, the brewer usually discards the yeast or uses it as a nutrient in the brew kettle. The brewer does not retain it for re-use because repitching early-flocculating yeast often results in lower attenuation with every re-use.

There are two locations in the fermentor where the yeast gathers in a quantity great enough for harvesting: the bottom and the top. All yeast strains eventually reach the bottom of the fermentor, if given enough time, and in most cases, it is easier for a brewer to collect yeast from the bottom. Collecting yeast from the top is not always possible, since not all strains are good top croppers and not all fermentor designs allow for top cropping.

Top Cropping

Ale strains are also known as top-fermenting yeast. During fermentation, the hydrophobic surface of the ale yeast causes the yeast flocculants to adhere to CO_2 and rise to the surface of the beer. In the past, brewers using ale strains always collected yeast by skimming it from the top of fermentations. It is quite likely this is why a brewery could reuse yeast for hundreds of years. As long as the brewers practiced good sanitation and collected the very healthy yeast from the top, the beers maintained their quality.

Today, bottom collection is the norm, with most brewers using cylindroconical fermentors that aid in cleaning and yeast collection. While these vessels help harvest yeast from the bottom, the quality of yeast collected is not as good as that collected from top cropping. Top-cropped yeast rises at a time in fermentation when it has a high viability, high vitality, and is relatively free from trub. When yeast drops to the bottom of a conical fermentor it mixes with dead yeast, trub, and bacteria. The length of time it takes for the yeast to settle to the bottom also puts the yeast under additional stress, and it is under hydrostatic pressure in tall fermentors. Mutations and dead cells build up faster under these conditions, so nowadays breweries only reuse their yeast an average of five to ten generations before starting from a new culture.

While there are some strain-specific exceptions, generally the more flocculent a yeast strain, the greater its tendency to rise to the surface during fermentation. After the first 12 hours of fermentation, many ale yeast strains rise to the surface and ferment from the top of the beer for three to four days during the height of CO_2 production. During this time the brewer can collect yeast from the top of the fermentor. Besides getting a great crop of yeast, the turnaround from pitching to collection is much quicker. You do not have to wait for the yeast to settle to the bottom before you can reuse it. The disadvantage lies in exposing the beer to the environment. If you have a sanitary, controlled fermentation room, then techniques like top cropping and open fermentation can be quite beneficial. Fermentor design is also a factor in top cropping. Large, flat, open fermentors make harvesting easy with buckets, shovels, or on a smaller scale with a cup or large spoon. Closed-top fermentors, with small openings for access, require specialized equipment to "vacuum" the yeast from the surface of the beer. Although few commercial breweries outside of Great Britain top crop today, the process is gaining a small but passionate following among craft brewers and homebrewers, because under the right conditions, top cropping is a very successful and effective yeast management technique.

Can you top crop your favorite yeast or not? While you can top crop most ale strains, the level of success depends not just on the yeast, but also on the equipment used, the timing, and the fermentor geometry. For example, White Labs English Ale (WLP002) is a very flocculant yeast. It looks clumpy even before fermentation. This is a great top-cropping yeast on the smaller homebrew scale, yet in the tall cylindroconical fermentors found in commercial brewing, several reports from the field state that the yeast fails to create a substantial enough head for successful top cropping and the yeast can only be harvested from the bottom of the fermentor. Perhaps it is bubble size, hydrostatic pressure, or some other factor, but it is important to remember that environment plays almost as big a role in top cropping success as does the yeast strain.

Even many lager yeast strains will top crop if the brewery has the right fermentors. Sudwerk Restaurant & Brewery in Davis, California, started production in 1989 with open fermentation equipment from Germany. In 1998, it changed most of its fermentation equipment to closed cylindroconicals but retained four open fermentors. The brewer successfully collect the yeast from the top by use of a stainless steel shovel two days into fermentation.

Other good top-cropping ale strains are Belgian-type and German *weizen* strains. These strains like to ferment from the top and are not very flocculant. Because they are not very flocculant, they are not good bottom-cropping strains. When a brewer repeatedly collects them from the bottom of the fermentor, he is collecting only the most flocculant of the cells. Over the course of just a few repitchings, the yeast population tends to become more flocculent, dropping out clear rather than remaining in suspension. Unless you are brewing a *kristallweizen*, that is certainly not a desired trait. By top cropping you can get many generations out of these unique strains with minimal drift in flocculation and attenuation levels.

Top Cropping Timing and Techniques

By day two or three of fermentation, top-cropping yeast will have risen to the top. If a strain is a good top cropper, it forms a thick head on top of the fermenting beer and is ready for collection. The yeast will remain at the surface for a large part of fermentation, but most top-cropping strains are not strong enough to stay at the surface until the end of fermentation.

At this time, you can collect the yeast by skimming it off the surface. The surface of the yeast head is high in protein, and so you will want to discard the first skim from the surface. The second or third skim and deeper usually contains the best yeast for re-use. To collect the yeast, you can use many different tools. In the past, brewers would draw a wooden board over the surface of the flat, open fermentor. Today, breweries that top crop from open fermentors use stainless steel. You can use almost anything to collect the yeast, such as paddles, shovels, buckets, or other devices. Whatever equipment you use for top cropping, ensure that it is cleaned and sanitized before each use and that the transfer from yeast surface to storage container happens in the most sanitary way possible.

When working with large fermentors, make sure that there is a stable and safe work platform. When dealing with larger volumes of yeast, consider using a sanitary centrifugal, positive-displacement (PD), or peristaltic pump. A pump is nice, because you can lower the inlet hose down below the protein-rich surface layer of the yeast and collect the cleaner and more desirable yeast just underneath. Move the inlet hose around just under the surface, vacuuming up the yeast. The pump outlet should go to a clean, sanitized container. A stainless pail with a loose-fitting lid works well.

On a small scale, such as fermenting in a 6-gallon (~25 L) plastic bucket or small stainless steel conical fermentor with a removable lid, the brewer can simply remove the lid and skim yeast using a large stainless steel spoon.

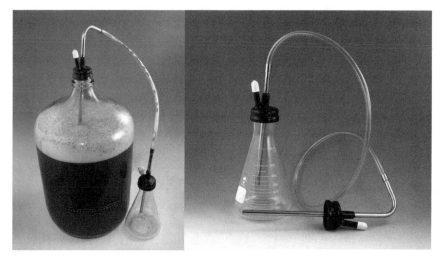

Figure 5.11: Homebrew top cropping device. Photos courtesy of Samuel W. Scott.

Keep in mind that when you remove the lid, the beer is subject to dust-borne wild yeast and bacteria dropping in from above. Try to open the lid only when there is no air movement, and do not remove the lid completely. Keep one edge in place so that the lid acts as a shield from dust dropping in from above. When working with a fermentor with a restricted opening, such as a glass or plastic carboy, the brewer needs to devise some method of vacuuming the yeast from the surface. Some brewers have successfully used a two-hole stopper or carboy cap, inputting sterile air or CO_2 through one hole and inserting a racking cane or other piece of stiff tubing into the other hole as a vacuum wand (Figure 5.11). The brewer attaches tubing to the wand, which runs to a sanitized container. Upon lowering the wand into the yeast, the pressure of CO_2 from fermentation forces the yeast out through the tubing into the collection vessel. Some brewers pressurize the vessel with supplemental CO_2 for faster collection, but this can be very dangerous, even fatal, unless the brewer knows what he is doing and exercises extreme caution. Any time you work with a pressurized vessel, there is the possibility of explosion and great bodily harm. Always use very low, precisely controlled pressures, and make sure the tubing never becomes blocked.

The yeast harvested from the top during fermentation is very active, so be sure to use a collection vessel that can relieve excess pressure before the vessel fails. Also, if you plan to store the slurry, de-gas it periodically, as the buildup of CO_2 can quickly kill the yeast.

Bottom Cropping

Most homebrewers and breweries in the United States collect yeast from the fermentor bottom. Even if the brewery is making ale using top-cropping strains, it seldom practices top cropping. It is a shame, since top cropping can result in an excellent crop of yeast for the next batch.

Bottom cropping has become popular because it is easy with the equipment that is in use today. Most commercial brewers ferment in cylindroconical fermentors, which are closed at the top. Inside the fermentor, the yeast may or may not rise to the surface when fermenting, but the brewer has little access to it if it does. Eventually, all yeast begin to settle and they drop and compact into the conical bottom of the fermentor, where the brewer can open a valve to dump the yeast. However, all of this ease comes at a cost: There is a high percentage of trub in bottom-collected yeast; as compared to top cropping, it takes longer before the brewer can collect the yeast; the yeast is under hydrostatic pressure; both bad and good yeast is present in the cone; and often there is inadequate cooling of the cone.

If bottom collection is so bad, why do it? Well, in some cases the yeast are not good top-cropping yeast, but are still quite good at producing the beer profile desired. In other cases, the equipment design requires bottom collection. In these cases, it is necessary to optimize the timing and process of harvesting yeast from the bottom of the fermentor to ensure optimal beer quality.

Bottom Cropping Timing and Techniques

In most commercial settings, it is important to collect yeast as quickly as possible. Once fermentation is complete, yeast begin the process of using up their reserves and breaking down. Environment and the health of the yeast play a big role in how fast the depletion of reserves and breakdown of the cells can occur. With large cylindroconical fermentors, where the yeast is packed into the cone, the breakdown can be very quick. The best time to collect yeast from the bottom of the tank is one to two days after initiating chilling. Under these conditions, waiting just 24 hours longer can drop yeast viability by as much as 50 percent. This is in direct contrast to small, homebrew-sized fermentors. With healthy yeast spread out across the broad bottom of a bucket or carboy in an average-strength beer, the yeast viability declines at a slower rate. Regardless of that fact, it is always best to harvest the yeast at the earliest opportunity that still respects the needs of the beer.

Figure 5.12: Yeast layers in a conical fermentor after settling.

Top Layer, dropped last, dusty, least flocculent, possibly contains respiratory mutants

Middle layer, average flocculation and attenuation

Bottom layer, dropped first, low attenuating, most flocculent, early death

The main issue with cylindroconical fermentors is heat buildup; it is best to have jacketed cooling on the cone. It is even better to have a separate temperature control for the cone jacket, so the brewer can set the yeast temperature cooler than the beer. Yeast is a surprisingly good insulator, and the yeast temperature in the center of the cone can be 10° F (5° C) higher than the cooling jacket's set point (Lenoel, et al., 1987). The yeast you want to collect is in the center of the cone. These yeast cells are not the most or least flocculent, they attenuate fully, and they do not have excessive bud scars. Holding the yeast you want to collect at a higher temperature does not help with preserving viability.

This temperature gradient is not an issue with fermentors such as carboys, buckets, and round-bottom commercial fermentors, since they have large, relatively flat bottom surfaces. The yeast settles in a broad, thin layer that tends to dissipate heat well and allows more of the yeast to remain in contact with the beer. While it varies by strain, a homebrewer who starts with top-quality, healthy yeast usually does not have to worry about autolysis for a considerable amount of time. Yeast breakdown in the average homebrew vessel is minimal, even after two to three weeks at fermentation temperatures, and even longer if chilled. Of course, if the brewer wants to reuse the yeast, it is still best to collect it eight to 12 hours after fermentation is complete.

Collection of yeast from a conical fermentor is relatively easy. First, ensure that the tank either has adequate carbon dioxide top pressure or has some other method to make up for the lost volume, such as venting. Sanitize the bottom valve, and make the appropriate connections to route the yeast to the collection vessel. Open the valve, and discard the first third of the yeast. As you drain it from the fermentor, you will see that the initial yeast is full of trub. This is the most flocculent yeast—cells that died early, cells that do not attenuate fully, and cells with other undesirable traits. As you continue draining the yeast, the slurry will lighten in color and, depending on the strain, it may take on a creamy consistency. This is generally the second third of the yeast mass and is the portion considered the best for repitching. This is yeast with fewer bud scars, yeast with average attenuation, and yeast with few mutations. Once you collect the yeast for re-use, the remaining third can be discarded. This last portion of yeast are the slower performers, and they may be low-flocculating, excessively dusty, and excessively attenuative.

If the fermentor is fitted with a racking arm, you can use it to harvest the desired yeast. Rotate the arm until it is within the ideal yeast layer, collect the yeast, then dump the rest via the bottom drain. Without a conical fermentor, it is not as easy to collect the magical middle yeast layer, but you still can collect good yeast. When working with large fermentors, transfer the beer first and then use a shovel to skim off the top layer of yeast, followed by collecting the preferred layer of yeast from the middle. While round-bottom or flat-bottom fermentors often have dump valves, draining the yeast from them tends to mix the yeast layers.

When working with homebrew fermentors such as buckets or carboys, the only option is to harvest the entire yeast cake and then try to separate out the good from the bad. Once fermentation is complete, allow the yeast to settle out, either at fermentation temperature or colder. Transfer the beer via sanitary siphon methods to keg or bottling bucket, leaving about 1 quart (1 L) of beer with the yeast. If you do not want to leave any beer behind, you can add back some sterile water once you complete the beer transfer. More liquid in the fermentor makes it easier to break up the yeast cake, but it also results in the need for a larger collection vessel.

Shake the fermentor to break the yeast free of the bottom. It might take significant shaking to turn the yeast cake back into slurry. Wipe the opening of the fermentor with a 70 percent alcohol solution. If you are using a glass carboy, you can also briefly flame the opening. Pour the resulting yeast slurry into a sterile, or at least sanitary, container. Wide-mouth, autoclaveable plastic containers are best. If you use a glass container, do not seal the container tight. Instead, use foil or a loose-fitting top, to avoid shattering the container if the yeast builds up pressure.

Before you use the harvested yeast, you will want to rinse it to separate out the trub and dead cells. Refer to the section on "Rinsing" (p. 168) for details.

In homebrewing the concept of "secondary fermentation" was quite popular for a number of years. The belief was that transferring the beer from one fermentor to another would do a couple of things for the beer.

The first was that it would get the beer off the yeast at the bottom of the fermentor, before the yeast broke down and caused off-flavors in the beer. The second was that transferring the beer made it clear faster. Both of these points are not completely valid. In a homebrew-sized batch, with healthy yeast spread out across a broad-bottom fermentor, there is little risk of autolysis flavors in the beer unless you leave it sitting warm for a couple of weeks past fermentation. Although the shelf life of yeast is strain dependent, every strain should be good for at least a week. Of course, you should not leave the beer on the yeast for longer than necessary, but waiting an extra few days for the beer to clear should not be a problem. If you are planning on making sour beers or doing any dry-hopping, fruit additions, or oak aging (anything that will require either yeast-free beer or longer warm-storage time), then transferring the beer to a clean vessel is worthwhile. The second theory, that beer clears faster after transferring, also is illogical. Unless flocculation somehow increases after transfer, the time it takes for the beer to clear should increase, not decrease. Transferring remixes the particles that were slowly drifting down through the beer. If anything, this slows the process of clearing the beer. Also, keep in mind that the large yeast surface at the bottom of the fermentor is not inert. It still has an impact on the maturation of beer flavor. Removing the beer from this yeast can slow the utilization of compounds like acetaldehyde and diacetyl.

Why does this secondary transfer possibly make it more difficult to collect the best yeast for re-use? If you make the transfer while there is still yeast in suspension and harvest the fallen yeast, you are selecting for the most flocculent cells in the population. These are the lower-attenuating and less active cells. Subsequent re-use can result in beers that do not attenuate as expected. If you dump that yeast and wait to harvest the yeast from the second vessel, you are selecting the least flocculent and most attenuative cells. Reusing this part of the population can result in beers where the yeast never settle. If you want to reuse the yeast, think about what sort of selective pressure you are putting on your yeast population. Harvesting early or late selects for the attributes that make the yeast behave that way.

Yeast Storage and Maintenance

Yeast is a living organism, and it is most healthy when feeding on wort sugars. When fermentation is complete, the cells flocculate, eventually drop to the bottom of the fermentor, and go into a resting state. Yeast at this point, stored under beer, is stable. Many brewers agree that as long as it is not a high-alcohol beer, the best place to store yeast is under the beer it fermented. Does that mean the best storage is in the fermentor? No. You should remove the yeast from the beer once it has done its work. Even if you top crop your yeast for re-use, you still need to remove the yeast from the beer or the beer from the yeast at the end of fermentation.

Storage Vessels

Ideally, you would use harvested yeast immediately. This allows little time for the cells to weaken and die and for bacteria to grow. Yet brewing the same day is not always possible, as you may not have the resources to brew another beer immediately. A common method for storing yeast at breweries is in 5-gallon, stainless steel soda kegs. They are readily available, the size is convenient for many breweries, you can modify the lid to fit your needs, and since they are constructed mostly from stainless steel, a brewer can clean and sanitize them using existing supplies. While soda kegs work well for the most part, they are not the ideal yeast storage vessel. They have two significant flaws. One is that they have small parts and gaskets, which can harbor bacteria and may prove difficult to clean perfectly. The other is that the lids do not vent pressure until it reaches a very high level. Carbon dioxide can build up quickly in yeast slurry, and pressures as low as 20 pounds per square inch can prove fatal to yeast. It is necessary to leave the pressure valve open (and covered with foil) or to vent and shake the keg at least once a day to purge the excess pressure manually.

A better vessel might be a stainless steel bucket with a lid that fits over the rim of the bucket, which keeps airborne particles from collecting where they can fall into the bucket when the brewer opens it. Homebrewers can sometimes find smaller versions of such vessels in well-stocked kitchen supply shops. The advantage to these types of storage containers is that they are also made of stainless and they vent excess CO_2 easily. As long as the lid is not too heavy or sealed via a fastener of some kind, the pressure buildup is minimal. The disadvantage is that these vessels may be difficult to store or carry, and it is far easier to knock the lid off accidentally and possibly contaminate the pitch.

A brewery can use other vessels for yeast storage. Some brewers shun plastic, because it scratches easily and scratches can harbor bacteria, but it can actually be a good choice. Be sure to use a high-quality, food-grade plastic, such as polyethylene or polypropylene, and be sure to use the vessel only for yeast storage. The advantage of plastic is that a cross-section of the yeast slurry is visible, so you can evaluate the condition and quantity of yeast by sight. For example, if you pull off yeast slurry and it is very runny, you won't know how much yeast to use in the next batch without counting under a microscope. By using a transparent or translucent plastic container to store the yeast, you can see how much yeast settles out and pitch accordingly. Of course, when using plastic buckets with lids that seal, you will need to vent them just as you would when using kegs.

For the homebrewer, smaller half-liter, 1- , and 2-liter wide-mouth polypropylene containers have an advantage in that they are inexpensive and the brewer can sterilize them in an autoclave. Many homebrewers use glass Mason jars or gallon jugs for storing yeast. They are cheap, easy to sanitize, and viewing the slurry in them is far easier than through plastic. However, the big drawback to glass is that it is so easy to break; under pressure, it can be downright dangerous. If you use any vessel with a screw-on lid, leave the lid loose. Engage only the first couple of threads, which allows any pressure to escape easily but is secure enough that the lid will not fall off. In all cases you can gain some additional protection by covering the top of the container with a piece of aluminum foil.

No matter which type of container you use, designate it as a "yeast only" container. Use a separate container for each strain and label each clearly. Store the yeast in a clean, refrigerated area. If you can, avoid using the food walk-in or the family refrigerator. It seems like every curious cook, bartender, or family member will open any container that says, "DO NOT OPEN." A dedicated refrigerator, even a used one, is a good investment.

One important step that many brewers skip is documentation. Document everything and keep good records. You should pay particular attention to fermentation temperatures, times, flocculation patterns, and attenuation from beer to beer, and keep that information along with the harvested yeast. Do not forget to record data such as sensory qualities of the beer, source of the yeast, number of generations, storage temperatures, storage time, etc. Trust us; you will forget which yeast that is and when you harvested it, let alone whether the beer attenuated properly.

Shelf Life

Every brewer asks, "How long can I store my yeast before it is too far gone to reuse?" That depends on many factors. Often brewers will ask, "I harvested this yeast "X" weeks ago from our pale ale. Is it OK to reuse today?" You really need to be able to answer a number of questions before you can guess at a ballpark idea of the yeast condition:

- What was the condition of the yeast at the time of collection?
- Was it top or bottom cropped?
- What beer did it fermented previously?
- What strain is it?
- What were the storage conditions?

The reality is that there is no way to know the real condition of the yeast and its ability to ferment another beer without testing for viability, cell count, and purity. (See "Your Own Yeast Lab Made Easy" for details on how to perform these tests.) Certainly, in a commercial setting where thousands of dollars are at stake, it is worth testing every pitch for viability and purity before re-use. A homebrewer can take more of a risk, as the loss of a batch of beer does not carry as high a price tag—although the emotional price tag may be high. The longer a brewer stores a pitch of yeast, the greater the importance of testing the yeast first to make sure it is healthy and active enough for fermentation. Yeast viability and health drops in storage, and the longer the yeast is stored, the lower the viability and health of the pitch. At the same time, any bacteria present has the opportunity to grow, especially with warm storage conditions.

Many other factors affect the viability of a pitch of yeast. For example, high levels of isomerized alpha acids affect viability. Many brewers are fond of stating that high hop bitterness protects a beer from bacterial spoilage. That is true to some extent. The coating action of hop compounds on cell membranes inhibits some bacteria from replicating. However, the same is true with yeast. Yeast harvested from highly bitter beers will have lower viability levels. Alcohol can also pose a problem for yeast. Alcohol is toxic to yeast, and the higher the level of alcohol in a beer, the greater the impact on the health and happiness of the yeast. All of these beer conditions affect the subsequent health of the harvested yeast, but even more important is the time between repitching and the storage conditions. No matter how healthy your collected yeast, you can quickly drive it into an unusable state with improper handling and storage.

Brewers often ask, "What is the best storage medium for yeast?" It depends on many factors. If you are going to reuse the yeast quickly, and the alcohol content of the beer it is mixed with is around 5 to 6 percent by volume or less, then that is the best storage medium. If the beer is a high-alcohol one, then it is better to get the yeast out of the alcohol. Some suggest using fresh wort, while others suggest sterile distilled water. The problem with using wort is that you are also providing food for any bacteria present, and it is better for the yeast to be dormant during storage than active.

Store collected yeast cold, in the range of 33 to 36° F (1 to 2° C), and ideally reuse it within one to three days. Most small-scale brewers do not follow this rule, especially if they need to manage multiple strains for multiple products. In practice, when starting with reasonably healthy yeast, one week of storage is acceptable for all yeast strains, and many strains are still viable enough for direct repitching after two weeks of storage. Everything gets a little iffy past that point, with some strains maintaining viability longer than others do. In general, the clean ale strains do quite well, as do the lager yeasts, the fruity and highly flocculent strains are a little less stable, and the worst seems to be the German *weizen* strains. After four weeks, the yeast viability is usually 50 percent or less. Ideally, you do not want to pitch yeast that has dropped below 90 percent viability.

Shelf Life of Dry Yeast

Dry yeast is only dormant, not dead or inert. Storing dry yeast at refrigeration temperatures greatly increases its shelf life. Stored at 75° F (24° C) dry yeast loses about 20 percent of its viability per year. Stored under typical refrigeration temperatures of 38° F (3° C) it only loses about 4 percent of its viability per year.

Near the end of fermentation yeast attempt to build a reserve of glycogen, to carry them through the lean times ahead and to use as energy for future replication and fermentation. As yeast sit in storage, they slowly consume their glycogen reserves to stay alive. Glycogen deprivation weakens their cell walls and makes them more susceptible to rupture. Cold storage temperatures retard this process, and a side benefit is that it also retards bacterial growth. However, you want to avoid freezing yeast, as ice crystals will rupture cell walls. Ruptured cells release their contents into the slurry, providing nutrients for bacteria to multiply. Some breakdown of cells is inevitable, so your collection of the yeast slurry and your storage method needs to be as free from contamination as possible. To be certain a pitch of yeast is acceptable, you should test the yeast for viability, vitality, and possible contamination after storage and before use.

No matter what, fresh is best. Yeast repitched the same day as harvested is the goal. You should store yeast at 33 to 36° F (1 to 2° C) and use it within seven days. Consider 14 days the maximum storage time, discarding any older slurries.

Reusing Yeast

Brewers have always reused (repitched) yeast, long before they knew yeast was responsible for beer production. In fact, brewers' continual re-use of yeast eventually led to the impressive genetic variety of brewing strains, and to their suitability for brewing. With careful attention to harvesting and re-use, a brewer should get at least five to ten generations of high-quality yeast from every initial culture. The key to reusing yeast successfully is to collect it at the optimal stage for that strain and to pitch a consistent cell count or wet cell weight. Consistency helps identify problems before they become significant.

When brewing beer, first-generation fermentation with yeast taken from the laboratory usually takes one to three days longer to complete than a repitch of healthy yeast. The new laboratory culture has to adapt to new surroundings. The switch from a laboratory culture to a brewery fermentation culture takes a couple of generations. Most brewers report the yeast "settles in" and performs best by the third generation. One key reason for this is that when reusing yeast, one generally does so with more cells, producing a shorter lag phase and faster overall fermentation. The laboratory culture often has fewer cells, but the viability and vitality tends to be much higher. Brewers repitch with more cells because of two issues. The first is that harvested and stored yeast often have lower viability than a lab culture, especially if the brewer bottom crops his yeast. The second possible issue is contamination, since harvested yeast are rarely as clean as a laboratory culture. Since sterile conditions rarely exist in a brewery, the pitch can increase in bacterial and wild yeast count with every subsequent pitch. By pitching a higher cell count, the fermentation proceeds faster, but it also affects flavor. Large breweries often blend the first-generation beer with other batches to maintain consistent flavors, but most smaller breweries find any flavor differences with first-generation beers to be within overall tolerances.

Brewers reuse yeast not just to save money or time, but also to create better and more interesting alcoholic beverages. Many academics say people started reusing yeast in the twelfth century, but it seems unlikely that people made beer for 7,000 years without reusing yeast; perhaps it was just that nobody documented it. The uniqueness of today's brewing yeast indicates a much more ancient practice of reusing yeast. How long does it take to domesticate wild yeast into brewer's yeast? It must have taken thousands of years of repitching. Michael Lewis, brewing professor at the University of California, Davis, once said he thought it would be an interesting thesis for a student to determine how long it takes to domesticate brewer's yeast. (Personal conversation with Chris White.) If you were to start with yeast collected from a plant in your yard, how many generations would it take for those wild yeast to take on the characteristics of today's brewer's yeast? Perhaps we will find out someday if someone takes Lewis up on his thesis suggestion, but for now, we must make an educated guess.

It seems reasonable to believe that earlier civilizations found that some of the best beer comes during the second and third generations of yeast, because the yeast has gone through a process of natural selection where the stronger cells survive. Back then, the first decent beer a brewer made was probably when he found out he could restart fermentation by reusing some of the beer from his last batch, even though he had no concept of live yeast.

So how many times can a brewer reuse a pitch of yeast? The life of a yeast culture depends in part on brewing conditions and the strain involved. For instance, a brewer using today's fermentors can generally reuse ale strains eight to ten times, while lagers go three to four generations. Tall stainless steel tanks with conical bottoms make it easy to collect yeast, but they put pressure on the yeast, reducing the effective number of re-uses. These days, even though we do not use yeast for hundreds of generations because of modern equipment, we still want to get the best beer possible by reusing the yeast.

While many brewers find that by the third generation their yeast is at its best, some may find that their yeast stops working. Often, the issue is with improper collection or storage techniques. That is not to say that the yeast itself cannot be an issue. If the yeast culture was unhealthy or unstable from the lab propagations, it can show problems later in fermentation. This is why laboratories need to be careful when doing yeast propagation. They must pay strict attention to selection, growth conditions, time in propagation, and purity after propagation. When a lab fails to respect the needs of the yeast, fermentation may proceed normally in the first generation but will exhibit problems just a couple of generations later. Yeast do work well for generations, but flaws or potential weakness in a brewery's yeast-handling procedures can also show after only a few fermentations. There is not just one set of best practices, and most brewers are doing a good job, otherwise more breweries would be having much more frequent and severe problems. Still, yeast problems after several generations are often due to something under the brewer's control, such as storage time, storage conditions, or harvest techniques.

Homebrewers can also reuse yeast with excellent results, and for some beer styles, repitching is the only way to ferment them properly. Many homebrewers get into yeast re-use not to save money, but rather because repitching and proper fermentation can make the difference between good beer and great beer. Of course, if you do not pay strict attention to the fundamentals of sanitation, collection, storage time, and pitching rates, yeast re-use is just as likely to end in failure as it is success.

The place where the vast majority of beginning homebrewers go wrong is a lack of sanitation. They believe their technique is flawless, but the reality falls far short. In many cases, the difference between bad and good homebrew is just sanitation. (This applies to plenty of startup craft breweries as well.) Do not blame it on your yeast, equipment, or recipe if the problem is your sanitation. Even if you think that sanitation is not the culprit, start by reviewing your sanitary procedures and pay strict attention to detail.

Collection technique is another trouble area for many homebrewers. Harvesting yeast too early, collecting only the highly flocculent yeast is a common mistake. Other homebrewers discard the bulk of the yeast in a "transfer to secondary" and then only collect the least flocculent and most attenuative yeast. The result is a culture that on the next re-use will not flocculate at all. Think about what selective pressure you are introducing when you collect yeast for re-use. (Refer to "Yeast Collection," pp. 148-156.)

Storage time is also critical and a common area for homebrewers to stumble. It is very easy to delay brewing for a week or two when you do not brew for a living. Remember that yeast are living organisms. Leaving them starving for a month or more is not the best way to treat them. If you want to reuse yeast, force yourself to brew again within two weeks, if not sooner. Your yeast and your beer will appreciate it.

A number of homebrewers have adopted the practice of transferring the beer from a fermentor at the end of fermentation and then adding a new batch of wort on top of the yeast cake. This is a bad practice. Can this practice make good beer? Absolutely. Will it make the best beer possible? Absolutely not. The yeast at the end of fermentation is not just healthy yeast. There are plenty of dead cells present, as well as all the break material and hop bits from the previous wort. You must collect the yeast, look at the population, remove dead cells and nonyeast material by rinsing, and then reuse only the proper quantity of cells in the next batch. Do not be lazy. Always clean and sanitize your fermentor between batches, and always ensure you are pitching the correct number of cells for the beer you are brewing. Yeast growth is important to beer flavor, and overpitching (especially with excessive trub) can have a negative effect.

Ideally, you only want to reuse yeast that is more than 90 percent viable, but most brewers just compensate for lower viability by using more slurry. This may be successful, but it can also lead to problem fermentations. The overall health of the yeast may be low, so the slurry may not produce the expected range of flavor and aroma compounds and may not attenuate correctly regardless of how much yeast you add. To check for viability, a brewer needs a microscope, but even without one, you can at least perform a quick and easy test. Starting the day before brewing, add 10 milliliters of thick yeast slurry to 1 liter of wort. Pay attention to the start of fermentation; you are checking to see if the fermentation starts with a normal lag time for that strain (4 to 12 hours).

If the lag time is longer than you have seen in previous fermentations with that strain in your brewery, you can try to compensate by using more yeast. Of course, using this approach will also affect fermentation character. Reusing a low-viability culture adds a significant number of dead or dying yeast cells, which can affect beer character. If the test shows a very long lag time (more than 24 hours), it is better to reculture than to try to add enough yeast to compensate. You should always keep extra, unused, healthy yeast on hand in case you encounter a problem with the yeast you intend to use.

Another good practice is to monitor the pH of your stored slurries. If you have measured a rise of more than 1.0 pH since harvesting the yeast, it indicates significant cell death, and you should discard the slurry.

To test for contamination, you need to plate the slurry on specialized media three to five days before brewing. You should check the slurry for aerobic bacteria, anaerobic bacteria, and wild yeast. Of the three, anaerobic bacteria are the hardest for a brewer to eradicate. The most common anaerobic bacteria are the lactic acid bacteria *Lactobacillus* and *Pediococcus*. If bacteria counts are higher than 1 per milliliter, and wild yeast is more than 1 per 0.1 milliliters, you should not brew with that yeast culture. We cover the procedures for these tests in "Yeast and Beer Quality Assurance" (p. 209).

If you have stored the yeast for two weeks or more, but it still tests clean, you might want to consider revitalizing the yeast before using. See the section on "Revitalizing" (pp. 167-168) for details.

Viability and Vitality

How do brewers measure the quality of yeast? Brewers use two terms to discuss the health of yeast: viability and vitality. We use the term viability to refer to the yeast being either alive or dead, and we express this as a percentage of live cells within the population. If every cell in a yeast culture is alive, we call that 100 percent viability. If half of the yeast in a culture is alive, that culture is only 50 percent viable.

We mentioned earlier that, due to flavor considerations, you should not reuse yeast unless the viability is 90 percent or higher. It is important to note that some methods to test viability are inaccurate when viability is lower than 90 percent, so the actual viability of an old culture may be questionable. What does viability tell us about the condition of the yeast cells in a population? Does it tell us if the yeast is healthy or not? No, it just tells us if the yeast is dead or alive.

If we want to know the condition of yeast, we call that vitality. Vitality is a measurement of the metabolic activity of the yeast. If a yeast culture is very healthy, strong, and ready for fermentation, we call that high vitality. If the cells are old, tired, starved, and not capable of good fermentation, we call that low vitality. Vitality correlates with fermentation performance. You want high-vitality yeast for fermentation. While you can overcome less than ideal viability with an increase in the quantity of yeast, you cannot overcome low viability with more cells. Before using low vitality cells, you should make an effort to return them to a healthy state.

Methods for testing cell viability and vitality center around three general principles: loss of replication capability, loss of metabolic activity, and cell damage. We will cover the procedures for accessing viability and vitality in "Your Own Yeast Lab Made Easy," but it is important to introduce the concept here because you must factor in the health of the yeast when repitching. Depending on the level of yeast health, you may need to pitch more yeast at the beginning of fermentation, oxygenate more, or perhaps perform a yeast starter or propagation to revitalize the cells.

Viability	Vitality
Methylene Blue	Acid Power
Alkaline Methylene Blue	Intracellular pH
Citrate Methylene Blue	Fermentation Test
Plate Count, CFUs	Alkaline Methylene Blue
Capacitance	Magnesium Release
Fluorescent Stains	Fluorescent Stains

Figure 5.13: Methods for viability and vitality testing.

Challenging yeast cells with vital dyes is the standard for viability testing. Vital dye staining tests the integrity of the cell wall as well as the ability of the cell to reduce or extrude the dye and remain colorless. The standard for assessing yeast viability since the 1920s has been methylene blue staining. However, researchers question if this is the best method, given its poor reproducibility and inaccuracy with viabilities below 90 percent. Some researchers have introduced other dyes, such as methylene violet, as an improved staining alternative, while others have explored modifying the methylene blue method by adding citrate to enhance accuracy.

There may be instances where you measure a viability of more than 90 percent in your pitch, but you still encounter a fermentation that slowly creeps along. How is that possible? It is quite possible for a pitch to measure high viability only to have a weak fermentation. Do not forget yeast can have a high viability but still have a low vitality. If the physiological condition (vitality) of the yeast is poor, you will most likely have poor fermentation. Unfortunately, most vitality tests are still expensive, time consuming, controversial, and not user friendly. A crude method for determining if a pitch of yeast is viable is to pitch a portion (at the appropriate pitching rate) into a lab-sized test fermentation. If fermentation begins within the expected time, then the yeast is most likely of sufficient vitality for use in a batch of beer.

Revitalizing

If testing reveals that your yeast is low in vitality after storage, you can revitalize it with fresh wort. Generally, we do not recommend revitalizing yeast depleted by poor storage conditions or long-term storage. A commercial brewery should always obtain a fresh culture of high vitality instead. Certainly, a homebrewer has a little more leeway if he or she is willing to accept less than ideal results. To revitalize a yeast culture:

1. You can start this process the morning of brew day. First, determine how much yeast you need to pitch and put it in a suitable container, such as a stainless vessel.
2. Let the yeast temperature rise to 70 to 75° F (21 to 24° C). If you need to apply heat, avoid applying high or uneven temperatures.

3. Aseptically add sterile (or as close to sterile as possible), high-gravity (1.080 SG, 20 °P) wort at a rate of 0.50 milliliters for every 10 milliliters of yeast slurry volume. For example, you would add 10 milliliters of wort to 200 milliliters of yeast slurry.

4. Hold at 70 to 75° F (21 to 24° C) for 4 to 12 hours without aeration or stirring.

5. The live, active yeast should turn the wort milky. Dead cells and other nonyeast matter should drop to the bottom of the container. Decant the active, milky portion into your wort, leaving behind any cells that sank to the bottom.

Rinsing

The question many homebrewers have is, "How do I select only the best yeast if harvesting the entire contents of the fermentor?" The answer lies in yeast rinsing. While it cannot completely replace selecting the ideal yeast with a shovel, it can help separate out the trub, dead cells, and alcohol from your pitch.

Rinsing can also be worthwhile in commercial settings, especially for yeast harvested from a high-gravity beer. Yeast do not store well in a high-alcohol environment. While you generally do not want to reuse yeast

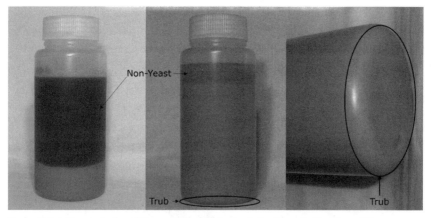

Figure 5.14: Yeast rinsing with a relatively clean pitch of yeast. Starting with a harvested slurry that has settled (left) decant the beer, add back sterile water, shake vigorously, and then let stand for 10 to 15 minutes. A layer of nonyeast material forms at the top and below it a large layer of clean yeast (middle). On the bottom, a layer of dead cells, hop bits, and other trub settles out (right). Decant the top layer and pitch the middle layer into your wort.

from high-gravity beers (above 1.070), some Belgian breweries and small commercial breweries have no choice because that is all they make!

Once you have harvested the yeast, place it in a sterile or sanitized container large enough for the yeast solids plus at least four times as much sterile water. Taller, narrower containers allow for better separation. The greater the ratio of water to yeast solids, the easier it is to separate the yeast. Add cool, sterile water to the yeast solids, but retain about 10 percent headspace in the container. This headspace helps to break up the yeast flocs and to mix the yeast with the water. Seal the container and shake vigorously. The idea is to break up the flocs. After a few minutes of shaking, set the container down and let the yeast and trub settle. Within minutes you will see a small layer of dead cells, brown yeast, and hop bits settle to the bottom. The layer above that should be the largest, with a creamy layer of yeast and water. If you wait longer, a layer begins to form on the top that is mostly water with the lightest of cells, proteins, and other matter. Once you see some stratification, usually within 10 minutes, discard the watery top layer, decant the middle layer of good yeast to another sterile or sanitized container, and discard the bottom layer. If you find that the yeast still appears to have excessive amounts of trub, you can repeat this process as many times as needed. However, avoid overworking your yeast without reason. The greater the number of transfers, the greater the contact with more containers, the more exposure to airborne contaminants, the more bacteria and wild yeast you are adding to your pitch.

Washing

Washing is very different from rinsing. In yeast rinsing, you are using dilution of a slurry to encourage better stratification of trub and yeast, allowing you to separate the two. In yeast washing, you are using acidification or other chemical means to reduce the number of active bacteria, while not damaging too many yeast cells. Acid washing has different effects on different yeast strains, and it does reduce yeast performance and viability. We recommend restarting from a fresh culture when confronted with a contaminated pitch.

Acid washing does not completely remove bacteria. It is not a complete solution, and you should not rely on it to clean up a contaminated pitch. Consider it only as a preventative measure against small amounts of bacteria. It is often less effective against lactic acid bacteria and ineffective against wild yeast and mold. After one or two repitchings, the number of bacteria can once again reach levels that affect flavor.

These are the steps for acid washing:

1. Bring the yeast to 36 to 40° F (2 to 4° C), and maintain that temperature throughout the process.
2. Determine how much yeast you need for fermentation, and place it in a suitable container, such as a stainless vessel. Start the acid washing procedure 120 minutes before the time you will pitch the yeast.
3. Add food grade phosphoric acid, mixing thoroughly, until the pH of the slurry is between 2.0 and 2.5 pH. You want to hold the yeast at this pH for 60 to 90 minutes, stirring continuously.
4. Add the entire mixture to the fermentor. You want to feed the yeast with wort as soon as possible.

Adding cold yeast to warm wort can result in temperature shock, but it is important that you keep the acid wash cold or it will damage the yeast. Proper acid washing in itself already causes yeast damage, but letting the temperature rise magnifies the impact on the cells.

Acid washing has been around for quite some time, but a newer, more effective alternative is washing with chlorine dioxide. Most breweries use BIRKO's DioxyChlor or Five Star's Star-Xene. Some homebrew shops have begun carrying chlorine dioxide tablets, which are a convenient form for homebrewers. Regardless of the product you use, you should follow the manufacturer's instructions for yeast washing. Here is a general overview:

1. Again, working at a temperature of 36 to 40° F (2 to 4° C), acidify water to pH 3 using a food-grade acid.
2. Add DioxyChlor Star-Xene to the acidified water. You are targeting a concentration of 20 to 50 ppm sodium chlorite once mixed with the yeast slurry you are treating.
3. After 15 minutes, add to the yeast slurry you plan to pitch, mixing thoroughly.
4. Allow to sit for a minimum of 30 minutes.
5. Add the entire mixture to the fermentor.

Transporting Yeast

For most brewers, a critical factor they rarely think about is "what happens to their yeast in between the laboratory and the brewery?" Obviously, yeast is alive and healthy when it leaves the laboratory, but it begins to deteriorate and die in transportation. Transportation takes time, and delays sometimes happen, which is never a good thing for a live culture. Temperature is also a factor in transportation, with hot temperatures accelerating the metabolic process of the yeast and very low temperatures possibly freezing the cells. All of this makes getting yeast to the beer production facility critical for breweries of all sizes whether the yeast comes from your own lab or a third party.

Large breweries address these issues in a number of ways. Anheuser-Busch, for instance, stores and grows up all of its yeast at one location, in part for security purposes, and ships the liquid yeast out to satellite breweries around the world. Other large breweries propagate yeast at multiple facilities, making transportation less of an issue but creating the potential for varying yeast quality from place to place.

Yeast propagation laboratories send out yeast to multiple and varied clients around the world, making transportation not just a critical aspect of business but also an unbelievable headache, at times. Success in transporting yeast depends on several factors, including speed of delivery, crossing international borders, regulations of the state and/or nation, and the rate of yeast attrition, which depends on the strain and the initial health of the yeast.

If you need to ship yeast, there are steps you can take to ensure its chances of successful transport. Start with the healthiest yeast possible. Yeast with higher glycogen reserves will use that glycogen to help withstand the rigors of shipping. Leaving your yeast in the propagation step or fermentation for an additional eight to 12 hours after terminal gravity is reached will allow the yeast to rebuild their glycogen reserves.

Try to ship the smallest amount of cells possible and have the destination grow the yeast. The fewer cells you ship, the cheaper the packaging and shipping. Shipping slants or plates can be successful, because the yeast have a ready food supply to help them through the trip, and the overall weight is minimal and not likely to leak. Thoroughly insulate your shipments against temperature fluctuations. In anything other than cold weather, add enough freezer ice packs or chemical cold packs to maintain as low a temperature throughout shipping as possible. It is best to avoid the use of dry ice, as it will freeze the yeast. As you can imagine, keeping a large slurry cold can be problematic. The larger thermal mass does help the slurry stay cool, but dense concentrations of yeast quickly build up internal heat.

Temperature is such a big issue with shipping yeast that you might want to attach a time-temperature or a freeze indicator to the yeast container. It can tell you what sort of temperatures the culture experienced on its transit. The time-temperature indicators show how long it was at a temperature higher than the control point. Freeze indicators show low temperatures for a set amount of time, so you can see if it was enough to freeze the yeast or not. The value of these indicators, at a dollar or two each, is that they will tell you if the culture is questionable before you lose a batch of wort. If you have a positive reading, you should validate the health and viability of the culture before use.

We recommend packaging all yeast cultures in nonbreakable containers. We prefer plastic, as stainless steel can dent, leak, and is heavy to ship. Secure the container opening for transport, and put it inside a plastic bag to catch any inadvertent leaks during shipping. Use the most rapid form of transportation possible. If your shipper permits it, use "Live Culture" and "Protect from Freezing and Heat" stickers on the box. If the plan is to transport via your own vehicle on a regular basis, then investing in thermoelectric "self-cooling" ice chests, which run on 12-volt power, might be worthwhile. Just 30 minutes at elevated temperatures, such as a car parked in the sun, can dramatically reduce the culture's viability.

6

Your Own Yeast Lab Made Easy

Quality From the Beginning

Whether you brew beer for yourself or brew to sell to thousands of consumers, you want to make the best beer possible. When Sierra Nevada Brewing Company built its first brewery in 1980, it did not have a lot of money or sophisticated brewing equipment. The brewery only made a small amount of beer in the first year, but one thing it did not skimp on was quality—it had a laboratory from the beginning (Grossman, 2009).

Many small breweries consider a laboratory too advanced or unnecessary when they open. They tell themselves they will add it later. But when? When they reach 3,000 barrels, 10,000 barrels, 100,000 barrels? Sierra Nevada realized that if it paid attention to quality from the beginning, it would make better beer. Early on, the brewery measured contamination and oxygen pickup but used that as a base to add new quality control steps as it grew. Sierra Nevada now has three labs and continually reinvests in high-end lab equipment and personnel.

Over the years, we have heard from many brewery startups that they want to make a beer as good as *Sierra Nevada Pale Ale,* but they rarely succeed. Why? One reason is that most do not match the strict quality control practiced at Sierra Nevada.

Setting up a lab and developing a robust quality-control program does not have to be complicated. In fact, some very simple laboratory practices can dramatically improve your beer quality without costing a lot of time or money.

Setting Up Your Lab

There are two main roles for a brewery laboratory: microbiology and analytical analysis. Microbiology in the brewery lab focuses on yeast culturing and quality assurance for both yeast and beer. Analytical analysis involves testing the raw ingredients and finished beer for parameters such as freshness, hop levels, color of the beer, and more. Most large breweries have their microbiology perfected and focus additional lab space and personnel on analytical analysis. They need to make sure they are keeping the same consistency from batch to batch and from package to package. Once you have mastered the microbiological needs of your brewery, consistency depends on analytical analysis.

Craft breweries and homebrewers tend to focus more on microbiology, because this has more of an impact on their beers. Consumers can accept some variability with craft beer from batch to batch, but not flaws in microbiology. Control over microbiology can be more difficult when brewing beer in restaurants, kitchens, open warehouses, or your backyard.

Environmental Considerations

The environment of a yeast lab is critical to producing quality cultures and reducing the risk of introducing contaminants. The most important aspect is creating a space with a clean air setting. An advanced laboratory is often set up as a "clean room": It is enclosed, and the air is supplied through HEPA or ULPA filtration units that remove airborne microorganisms and provide a positive pressure, keeping out unfiltered air. Laminar flow hoods offer similar protection in a smaller package, providing a workbench continuously bathed in clean air. When you cannot employ a clean room or workbench, you can still take measures to improve your laboratory environment.

Many craft brewers and homebrewers do not have a dedicated lab space. While this is not ideal, it is often possible to find a location in the home or brewery and make it acceptable. Your lab can be almost any-

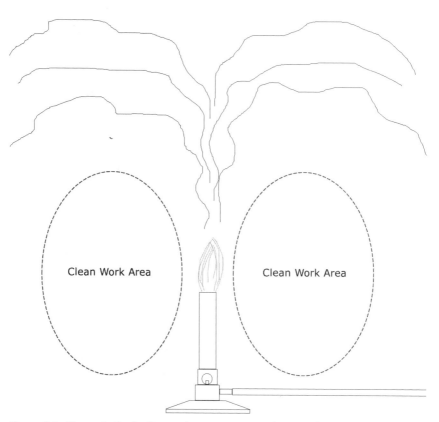

Figure 6.1: The updraft of a Bunsen burner creates a clean work area.

where, provided you are aware of possible contaminants and can control their source. Drafts, blowing fans, dusty overhead cabinets, and filthy countertops are all threats to pure culture techniques. All lab surfaces should be clean enough to eat off and free of things that will get in the way. It does not always need to be dust free, as you can wipe down the area with 70% isopropyl alcohol before working, but use caution, since you will also need to work with an open flame.

Before bringing out any cultures and starting to work, ensure that you have removed the source of any drafts. Fans and wind can blow airborne contaminants into the work area. Shut windows and turn off any fans in the area, including central heating and air. Even though you have now eliminated air movement, bacteria and wild yeasts are still descending constantly. To counter this, light a flame, such as an alcohol lamp or a Bunsen burner, and work near the updraft it creates (Figure 6.1). This is an inexpensive and effective barrier that pushes airborne bacteria and yeast up and away from sterile cultures and media.

Fire is a very useful tool, because it can kill microorganisms on contact. Flaming the opening of a glass vessel by passing it through a flame kills the microbes on and around the opening. You should get in the habit of flaming both the cap and the opening of a container immediately after opening and immediately before resealing.

Use caution when working with an open flame, and do not overdo it; a few quick passes through the flame will do the trick. Glass test tubes and Erlenmeyer flasks are often made of Pyrex or Bomex and will withstand heating, but be careful with other glass and plastic parts and your fingers!

Of course, there are other considerations to how you approach your lab space and work. Make sure you have adequate lighting, because much of the work you will do is with small cultures. Keep hair and clothing back away from the work and any open flames. A proper-fitting lab coat is not just a fashion statement. It keeps lab materials off your clothes and keeps material from your clothes off the work surface. You also want to set up in an area where there is minimal foot traffic, vibration, and noise. People walking through an area generate drafts, swirling up dust from surfaces. Vibration and noise make it difficult to work. Excessively high or low temperatures not only make it uncomfortable to work but can also make it difficult to work with certain media.

Let us recap the important aspects of your lab space:

- Overall cleanliness
- No or very low airflow
- Minimal foot traffic, noise, and vibration
- Wear appropriate clothing and keep hair back.
- Adequate lighting and ambient temperatures
- Wipe down surfaces before starting work.
- Provide a microbe-free environment within the workspace.

Lab Safety

During the handling and transfer of live yeast cultures, sanitary working techniques often require the use of flame and/or chemicals. Paying strict attention to safety is not just for the benefit of the yeast but also for the individual working in the lab. Lack of attention to safety in the lab can quickly lead to injury or death. If you are uncertain of how to work safely, you should not attempt the work.

In the brewery and lab, we commonly use several chemicals to sanitize containers and equipment before culture transfer. These may include io-dophor, chlorinated and brominated solutions, peracetic acid solutions, and alcohols (isopropanol or ethanol). For the same reasons that these chemicals are effective as sanitizers, they can be hazardous to humans. It is important to follow the label instructions to use these chemicals safely and to assure their maximum effectiveness as sanitizers. Consider the following:

- Only use properly labeled chemicals. Read labels or material safety data sheets (MSDS) to understand the health effects of sanitizers used in the lab. Some are inhalation hazards; others can cause irritant or corrosive effects to eyes and skin. Ensure adequate ventilation and use of personal protective equipment. Maintain copies of MSDS for all chemicals.
- Read labels to avoid mixing incompatible chemicals and to avoid storing them in containers with which they are not compatible. If you transfer any amount to a secondary container, ensure that you properly label that container as well. This avoids confusion and allows segregation of incompatible materials.
- Follow the manufacturer's instructions for dilution. Use of some chemicals at full strength can be more hazardous, may not increase effectiveness, and can increase costs.
- Ensure proper disposal of containers and used sanitizing solutions. These requirements will vary depending upon the legal requirements by location.

Handling flammable liquids requires some special considerations:

- Ensure that you keep bulk liquid containers in a separate location from the working stock. An approved storage site is critical when working with larger volumes.
- Ensure that you have appropriately rated fire extinguishers at the ready in areas where you use or store flammable liquids. Know the procedure for activating the fire extinguisher before a fire occurs.

- Work on a sealed, fire-resistant surface without low cupboards or other flammable material overhead.
- Metal containers are preferred for handling and storing of most flammable liquids, since they can be grounded to avoid static sparks during liquid transfer, and they are not as susceptible to the effects of an external fire.
- Ensure adequate ventilation when dispensing or using flammable liquids. This helps protect the user from inhalation of vapors and reduces the likelihood of building up vapor that may result in a flammable atmosphere.
- Sources of ignition, such as sparks or open flame, should not be present where you use or dispense flammable liquids. You must take special care if flame sterilization and flammable liquid sanitizers are used in close proximity.
- Eliminate or reduce the presence of combustible materials such as curtains, tablecloths, lab bench absorbent pads, wipes, waste containers, etc.
- Ensure proper storage and disposal of materials used to work with or clean up flammable liquids. Flammable solvent-soaked rags or paper towels in a wastebasket are a serious fire hazard.

You must use personal protective equipment when handling hazardous materials. Consider the following:

- Do not skimp on proper safety equipment.
- Properly designed chemical goggles keep liquids from splashing or dripping into the eyes. Safety glasses alone, even with side shields, do not offer as much protection against a liquid splash.
- The purpose of a face shield is to protect the parts of the face other than the eyes. When using a face shield, it still requires additional eye protection.
- Gloves come in many sizes, lengths, and materials of construction.
  - Latex gloves are ineffective for protection against solvents such as alcohols.
  - Nitrile or neoprene gloves are a better choice for working with water-based and flammable liquid sanitizers.
  - Inspect gloves regularly to ensure that they do not have leaks.
  - Gloves should fit appropriately—not too large, not too small.

- A chemical-resistant body covering such as an apron is recommended when handling chemicals in excess of small quantities.

Whether in the homebrew environment or commercial setting, a supply of fresh running water should be readily available. If an individual is exposed to a chemical on the skin or in the eyes, in most cases, the product manufacturer will recommend rinsing the affected area for 15 minutes with clean running water. In a commercial/industrial setting, an eyewash/safety shower should be present, properly tested, and maintained. In the home setting a sink, shower, or garden hose should be available for this purpose. Always read the safety precautions for the materials you use, have a plan in place to deal with emergencies, and have the equipment to carry out that plan before you begin to work. Always seek medical advice after any accident that involves exposure to chemicals.

Working safely is a matter of recognizing and anticipating hazards, avoiding or eliminating them, and having a plan of action in case things get out of control.

Lab Equipment

Lab Setup
- Balance, triple beam or electronic, when working with sub-gram amounts
- Weigh paper or weigh boats
- Orbital shaker or stir plate with magnetic stir bars
- Microwave
- Propane torch
- Bunsen burner w/gas source, alcohol lamp, or propane torch
- Inoculating loop for transferring small amounts of cells from one medium to another. Available as sterilized, one-time use or as a reusable wire loop made of stainless steel, nichrome, platinum, or other wire. You sterilize the metal loops by flaming before each transfer. Metal loops require cooling prior to transfers, which can be done by immersing the loop in sterile water or by touching the hot loop to an agar surface before picking up a colony. Loops come in different sizes and wire thicknesses. Thinner wire heats and cools faster than thicker wire. Some loops have two different sizes on the opposite ends of a single handle. In general,

you would use the larger loops for plates and the smaller loops or wires for slants.

- Test tube racks
- Screw-cap test tubes (glass and sterile disposable, 16 x 120 mm, 16 x 150 mm)
- Sterile Petri dishes (100 x 15 mm and 60 x 15 mm)
- Erlenmeyer flasks (50 ml, 100 ml, 250 ml, 500 ml, 1 L)
- Pyrex glass bottles (500 ml and 1 L)
- Graduated cylinders (100 ml, 500 ml)
- Graduated beaker (1 L)
- Breathable cotton or foam stoppers
- Sterile pipettes (1 ml, 10 ml)
- Glass Pasteur pipettes or sterile transfer pipettes
- Pipette bulb or Pipetter
- Lab thermometer
- Laboratory swabs
- Parafilm—laboratory wrap used to keep plates and slants from drying out
- Aluminum foil
- Apparel (lab coat, shoe covers, hair cover, face mask, eye protection)
- Nitrile gloves
- Safety glasses
- Heat-protective gloves
- Autoclave or pressure cooker. Used to sterilize the equipment and media used in culturing
- Sterilization indicator tape
- pH meter or pH strips (pH meter requires calibration solutions and cleaning/storage solutions)
- Microscope (10X, 40X, and 100X oil immersion objective with 10X or 16X eyepieces)
- Slides
- Cover slips
- Immersion oil
- Lens cleaning kit
- Agar. Used to solidify wort media in slants and plates. Lab-grade agar is not terribly expensive, but if you are on a tight budget, the agar powder sold at specialty markets and health food stores works fine.

- Culturing medium (malt-based, sterilized 1.040 wort)
- Incubator (commercial or improvised such as Styrofoam box with heating pad and computer fan)
- Water bath (commercial or alternatives such as baby wipe warmer or aquarium heater)
- Fire extinguisher
- First aid kit
- Eye wash station
- Material safety data sheets (MSDS) on all products in use

Contamination Detection

- Membrane filtration apparatus
- Membrane filters (pore size 0.45 microns for testing, 0.2 microns to sterile filter)
- Membrane pads
- Vacuum pump (can be an inexpensive manual hand pump)
- Metal forceps
- Metal spatula
- Selective testing media (various, based on test)
- Wash bottle for isopropanol and water
- Sterile Petri dishes (100 x 15 mm)
- Sterile sampling bags or containers
- Agar
- Culturing medium (malt-based, sterilized 1.040 wort)
- Cell spreaders
- Gram stain kit (requires microscope, slides, and cover slips)
- Anaerobic chamber (or anaerobic packs in a large, airtight container). While anaerobic media exist, an anaerobic chamber is the preferred method for regular testing for anaerobic organisms.

Cell Counting, Viability, Vitality

- Methylene blue (optional: citric acid, 0.1 M glycine buffer solution at 10.6 pH, methylene violet 3RAX)
- Hemocytometer with cover slip
- Pipette
- Screw-capped culture tubes to perform serial dilution
- Microscope (10X eyepiece, 10X, 40X, 100X oil immersion objectives)

- Lens cleaning solution and appropriate swabs
- Handheld counter
- pH meter
- Deionized water
- 50 ml conical centrifuge tube
- Conical stir bar
- 20% glucose solution

Yeast Storage and Propagation
- Agar
- Culturing medium (malt-based, sterilized 1.040 wort)
- Shaker or stir plate
- Erlenmeyer flasks (50 ml, 100 ml, 250 ml, 500 ml, 1 L, 2 L)
- Screw-cap test tubes (16 x 120 mm, glass and sterile disposable)
- Sterile Petri dishes (100 x 15 mm)
- Sterile pipettes (1 ml, 10 ml)
- Pipette bulb or Pipetter
- Centrifuge, 1.5 ml microcentrifuge tubes, glycerol, and small ice chest (for freezing cultures)
- Sterile mineral oil

Fermentation Testing
- Culturing medium (malt-based, sterilized 1.040 wort)
- Pyrex glass bottles (500 ml and 1 L)
- Erlenmeyer flasks (50 ml, 100 ml, 250 ml, 500 ml, 1 L)
- Graduated cylinders
- Sterile pipettes (1 ml, 10 ml)
- Pipette bulb or Pipetter
- Shaker or stir plate

How Much Lab Does My Brewery Need?

How much should you invest in a laboratory for your brewery? It can range from simple (less than one hundred dollars) to complex (costing many thousands). The amount you invest depends not only on what you want to accomplish, but also on the size of your operation, philosophy, and more. Large breweries have no real choice if they are to be successful. Smaller-scale breweries that have much tighter control over distribution, such as brewpubs that do not distribute outside the restaurant, have more flexibility. Homebrewers have the greatest flexibility, because they are not selling their beer and have the ultimate control over who drinks it. Even so, a surprising number of homebrewers show more interest in setting up a lab and controlling beer quality than many small commercial breweries. The fact is that many small breweries throughout the world have no formal quality assurance. Small breweries are often one-person operations, and the brewer feels there is not enough time for quality analysis. Does this mean they will produce bad beer? Not necessarily. The beauty of the brewing process is that if you follow good practices and are a skilled brewer, you can make good, stable beer. Of course, if you do not test your products, problems can slip past you before you have a chance to recognize them, and the first sign of trouble comes only after customers complain or declining sales hurt the brewery.

This always seems shocking to us, because quality assurance measures have important consequences for beer quality and customer satisfaction. Making inferior-quality beer or beer that turns poor quickly during distribution negatively affects sales and growth. If allowed to continue, this will eventually threaten the survival of the brewery. Consider the value of the brewery's reputation, and compare that to the cost of funding a modest lab.

So where do you start? Any brewery, no matter how small, should run basic forced wort and forced ferment tests. They are simple, inexpensive, easy, and can tell you a considerable amount about both the hot and cold side of your brewery. You can add other simple, inexpensive tests, such as diacetyl force and fermentation trials.

Another valuable, but inexpensive practice is sensory analysis. Sensory analysis can be as simple as tasting the beer on a regular basis and keeping notes, or can include a formal panel of experts. Regardless of the complexity, you should always treat tasting seriously, not just as an excuse to drink beer. You should design a sensory program that is consistent and regular, such as tasting all beer in the tanks at 10 a.m. each weekday. We have seen many cases where a problem developed in a fermentor, and without regular checks in place, many more batches of beer were lost. Without a regular tasting program, brewers often get too busy to remember to sample the beers and think about beer quality.

Performing cell counts and checking yeast for viability and vitality is the next step. It is not very expensive or difficult to master. The time required to perform these types of tests on a pitch of yeast is minimal, especially when compared to the time invested in making a batch of beer.

Any brewery that packages and distributes beer should, at a minimum, plate its beer, water, fermentors, and other equipment for possible contamination. It should design and follow a regular procedure for sampling, including bottles or kegs and locations throughout the brewery.

Packaging breweries should also consider VDK testing (which includes diacetyl) a requirement, because the precursor is flavorless. Once the beer reaches the market, diacetyl can appear when the precursor oxidizes. While the inexpensive diacetyl force test is a good first step, it cannot tell you the quantity present. VDK testing requires either a distillation apparatus and a spectrophotometer or a gas chromatograph, so the brewery needs either to invest in the equipment or send out samples to a lab.

The lab can grow from there, taking on oxygen measurements (on wort and final beer), tracking and maintaining the health of the yeast, starting new propagations when conditions require it, and conducting even more analysis of the beer.

There is no upper limit to what your lab can accomplish, but every brewery should strive to perform at least some basic testing in-house. While it may require a time investment, having testing on site means being able to obtain quick information to make critical decisions about beer quality.

Sterilization

While many brewers frequently use the word "sterilize," they are often using the word incorrectly (Figure 6.2). When brewing beer, we rarely sterilize anything. Instead, we clean and sanitize. However, the yeast lab requires a higher level of purity, and we do need to sterilize. You do not want to grow a yeast culture only to find out you have also grown bacteria or wild yeast at the same time. One key point to keep in mind is that you cannot sanitize or sterilize something that is not clean. A successful lab is a clean lab. You should have protocols and procedures in place that force you to maintain clean and sanitary operations in your lab and brewery.

Clean	Cleaning is the removal of dirt, oils, protein, and other material until the surface is free from the presence of foreign substances. It is not possible to sanitize until the surfaces are clean.
Sanitize	Sanitizing is the reduction of microorganisms, usually with heat or chemicals, to a point considered not harmful to humans. It does not guarantee a kill rate of 100 percent, but rather to a minimum kill ratio of 99.9 percent. The products for sanitizing are often no-rinse at proper concentrations.
Disinfect	Disinfection is a reduction of microorganisms to a minimum kill ratio of 99.999 percent. The chemicals used in disinfection are often unsafe for consumption, requiring a rinse after use.
Sterilize	Sterilization is the complete inactivation of all organisms: fungi, bacteria, viruses, and spores. Steam requires a minimum of 15 minutes at 250° F (121° C) or 3 minutes at 273° F (134° C). Dry heat requires at least two hours at 320° F (160° C).

Figure 6.2: Levels of sanitation.

Wet Heat

The most common sterilization method is some form of heat: wet, dry, or flame. The type of object you are sterilizing often determines the best method. One of the best tools for this is the autoclave. An autoclave uses steam under pressure to achieve temperatures in the 250 to 273° F (121 to 134° C) range. At minimum, an object requires a holding time of 15 minutes at 250° F (121° C) or 3 minutes at 273° F (134° C) to sterilize it. Holding time starts when the chamber and the items in it have reached the target temperature, so your total time will exceed the holding time. Certain items, such as liquids or dense or bulky items, may require longer hold times to ensure that objects have reached the correct temperature and minimum time.

For the average lab at a small brewery, you only need to sterilize on a relatively small scale, which you can do in a benchtop pressure cooker. You can use a pressure cooker for small-scale laboratory supplies, such as lab ware or media for plates, slants, and yeast propagation. These pressure cookers are ideal for home brewery use, since they are inexpensive and easy to use. True autoclaves come in all sizes and tend to be considerably more expensive as they get larger and more automated. The key advantage to these larger autoclaves is that they have larger chambers, allowing more or larger items to go through a cycle at one time. They often come with some level of automation or special cool-down cycles that makes it possible to run more cycles with less effort. When selecting an autoclave, determine the largest item you believe you will need to sterilize, and then find a unit with a chamber size that will accommodate it.

For effective sterilization, the steam needs to get into every nook and cranny. An overcrowded autoclave is an ineffective autoclave. If you are using a simpler autoclave or pressure cooker, you will need to purge air manually from the chamber at the beginning of the cycle. It is important that you properly prepare the objects going into the autoclave. All tight-sealing containers need their lids left ajar, as they might implode or explode with the pressure changes of the autoclave. In addition, if you are sterilizing liquids, at the end of the cycle you do not want to vent the autoclave rapidly, since it will cause the liquid to boil rapidly and gush out of the containers. You need to clean all objects properly, as any grime has the potential to shield organisms. If your autoclave has meters or charts, record the data from every run or include the printout along with any other documentation, such as the daily lab logs. You can also use color-changing indicator tape to mark items prior to autoclaving. It is handy, as it gives a quick, visual indication that an object is sterile. However, get into the habit of removing the tape on use, so that someone later does not think a nonsterile vessel is sterile.

Dry Heat

Dry heat is another option for sterilizing objects, but it requires higher heat and longer hold times, which are often unsuitable for some materials. Dry heat requires at least two hours at 320° F (160° C) to sterilize an object. The higher heat and longer times are needed to transfer enough heat energy to inactivate any organisms present. Contact with steam is far more effective in transferring the energy needed to inactivate an organism. Have you ever accidentally put your hand over a boiling pot of water? Have you ever reached into an oven at 212° F (100° C)? If you have, then you will be familiar with how much hotter the steam is to your skin, because of the energy contained in the vaporized water. When the steam turns back into liquid on your skin, it releases tremendous amounts of heat.

Still, dry heat has some advantages. For many on a shoestring budget, dry sterilization has its advantage in cost and the ability to sterilize large objects, as you can use a common household oven. If you are using such a device, realize that the temperature setting can be wildly inaccurate. Any time you use a household oven, back it up with a good lab-grade thermometer. Of course, that savings in initial equipment costs is often quickly lost in the additional time required for each sterilization cycle. It is possible to use shorter times with forced ventilation ovens or higher temperatures.

Incineration

Some objects do not require complete sterilization. For example, when using an inoculating loop you only sterilize the length of the wire, not the handle. In the lab, flaming is the method of choice for inoculating loops

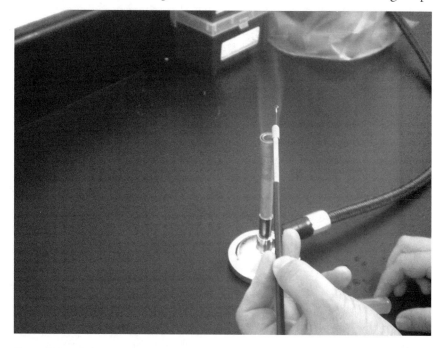

Figure 6.3: Prior to every transfer, flame the inoculation loop until it glows red to sterilize it.

and straight wires, but you could theoretically use it on any small object not destroyed by the flame. When flaming a loop or straight wire, work from the tip back to the handle and then back to the tip, ensuring that the portion under flame glows red. If there is a lot of material on the wire and you place it directly into the flame, it can "pop" as the liquid inside boils. Besides being a hazard for the user, this can send the material flying onto other surfaces, which is not good aseptic technique. It is a good idea to clean your wire before flaming, or first hold the loop above the flame until any material on the loop dries before lowering it into the flame. Once flamed, you can cool the loop by touching it to the sterile medium before taking a yeast or other sample.

Another practice involving flame is to dip the object or wipe 70% alcohol on it, then ignite the alcohol, burning it off. This leaves less residue than flaming the object until red. However, use the utmost caution when working with alcohol and open flame, as the results can be deadly.

Tyndallization

New brewers often think they can sterilize something by boiling it for 15 minutes. Boiling an object in water or boiling a liquid for 15 minutes kills most vegetative bacteria and can inactivate viruses, but it is ineffective against many bacterial and fungal spores. Boiling is not sterilization, but it can kill most of the microbes that concern brewers. If you have more time on your hands than money, you can try Tyndallization, a process in which you boil for 20 minutes one day, then again the next day, and so on until you have boiled the liquid four times. The incubation period between each boil gives any heat-resistant spores present a chance to germinate, and the next boil kills them. Unfortunately, this will not sterilize water, as the boiled medium would need to support the growth of the organism. Go buy a nice stovetop pressure cooker instead.

Autoclave Testing

Being able to sterilize media is a critical function of a laboratory. It is important for the lab to check periodically that the autoclave is performing correctly. The most common way to do this is by using a biological indicator, usually an organism (supplied in a glass capsule) that is very difficult to kill. The user runs the capsule through a sterilization cycle to see if it was successful.

Materials
- 3M Attest Biological Indicator capsule (or similar product)
- Autoclave or pressure cooker

Procedure
1. Place 3M Attest Biological Indicator capsule into a test bottle of medium. You may also include an indicator capsule in any of the other items being autoclaved.
2. Allow the full autoclave cycle to run.
3. When the cycle is finished, wait until the pressure gauge reads 0 psi and carefully vent the autoclave. Allow contents to cool for at least 10 minutes.
4. Carefully remove the biological indicator from the liquid bottle and/or wherever else it was included.
5. Check the indicator vial label for a color change from rose to brown or whatever the manufacturer specifies.
6. Bend the capsule gently to break the inside and release the liquid. Do the same to a non-autoclaved, labeled control for bacterial growth.
7. Place the biological indicators into a 133° F (56° C) incubator.
8. Examine the indicator tube at 8, 12, 24, and 48 hours for any color change. A yellow color change indicates bacterial growth.
9. Compare vial to the non-autoclaved control at each time point. You want the capsule to remain the original color, indicating that the cycle killed the bacteria.
10. After you check the results, discard all of the material used in the test run.

Yeast Culturing

Anytime you work with live yeast, you are working with a yeast culture. When you ferment a batch of beer, you can consider that a yeast culture. When you propagate yeast, you are culturing yeast. However, many people use the term yeast culturing to mean the smaller steps from slants and plates that you would perform before propagation.

Keep in mind that isolating and propagating yeast from small colony sizes requires sterile conditions and sterile media. Either you will need to purchase presterilized media, or you will need a pressure cooker or autoclave.

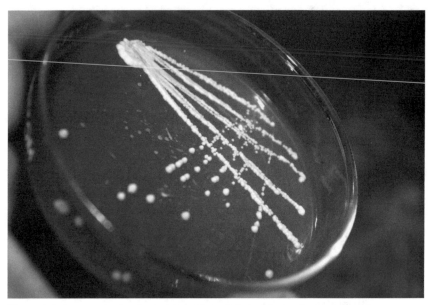

Figure 6.4: A properly streaked plate will result in isolated colonies grown from a single cell. Photo courtesy of Samuel W. Scott.

Plates and Slants

Labs use plates and slants in all bacteria and yeast work. Traditionally, labs made plates with glass Petri dishes. Today most labs use presterilized disposable plastic Petri dishes that come 20 to a sleeve. You can buy them in various sizes from 60 to 120 mm in diameter. We have found 100 mm is a convenient size for most work. Plates and slants are made with agar, a gelatinlike substance that is liquefied at temperatures above 107° F (42° C) and forms a gel under 99° F (37° C). Once solidified, the yeast or other organisms can grow upon the surface.

A plate and slant have the same material inside, but a slant has a longer shelf life because it has a screw-cap lid and does not dry out as fast. The caps with gaskets seal better than those without, extending storage life. You should seal non-gasket caps with either vinyl tape (electrical or insulating tape) or Parafilm. An unsealed plate has a shorter shelf life, especially in low-humidity storage. You can extend the shelf life of a plate by sealing it around the circumference with vinyl tape or Parafilm. Vinyl tape is much cheaper and comes in a variety of colors, which you can use to help color code your work. Another benefit of sealing plates with vinyl tape is that it holds the plate together, reducing the likelihood of contamination when handling the plates.

A slant (also called a slope) can last up to one year, but you should re-culture slants every four to six months to avoid mutations. A slant is your mother culture, which should remain pure due to its infrequent usage. When you contaminate a slant, you lose your mother culture. You may make backups or new slants from older ones by following sterile transfer techniques.

Long-Term Storage

You can use other storage techniques to protect cultures over the long term. Commercial and university labs use deep-frozen cultures as permanent mother cultures, but this is beyond the means of most small brewers or homebrewers. Some homebrewers report success with freezing cultures in a standard freezer, although the length of time you can store a culture this way may not be any longer than with a well-prepared slant; it depends a great deal on your technique and the strain. You can also store a slant under oil, which was the method labs used before freezing and is a decent option for the small brewery. In Figure 6.5 we list the estimated shelf life of each method. The difference between maximum shelf life and reliable shelf life is the rate of mutation. While it is possible to store a culture warm for many years and have live cells, that is not the true goal of long-term yeast storage. What you are striving for is a mutation-free culture. The warmer you store a culture, the more a culture grows, the greater the rate of mutation. Warmth, oxygen, and available nutrients all increase the incidence of mutation, and that is what prevents most of these methods from being true long-term storage options. Desiccation is not a good option, as the process itself may introduce mutations.

Method	Reliable Shelf Life	Maximum Shelf Life
Harvested slurry (38° F /3° C)	2 weeks	6 months
Agar plate (38° F /3° C)	1 month	1 year if sealed
Agar slant (38° F /3° C)	3 months	1-2 years
Agar stab (38° F /3° C)	4 months	2-3 years
Water immersion (38° F /3° C)	6 months	3-5 years
Oil immersion (38° F /3° C)	4-6 months	10-14 years
Desiccation (38° F /3° C)	—	3-6 years
Home freezer (-2° F /-19° C)	0-2 years	5+ years
Professional frozen (-112° F /-80° C)	Indefinite	Indefinite

Figure 6.5: Summary of methods for yeast storage. The problem with long-term storage is not viability, but maintaining a mutation-free culture.

The plate is your working culture. It also provides a look at the purity of your yeast, since microorganisms other than yeast that will contaminate your beer can also grow on the plate as a visible colony. This allows you to identify the presence of possible contaminants without a high-power microscope. Of course, this method will not ensure the purity of a culture, but if you see more than one type of colony, you can be certain the culture is not pure. If you detect any foreign growths on your plate, it is contaminated and you should discard it.

Preparing Agar Slants and Plates

You can buy prepared slants and plates, but beware of the inexpensive variety. Test any plates or slants you purchase or make by incubating a random sample. If there is growth, then all the plates or slants from that batch are suspect. If you are serious about your lab work, we recommend learning to make your own plates. You can easily recoup the initial cost in equipment and supplies over time, and the labor involved is not excessive.

You prepare plates using 1 to 2 percent agar mixed with other materials that provide yeast food or other special capabilities to the medium—10 to 20 grams of agar along with 1 liter of liquid. Slants require a slightly firmer medium. The more agar you use, the firmer the medium becomes. Some labs prefer to work with a softer surface, while others prefer a firmer one. For culturing and growing brewer's yeast, you will want to use a malt-based sugar both for your solid medium used on plates and slants and for your liquid medium when you propagate a culture.

You can buy just about any medium you want as a pre-mixed powder, or you can mix your own. The basic process involves mixing the powder with distilled water or wort, heating until it dissolves, sterilizing, and then pouring into plates using aseptic technique. If you are making slants, the process is the same, except you fill the slants from the melted medium, and then sterilize them.

Here is the process for creating your own medium. You are going to be making both plates and slants in this procedure:

1. Prepare 1 liter of 1.040 SG wort, without hops and with any nutrients you would like to add, like Servomyces. Boil the wort until hot break forms, cool, and filter out the break material.
2. Measure out 15 grams of agar powder, and sprinkle on the wort surface. Allow the powder to hydrate for a few minutes. Do not stir until the agar appears fully hydrated.
3. Stir or swirl to mix, then heat in a microwave oven or slowly on a stove to melt the agar and boil for a couple of minutes until the agar is fully dissolved (check the bottom for translucent grains of agar).
4. At this point you can pipette the solution into suitable tubes for slants. You

want to add enough of the solution so that when tipped at an angle, it develops a good-sized working surface in the tube, but not so much that the agar is closer than a few centimeters from the tube opening. It is best to test first with water to determine what angle and how much volume you need per tube. Generally, the best angle is somewhere between 20 and 35 degrees, but it is not critical. Once you determine how much medium it takes, you can begin filling the tubes with a pipette. Don't worry about working sterile at this point, since the slants will go into the autoclave. Place the caps loosely on the tubes, place the tubes upright in a rack, and place the rack in the autoclave.

5. Transfer the remaining agar solution to a suitable container with a loose cap, or cover with foil, and place in the autoclave to steam sterilize.

6. After sterilizing, allow the mixture to become cool enough to handle but still pour easily.

7. Take the slants out and lay them down at an angle, with the cap end propped up to make the appropriate slope.

8. If you can hold the flask comfortably with your bare hand, hold it up to your cheek, and it should feel quite warm but not uncomfortable. At this point the agar is close to setting, and you need to act quickly. If you try to pour with the agar too cold, it will come out lumpy and not settle in the plates. If you pour with it too hot, the plates will end up with a lot of excess condensation under the lid.

9. Set out your sterile plates with the lids closed.

10. Working under the hood or using aseptic technique, quickly in succession remove the foil or cap from the flask, tilt the lid on one of the plates, and pour (usually 15 to 20 ml) into each plate.

11. You will notice that condensation forms on the lids. Once the plates have cooled and the agar has set, you can stack them several high, wrap a rubber band around them, and flip them over onto their lids. Do not wrap them in Parafilm or vinyl tape until the condensation dissipates. Place them in a warm area (80° F /27° C) for a day or two, and the condensation should evaporate.

12. The plates and slants are ready to use at this point. Tighten the caps on the slants before storing. If you want to store plates without drying out, wrap a continuous piece of vinyl tape around the edge or wrap the entire plate in Parafilm to seal it.

13. Store plates inverted in a closed container.

Streaking a Plate

Streaking an agar plate is a quick and easy way to isolate yeast and to check for purity. When streaking a plate, you dip a sterile inoculation loop into the yeast source and run the loop over the agar surface in a pattern, with a goal of having the last cells spaced wide-enough apart so that a single cell has enough room to grow into an isolated colony. By selecting only from normal-looking colonies grown from single cells, you are starting with a pure culture.

Procedure

1. To begin, clean an area and light an alcohol lamp or Bunsen burner.
2. Place the plate near the flame, with the cover on and the agar surface to streak pointing down. You always store your plates with the agar-filled portion on top; the agar surface for streaking pointing down. This keeps any airborne material from landing on the plate surface.
3. Select a sterile disposable loop, or sterilize your loop in the flame.
4. While keeping the loop in the clean area near the flame, open the slant or other yeast source and pass the opening through the flame.
5. Insert the inoculation loop into the slant tube, and touch it to the agar surface to cool the loop. Only touch the loop to the yeast colony, do not take a loopful. You want a tiny amount of yeast. Remove the loop, taking care to keep it in the clean area around the flame, but not so close as to damage the yeast.
6. Quickly re-flame and close the slant.
7. Set the slant down and pick up the agar side of plate, only turning it over in the clean area near the flame.
8. Run the tip of the loop back and forth many times in a small section. Flame the loop. Rotate the plate 90 degrees, and streak the loop through the section just streaked and streak a new section. Turn the plate again and repeat the streaking. The purpose is to first deposit the cells onto the plate, then to pull fewer cells out to another clear area, getting few cells farther apart each time. If you see yeast on the plate, then you took too much from the slant. You want to spread just a few cells, invisible to the naked eye, across the surface. Placing too much yeast in one area makes it impossible to grow and select from a single cell, which is your goal (Figure 6.6).
9. Turn the agar surface back down, and place back down onto the cover.

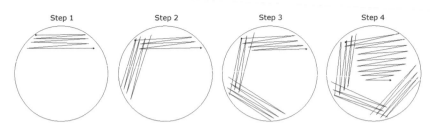

Figure 6.6: Streak, then rotate to end up with single cells spread out across the plate by step 4.

10. Grow the plate for two to three days at room temperature (72° F, 22° C), the agar-filled plate on top, the surface of the agar pointing down. A dense yeast culture will grow in the first area you streaked, getting thinner in the later streaks. If your process did not result in isolated colonies, you should streak a new plate.

11. Once you have enough growth, seal the edges of the plate with vinyl tape or Parafilm and refrigerate.

Streaking a Slant

To create new slants you need only a minute amount of yeast to transfer to the surface of the agar, so a small loop can be more efficient when you streak a new slant. When selecting yeast for a slant, you want to choose from a pure yeast colony, and a plate can provide a pure source of yeast. On a properly prepared plate, the colonies grow from a single cell. Before you select a colony to use for your slant, you should inspect them all to make sure they do not have an odd color, are translucent, or have an odd shape. If the perimeter of a colony is not smooth, even, and consistent, do not use that colony.

Procedure

1. Clean an area and light an alcohol lamp or Bunsen burner. Remember to follow the sterile technique, flame all openings, and work quickly in the clean area of an open flame.

2. Select a sterile disposable loop, or sterilize your loop in the flame.

3. Open the plate or other yeast source.

4. Touch the loop to the agar surface to cool. Use the loop to pick up yeast from a pure colony on the plate. You need only a pinprick-sized bit of yeast.

5. Set the plate down and pick up the slant.

6. Open the slant, insert the inoculation loop, and smear the yeast in a serpentine line down the middle of the agar surface. There is no need to break the surface of the agar or to smear every bit of the surface. Putting fewer cells into the slant and giving them room and food for growth can extend the life of the slant. A small amount goes a long way, so use very little yeast.

7. Re-flame and close the slant. Leave the cap loose while they are growing, and colonies should appear over two or three days at 72° F (22° C).

8. Once the growth is complete, tighten the cap, and the slant is ready for cold storage.

If you want to acquire a master culture from bottled beer, first streak it onto a plate. If the result is pure colonies, then you can make a slant from that plate. However, there can be more than one strain, and even wild yeast, in that beer. You will want to make several slants, selecting from different colonies. You should also do some small-scale fermentation trials from the yeast before committing a full batch to an unknown culture. To create a backup slant or to transfer from slant-to-slant, quickly dip your loop into the yeast on the surface of the first slant and deposit it on the second slant.

Procedure
1. Place two slants in a rack.
2. Loosen both caps.
3. Pick up and open the source slant, flame the opening, pick up yeast, cap and replace to rack.
4. Pick up and open destination slant, keeping loop within sterile area.
5. Flame the opening and deposit yeast on surface.
6. Recap loosely and leave at 72° F (22° C).
7. Put the original slant back in the fridge with the cap tight and sealed. Let the new slant grow, and place it in the fridge once a creamy white glob of yeast appears on the surface.

Stabs

Stabs are useful for organisms that do best under anaerobic conditions, such as some bacteria. A stab is a partially filled tube of agar, about 3 centimeters deep and left to solidify vertically. To inoculate a stab, use either a needle or a loop and stab it down into the center of the agar until it reaches the bottom of the tube. Pull the loop or wire back out and seal the tube. If you have trouble pushing your loop to the bottom of the stab, chances are you are using too much agar in your medium.

Oil Immersion

Oil immersion extends the life of slants. Before frozen-culture storage became widespread, this was the method a yeast lab would use for long-term storage. The idea is to overlay the surface of the slant with sterile mineral oil, so that it remains under oil and out of the reach of oxygen at all times. The shelf life increases to a minimum of two years, although there is information that states some samples of *Saccharomyces* have been viable after 14 years at room temperature storage. Of course, viability does not guarantee the culture is mutation free. The warmer the storage, the greater the incidence of mutation, so store your cultures cold (38° F /3° C).

Procedure
1. After inoculating your slants and incubating them, add a layer of sterile mineral oil.
2. Store around 38° F (3° C).

Water Immersion

Storing yeast under water, as opposed to under beer, is becoming more popular. Sterile distilled water storage puts yeast in a resting state, and some reports suggest yeast can be stored in this manner for years without refrigeration. You would generally only do this with small quantities of yeast, which you then propagate in your lab. However, it is possible that this will work with larger slurries. Some brewers are now trying this. The key is to use sterile distilled water and wash the yeast slurry several times in the sterile distilled water to remove any traces of beer.

Procedure
1. Add 2 to 3 milliliters of distilled water to a screw-cap tube, and sterilize in the autoclave or pressure cooker. Cool to room temperature before using.
2. Using a sterile loop, transfer a colony from a plate to the water. You only

want a small amount of yeast, about the size of a match head. Avoid picking up any of the solid medium underneath.

3. Cap the tube tightly. If the caps do not have a gasket, wrap the cap with vinyl tape or the entire tube in Parafilm to seal.

4. You can store these vials at room temperature for months, although refrigeration may extend storage even longer.

Freezing

You may have heard that professional yeast banks store their stocks frozen at -80° C, and they can store properly frozen yeast indefinitely. While -80° C storage is the best way to prevent mutation, it is also possible to store them at -20° C and get improved results over refrigerator temperature storage. Anecdotal evidence suggests that it is possible to achieve storage times of up to five or more years with minimal mutation. The difficulty is that the results can vary depending on the health of the yeast when frozen, yeast strain, temperature control, and many other conditions of storage. Your goal is to get yeast in the peak of health and to store them at -20° C with minimal damage.

The better the condition of the yeast when frozen, the better their condition upon thawing. Collect the yeast for storage from a clean lab propagation. You want to use yeast that are at their peak of health, with a large reserve of glycogen and trehalose. In fact, the cells' ability to tolerate freezing correlates with glycogen and cellular trehalose levels (Kandror, et al., 2004).

The higher the freezer temperature, the shorter the shelf life and stability of the culture. It is important that once you freeze your yeast, you do not let it thaw. If you do not have a -80° C freezer, you will need a reliable, well insulated, non-frost-free freezer. You can use a frost-free freezer, but it has a warming cycle to prevent ice buildup. Once you freeze your cultures, place them in a Styrofoam cooler inside the freezer. This will help stabilize any temperature fluctuations and improve storage life.

You will need to add some form of cryoprotectant to your yeast before freezing, such as glycerol. Cryopreservants such as glycerol work by preventing osmotic lysis. Normally, as the medium around the cells freezes there is less and less liquid water at the cell surface, which creates an osmotic gradient. This pulls water out of the cell by osmosis and kills the cell. Adding a cryoprotectant prevents this from happening.

It can be tricky to get good yeast freezes that will not die upon thawing after storage. Some labs quick-freeze microbes using liquid nitrogen, though not all yeast labs consider this necessary or beneficial when working with yeast and just place the cultures in the -80° C freezer. Some homebrewers have used dry ice/ethanol or dry ice/acetone baths to quick-freeze their samples before placing them in the freezer.

Using a frost-free freezer results in temperature swings that will freeze and thaw the culture, causing repeated damage to the cells. When storing at -20° C it may prove beneficial to increase the amount of cryoprotectant used, so that the culture does not freeze solid. This provides the benefits of the low temperature, but avoids loss of viability from freezing and repeated freeze/thaw cycles. In addition, adding 1 gram per liter of ascorbic acid as an antioxidant to prevent membrane lipid oxidation can improve viability as well (Sidari and Caridi, 2009).

Materials
- Sterile glycerol
- Sterile YPD solution
- Sterile CryoTubes or screw-cap microcentrifuge tubes
- Centrifuge
- Sterile pipettes
- Mechanical pipetter
- Freezer
- Styrofoam box (for -20° C storage)
- Ascorbic acid (for -20° C storage)

Procedure for -80° C Storage
1. Pick a culture and grow it in 10 milliliters of medium for 48 hours. Growth is done before this time, but the yeast build glycogen reserves after growth.
2. Move the 10 milliliters culture to a 40° F (4° C) environment, and hold for another 48 hours, to encourage the yeast to build trehalose.
3. Under the hood or near a flame re-suspend the yeast in the 10-milliliter culture and transfer 1 milliliter to a sterile 1.5 ml microcentrifuge tube. Label the tube with the strain name, number, and date.
4. Centrifuge the tubes for 3 to 4 minutes. Remove carefully and place in a rack under the hood.
5. Carefully discard the liquid, saving the yeast pellet at the bottom.

6. Add 1 milliliter of a 15 percent glycerol, 85 percent YPD solution to the tube, and gently re-suspend the yeast with a sterile pipette.
7. Seal tightly, wrap in Parafilm, and place in appropriate boxes within the -80° C freezer.
8. To revive the yeast, either select a portion of the culture with a pipette tip and plate it or thaw the entire culture by holding it in your gloved hand until it reaches room temperature, and then add to 100 milliliters of liquid growth medium.

Procedure for -20° C Storage

You can follow the same procedure as for -80° C storage, but it may be possible to increase dramatically the resulting viability by following this modified procedure.

1. Follow steps 1 through 5 from the -80° C procedure.
2. Prepare a solution of 50 percent glycerol and 50 percent YPD.
3. Add 1 gram per liter ascorbic acid to your solution.
4. Add 1 milliliter of the solution to the tube, and gently re-suspend the yeast with a sterile pipette.
5. Seal tightly, wrap in Parafilm, place the tubes upright inside a small Styrofoam ice chest and then place the ice chest into the freezer.
6. To revive the yeast, either select a portion of the culture with a pipette tip and plate it or warm the entire culture by holding in your gloved hand until it reaches room temperature, and then add it to 100 milliliters of liquid growth medium.

Picking Colonies

Proper colony selection is a vital part of yeast culturing. This is where it all begins, and if you are careless when choosing colonies, it can potentially lead to propagating unhealthy yeast. To begin, remove the agar plate from its storage and let it warm up naturally to room temperature. This is the same principle that you use when pitching yeast into freshly made wort. You always want to make sure the yeast is approximately the same temperature as the growth medium, which prevents temperature-related yeast shock.

After the culture plate reaches room temperature, carefully examine the yeast colonies. Look at the plate from both sides in a well-lit area.

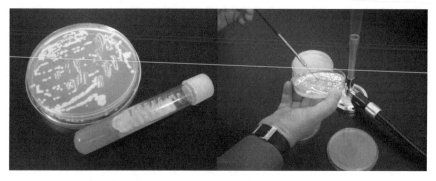

Figure 6.7: Examine the colonies on the plate or slant before transfer. Work in the clean area of the flame. Select only colonies that are separate from their neighbors.

Mentally select the colonies you want to grow. Scan the surface of the agar for unusual-looking colonies or any moldy areas. Mold sometimes appears as a clear substance sprawling across the plate, so it can be difficult to see. Other times mold is obvious and looks like a hairy growth, similar in appearance to those that grow on bread, cheese, and fruit. Still other times, the mold is a mixture of the two. If you notice any mold on your plate, you should start over with a different plate. If you insist on using that plate for some reason, carefully select a colony and re-streak on a new plate.

Bacteria are harder to identify, as they may look like yeast colonies at first but usually turn more translucent and sometimes colored. Shiny colonies are usually indicative of a bacterial infection, whereas misshapen colonies often turn out to be wild yeast. Yeast colonies grown from a single cell are round, creamy off-white- or milky manila-colored discs with a peak in the center. Different strains will display different morphologies and textures, and you should get familiar with the consistency and appearance of the strains you are working with so you are more likely to notice any changes. In general, avoid any abnormal-looking growths.

If you determine your plate is contaminant free, your next step is to choose which colonies to transfer. In most cases, you will want to choose more than one colony to start your culture to maintain genetic diversity. Each colony contains at least 1 million cells, all generated from the same mother cell. That means any mutations that cell had, aberrant or otherwise, exist in all of the budded daughter cells. When starting to grow a culture, you want to have a good amount of genetic variety present. In theory, the strongest yeast cells will survive and proliferate in the environment you provide them, and the ensuing culture will be healthier and more viable. Yeast cells go through many cell divisions in a short amount of time, which accelerates the process of natural selection. With yeast, natural selection occurs during a few days of propagation, as opposed to the centuries that it may require for other species.

We recommend that you select about ten individual colonies. In other words, pick ten colonies that you can easily distinguish as individual colonies that do not share any border with any other colonies. This helps to ensure that the colony was not nutrient-deprived during its growth. Colonies that share a border with other yeast colonies are in direct competition for nutrients from their neighbors. Their access to necessary nutrients is limited to the amount of nutrient the yeast can wrestle away from its neighbor. This is not an ideal growth situation for yeast cells, and colonies that grow without competition are less likely to be physically deficient.

The relative size of one colony to another is also an important part of your selection criteria. The colonies you choose should be neither too large nor too small, but be aware that when colonies are close together, they tend to be smaller. However, a colony that is too small compared to the others on a plate is indicative of a respiratory mutant. Respiratory mutants are cells that have a mutation in their respiratory pathway, and they cannot utilize oxygen. This causes them to form smaller colonies, since they cannot utilize nutrients in the same way as normal cells. These cells cannot grow as fast or compete for nutrients, and they will have trouble metabolizing the sugars and nutrients found in wort. This leads to all sorts of issues in fermentation, like slow or sluggish fermentation or incomplete attenuation, as well as low levels of yeast growth.

You should also be suspicious of colonies that are too big. These colonies may be large because they have merged with another colony or because they are covering a respiratory mutant colony that they have overtaken. In addition, these larger colonies are not as healthy because they have exhausted the nutrient supply around them and used up all of their resources. The yeast cells in these colonies have divided more times that those cells of medium-sized colonies and are weaker. The actual size of the colonies depends on many variables. Generally you will select from colonies that range from ⅛ to 3/16 of an inch (3 to 5 mm), but let experience be your guide. Pay attention to the colonies you select and what results you get from a propagation grown from them. Document everything (photos are a good idea), and use that information when analyzing the data from your taste panels.

Starting Propagation From a Plate

To propagate yeast from a plate, you are going to select a number of colonies from a plate and transfer them to a sterile liquid medium. You have options on what the best liquid size is, but we recommend 10 to 25 milliliters. This is a convenient volume for the readily available tubes. Prepare your sterile medium ahead of time using plastic transport vials. They come in a range of sizes, from 10 milliliters on up. A good size for the first step off a plate is a 30- to 50-milliliter container. When beginning propagation of a culture that you have stored for a long time or yeast harvested from a beer bottle, using a lower-gravity medium puts less osmotic stress on the cells. A specific gravity of 1.020 is a good choice. After the first growth, you can switch to a more concentrated medium, such as 1.040 SG.

1. To begin, clean an area and light an alcohol lamp or Bunsen burner. Remember to follow the sterile technique, flame all openings, and work quickly in the clean area of an open flame.
2. Identify the colonies you will harvest.
3. Select a sterile disposable loop, or sterilize your loop in the flame.
4. Working quickly in the clean area around the flame, open the plate and touch the loop to the agar surface to cool. Use the loop to pick up a colony from the plate. In this case, you are trying to pick up the entire colony, but you want to avoid digging into the agar or touching any surrounding colonies.
5. Set the plate down and pick up the transport vial.
6. Open the vial, flame the opening, dunk the inoculation loop into the liquid medium, and shake the yeast free. Repeat until you have harvested several colonies.
7. Close the vial. You can leave the cap loose while they are growing, or you can pierce a hole in the cap with a hot wire and cover it with a square of Parafilm.
8. Place the vial upright on a shaker table, if you have one. This helps aerate and mix the yeast with the medium. Hold the culture for one or two days at 72° F (22° C).

9. Once the growth is complete, the culture is ready for the next propagation step.

The culture might appear slightly turbid, and eventually a white yeast
sediment will appear on the bottom, giving you some assurance that the
culture grew. Many brewers ask how many cells are present at this point.
While we can estimate how many cells might be present, it is far better
for you to do a cell count. Small differences in process can create large
variations in cell counts at this stage. You should count to know what you
can expect from your process. Refrigerated, the results of this first step
will keep for up to seven days, but it is better if you immediately transfer
it to the next step.

The next recommended size is ten times your previous volume, 100
to 250 milliliters. If you want to reduce steps, you can go up in volume
to a multiple of twenty, but you will start to reach a level of diminishing
returns. You will also want to give the yeast 48 hours instead of 24 if you
make larger steps. Ideally, you will use sterile flasks and media during all of
these steps, until you transfer the culture to the brewery. A simple method
for sterilizing flasks is to cover them with a foil cap and place them in the
oven at 350° F (177° C) for two hours. You can prepare your flasks days
in advance; just avoid opening the foil cap. If you cannot steam- or dry-
heat-sterilize your equipment, use boiling water to pasteurize everything.
If you choose chemical means of sanitizing, you should follow it up by
rinsing with sterile or boiled water, especially in the smaller propagation
steps. Large amounts of residual sanitizer can impact the growth of your
culture. If you do not have a presterilized medium to add to the flask, you
can pour in a hot boiled medium instead. In either case, quickly drape
foil over the top, creating a loose cap that extends down the sides about 3
inches (76 mm). Once the medium is at room temperature, you can add
the culture from the previous step

Shake the vial to re-suspend the yeast into solution. Unscrew the cap
slowly, as there may now be pressure in the vial if you did not add a vent
hole. Flame the vial and flask opening, and quickly dump the vial contents
into the flask. Replace the foil cap, and either shake the flask or put it on
a stir plate or shaker table, if you have one, to aerate and to mix yeast into
the solution. Hold at 72° F (22° C) for one to two full days before use.
You should see activity within 12 to 24 hours.

You can repeat this process into larger sizes until you reach the size needed by the brewery or the size needed for your homebrew batch of beer.

Here are some tips for successful culturing:

- Review your entire process and have everything needed at hand before opening any containers.
- Work within 3 inches (7 cm) of the flame whenever working with cultures to maximize the shield provided by the flame.
- Loosen caps prior to making a transfer, so they are easier to open.
- Any time you transfer cultures or media from one container to another, flame the openings.
- Perform transfers quickly, leaving vials and plates open for as little time as possible.
- Always swirl the yeast into solution before transfer, as it will usually be sticking to the bottom.
- Aeration improves growth and yeast health, as does mixing. Shaking or stirring improves cell growth.
- Always write dates and names on cultures using a permanent marker. Having even a few unlabeled vials is a nightmare.
- Do not freeze your plates and slants. Store them in the refrigerator.
- Wrap plates with plastic wrap, Parafilm, or vinyl tape to prevent premature drying. Make sure you close the lids on slants tightly before you store them in the refrigerator.
- Do not panic. Have fun. At worst, you would need to start again.

Maintaining a Yeast Library

The best way to store a yeast library is at -80° C, but that is not practical for most breweries. Storage at any warmer temperature results in genetic drift over time. The warmer you store your cultures, and the more the yeast grow, the faster the drift.

Many homebrewers new to yeast culturing dream of storing every strain they come across. Unfortunately, every strain comes with a small amount of overhead—not just in storage space, but the work involved to confirm periodically that the culture has not deviated too much in storage and to re-culture for another period of storage. If you have the time and interest you can store as many as you like, but many homebrewers find it is best to store only the cultures that you cannot replace easily. By keeping fewer strains, you are more likely to re-culture them more frequently, resulting in a healthier, less mutated culture over time.

To create a yeast library of your collected strains, first purify and test the cultures you are going to store. Yeast strains from beer samples or fermentation samples need purification and testing. Purification by multiple rounds of plating on wort media plates is the recommended method. It can take many rounds of propagation and testing to obtain yeast that is free from contaminants.

Once you have a plate that you believe is a pure culture, pick ten individual colonies and perform ten trial fermentations. You are attempting to evaluate the diversity of the plate, trying to ensure that you have a pure culture. If the trial fermentation samples all test the same for all parameters (e.g., speed, attenuation, flocculation, taste, and aroma), your work is done. If the results are different, you need to determine which strain or multiple strains you should preserve and work to purify your culture. A good next step is to isolate colonies from the test fermentation that represent the ideal yeast behavior.

Having purified your culture, you can use any of the techniques outlined in this chapter for storage. Slants or oil immersion slants are perhaps the best combination of ease of use and storage time. Freezing is another possibility—although it may not work equally well for everyone.

Yeast Capture

We are pretty sure that we are not the only ones carrying around a couple of 50-milliliter sterile transfer vials just in case we run across a yeast we want to take home. In a beer drinker's life, there are many opportunities to pick up interesting yeast strains.

On the Road

When you are on the road, you need to be a little more guerrilla than you are in the lab. Carry a couple of vials, perhaps a few individually wrapped sterile swabs, and a cheap butane lighter. If you come across a surface that might have an interesting yeast or bacteria on it, just swab it and put it back in the wrapper. If the swabs are short enough, you can put it into one of the vials to keep it from drying out. If you think you will be swabbing a lot, you might include a few milliliters of sterile water in each vial.

If you come across a bottled beer with sediment, just harvest the yeast like you would back in the lab by swirling the sediment, flaming the openings, and quickly transferring to your vial. Once you get home, plate the contents so you can analyze the sample for purity and uniformity.

While there are many tales of sneaking a sample from this brewery or that brewery while on a tour, we do not consider it proper etiquette. Ask first, even if you think they will refuse.

Bottled Beer

Most beer sediment can be a good source of yeast. However, it can often be hit or miss depending on the beer, and you should always test it for purity before committing a batch of beer to fermentation. There are some challenges, like trying to retrieve yeast from a filtered or pasteurized beer. Even though filtered beer can have some yeast in it, it is hard to cultivate such small quantities. If you are determined, membrane filtration of one or more bottles might yield enough live cells to get started. If the beer is pasteurized, your chances are extremely slim. Even if there are cells in the beer, they are most likely dead.

Alcohol, pressure (CO_2), temperature, handling, contamination, and time all work against the survival of yeast and the chance of culturing them from a bottle. As yeast sit in a bottle of beer, they slowly strip the beer of any trace minerals, elements, and some residual sugars. Once the yeast run out, they resort to feeding off dead yeast cell material. If you measured the pH of a bottle-conditioned beer over time, you would notice a rise as the cells die and release alkaline compounds into the beer.

In addition to cell death, living yeast can mutate. Mutations happen when fragments of yeast DNA rearrange. Although brewer's yeast is fairly mutation resistant, mutations can build over time and eventually become noticeable in the yeast population. The result is that you should not always expect yeast harvested from a bottled beer to perform exactly the same as it did at the original brewery. It is very difficult to get commercial-grade-quality yeast from bottle-conditioned beer, but you can get some nice, diverse yeast to use in a few homebrew batches.

The process of culturing yeast from a bottle is easy when working with unfiltered or bottle-conditioned beer.

1. Refrigerate the bottle for one week to get a nice yeast sediment at the bottom of the bottle.
2. Remove the bottle from the refrigerator, sanitize the entire top of the bottle, especially the rim area, and have a sterile yeast collection vessel ready. Work at your lab bench in a clean environment.
3. Remove the bottle cap with a sanitized opener, flame the bottle opening, and carefully decant the beer into a glass, which you can drink after you are done.
4. Stop pouring when you get close to the sediment, swirl the remaining beer to stir up the yeast, reflame the bottle opening, and pour into your sterile collection vessel.
5. If the beer you are working with has a blend of yeast, you have two choices. You can grow up the culture as is and brew with that or plate it out and try to figure out which colonies represent the proper blend you are trying to copy.
6. If you are working with a single strain, plate it out and use the lab techniques in this book to purify and test the strain.

Yeast and Beer Quality Assurance

This section covers some common yeast and beer quality testing, enough to handle much of the yeast-related testing you will need. While the science of beer quality testing is far more extensive than checking for contamination and diacetyl, these are good starting points for a new lab. Once you have mastered the basics, your lab can grow to do more beer quality testing.

Type of Organism	Flavor Description
Anaerobic bacteria	Lactic acid
Aerobic bacteria	Enteric, vomit
Wild yeast	Phenolic, Band-Aid

Figure 6.8: Common beer spoilage organisms.

Ideally, a brewer wants zero colony forming units (CFU) of these organisms when the lab tests his or her beer. Brewers debate the level at which flavor problems begin, but the rule of thumb is 100 CFU per category is considered "clean." The issue with even low numbers is that the presence of just a few CFU can rapidly grow to several hundred CFU very quickly, hence the desire to maintain lab results of zero CFU at all times.

Over the last ten years, White Labs has tested about 10 percent of all U.S. craft beer for beer spoilage organisms. Eighty percent of the samples tested had zero CFU on all three tests, while 20 percent had levels ranging from one CFU to thousands. There was an even distribution of anaerobic bacteria, aerobic bacteria, and wild yeast as the spoilage organism. While not a certainty, we could hypothesize that one-fifth of the beer those breweries produced over that ten-year span needed some improvement in cleaning and sanitation procedures.

A sample of yeast can have a varying degree of health and a varying degree of purity. The only way to know the quality of the yeast is to perform laboratory analysis for contamination, cell count and health.

To test for contamination, you need to plate the slurry onto specialized media three to five days before use. While it may seem obvious that you need to check the yeast slurry for aerobic bacteria, anaerobic bacteria, and wild yeast, you should also test your water, wort, and brewery equipment.

Of the three types of organisms, anaerobic bacteria are the most common bacteria found in brewer's yeast slurry, and they are the hardest for a brewer to eradicate. The most common anaerobic bacteria are the lactic acid bacteria, *Lactobacillus* and *Pediococcus.*

Medium Name	Medium Type	Organism Cultured	Common Brewery Organisms
Universal Beer Agar (UBA)	Aerobic (can be used anaerobically)	Wild yeast, bacteria	*Lactobacillus, Pediococcus, Acetobacter, Enterobacter*
Wallerstein Differential (WLD)	Aerobic (can be used anaerobically)	Wild yeast, bacteria, molds	*Brettanomyces, Candida, Saccharomyces*-type wild yeast, *Lactobacillus, Acetobacter*
Schwarz Differential Agar (SDA)	Aerobic (can be used anaerobically)	Bacteria	Acetic acid bacteria, *Bacillus, Lactobacillus, Enterobacter*
Hsu's Lactobacillus and Pediococcus (HLP)	Anaerobic	Bacteria	*Lactobacillus* and *Pediococcus*
Lin's Wild Yeast Medium (LWYM)	Aerobic	Wild yeast	*Saccharomyces*-type wild yeast
Lin's Cupric Sulfate Medium (LCSM)	Aerobic	Wild yeast	Non-*Saccharomyces* wild yeast
MacConkey Agar	Aerobic, for water filtration sample	Enteric bacteria	*Escherichia, Klebsiella, Enterobacter, Hafnia* and *Citrobacter*

Figure 6.9: Common brewery tests for contaminants.

Sample to Test	Testing Frequency	Common Contaminants
Water (rinse water or incoming)	Weekly	Enteric bacteria
Wort (taken inline between chiller and fermentor)	Every brew	Acetic acid bacteria Lactic acid bacteria
Fermentor	Every start (after 24 hours and again after 5 days)	Acetic acid bacteria Lactic acid bacteria
Yeast Slurry (used when propagating or when harvesting and storing yeast)	All propagations & post harvest	Acetic acid bacteria Lactic acid bacteria Non-*Saccharomyces*-type wild yeast *Saccharomyces*-type wild yeast Yeast health & viability
Serving/Bright Tank (post filtration)	Once a week or after each refill	Acetic acid bacteria Lactic acid bacteria
Equipment (filler, crowner, lines, bottles)	Every start	Acetic acid bacteria
Bottles and Kegs	At least a six-pack of bottles across each bottling run or a sample or two from a kegging run	Acetic acid bacteria

Figure 6.10: Typical brewery testing regimen.

Sample Amount(s)	Max. Acceptable CFU	Media Options
100 ml membrane filtered	≤ 10	MacConkey Agar
Pour plates 1 ml aerobic 1 ml anaerobic	 0 0	UBA or WLN (no cycloheximide)
Pour plates 1 ml aerobic 1 ml anaerobic	 0 0	SDA or WLD HLP
1:100 dilution for testing using pour plates		SDA or WLD HLP
1 ml aerobic 1 ml anaerobic	0 0	LCSM or Lysine LWYM
1 ml aerobic 1 ml anaerobic	≤ 1 ≤ 1	Methylene blue
0.1 ml (microscopic evaluation)	Round to ovoid cells, > 90% viable	
100 ml membrane filtered 1 ml anaerobic	≤ 10 ≤ 10	SDA or WLD HLP
Swabs + 100 ml membrane filtered, aerobic	≤ 10	SDA or WLD
5 ml from sample into plate with 10-20 ml of medium (us- ing a heavy ratio of agar)	≤ 10	SDA or WLD

Plating Methods

When checking for contamination, the source and concentration of the sample determines the testing method.

When working with filtered beer or water, the best method is membrane filtration of a 100-milliliter sample grown on a plate. When the concentration of organisms is low, membrane filtration allows you to sample a larger volume. Plating out a few milliliters of already filtered beer or water without membrane filtration would be very hit or miss, and you would most likely not find any contamination.

When working with unfiltered beer, bottle-conditioned beer, or beer in fermentors, the yeast count is much higher and membrane filtration often will not work, since it will clog easily. In this case, the pour plate method is best, since you can sample up to 10 milliliters in a 100-millimeter pour plate.

When working with yeast slurry, typical testing involves removing a 10-milliliter sample, diluting it 1:100 with sterile water, and using the spread plate or pour plate method and a suitable medium. (If bacteria counts are more than 1 per milliliter, and wild yeast is more than 1 per 0.1 milliliter, you should not use the yeast slurry.)

Membrane Filtration

The best way to get a good idea of your beer or water quality is membrane filtration of about 100 milliliters. The apparatus for membrane filtration varies in cost. The initial cost for a reusable apparatus is about $100, and it requires the use of an autoclave for sterilization, but if you plan on lots of testing, the reusable unit is cheaper. Companies such as Nalgene make sterile, disposable units already outfitted with membrane filter and pad. Disposable units cost about $8 per use.

Materials
- 100 ml beer or water sample
- Membrane filtration apparatus
- Vacuum pump (hand pumps or water aspirator pumps are inexpensive options)
- Filter pad (47 mm diameter)
- Membrane (0.45 micron pore size)
- Media plates

- Metal spatula or forceps
- Antifoam
- Incubator (anaerobic chamber if testing for anaerobic bacteria)

Procedure

1. Remove appropriate media plates (refer to Figure 6.10 for selective media choices) from cold storage, and allow them to warm up to room temperature.
2. Assemble membrane filtration apparatus under a laminar flow hood or near a Bunsen burner.
a. If you are working with a reusable apparatus, use sterilized forceps and place a sterile pad and membrane on top of the filter base. If you are using a gridded membrane filter, place membrane grid side up.
b. If you are working with a carbonated beer sample, you may want to add a few drops of antifoam to the lower portion of the filter unit.
c. Carefully replace top filter portion on base.
3. For each sample, pour 100 milliliters of beer into the upper (graduated) cup on the filter unit. Mark the lid of filtration unit with sample type.
4. Place the lid back onto the upper cup.
5. Hook the vacuum pump up to the filter unit and turn it on. Allow your liquid sample to transfer from the top portion of the unit to the lower base.
6. Turn off the pump, and carefully release the vacuum. Remove the membrane filter with sterilized forceps, and place the membrane (not pad) grid side up, directly on top of your selected medium. Try to lay the membrane as flat as possible, and avoid trapping bubbles under the membrane. You can remove and reapply the membrane if necessary. Replace the lid on the plate, and label with the sample name and date.
7. Repeat the procedure with any other samples. You should use a new membrane filtration unit for each sample. To ensure your process and equipment is sound and sterile, you may wish to perform control runs with sterile water.
8. Once all samples are complete, invert the plates and place in an incubator. You can check the plates each day for growth. Usually it takes three to five days in the incubator for the enumeration of colonies.

Pour Plates

The pour plate method involves mixing a sample (typically 1 to 10 ml) in with the medium while it is still warm enough to be liquid, but not so hot that it kills the organisms you want to grow. Once the medium solidifies, the plate is inverted and incubated.

There are a few issues to watch for when making pour plates. The most common mistake is mixing the sample and the medium before the medium has cooled sufficiently, killing some or all of the bacteria and affecting the result. Another common issue is failing to mix the sample sufficiently with the medium. If you do not swirl the mixture enough, you will not get an even distribution of colonies, making it difficult to count accurately. You also want to avoid mixing a very cold sample with the medium, as it can drop the temperature enough to cause the medium to solidify around drops of the sample.

Materials
- Beer sample
- Sterile Petri dishes
- Medium in still liquid form, 113-122° F (45-50° C)
- Pipette
- Incubator (anaerobic chamber if testing for anaerobic bacteria)

Procedure
1. Prepare appropriate medium and ensure correct temperature (refer to Figure 6.10, p. 212, for selective media choices).
2. Pipette an aliquot of the sample into the plate. You can test 1- to 2-milliliter samples in 60-millimeter plates and up to 10-milliliter samples in 100-millimeter plates. If the concentration of organisms is high, it may require preparing a dilution of the sample to get an accurate count.
3. Pour the still-liquid medium into the plate to a depth of at least several millimeters while swirling the plate to distribute the sample evenly. Alternatively, you can mix the sample and medium in an Erlenmeyer flask and then pour into a plate.
4. Wait for the medium to solidify, and invert.
5. Place in an incubator (anaerobic if required), medium side up, at 86° F (30° C) for three days.
6. Record results, including number, type, size, and color of colonies ob-

served. Some bacteria may grow on the surface while others will form lens-shaped colonies within the agar. To sample submerged colonies, stab through the agar with a loop.

Spread Plates

The spread plate method involves diluting the sample and then transferring a small amount to the surface of an agar plate. You then spread the sample and any organisms evenly over the entire surface with a spreader. This technique is limited to the amount of liquid that the agar surface can absorb in a reasonable amount of time, generally no more than 0.1 milliliter on a 100-millimeter plate.

Materials
- Yeast slurry sample
- Media plates
- Sterile pipette
- Glass spreader
- Flame source
- 70% isopropyl alcohol in beaker deep enough to submerge spreader end
- Incubator (anaerobic chamber if testing for anaerobic bacteria)

Procedure
1. Dilute sample down to provide an appropriate concentration of organisms. You may need to prepare several dilutions to obtain properly separated colonies for counting. Pipette 0.1 milliliter of the sample onto the center of the agar surface.
2. Remove the spreader from the alcohol bath and pass briefly through the flame, burning off the alcohol. If you keep the rod in the flame for too long, it will get hot and can burn your hand. Allow the spreader to air-cool in the area around the flame or to touch the agar surface away from the sample.
3. Spread the sample across the agar surface with the spreader. Move the spreader back and forth from top to bottom across the plate several times. Unlike streaking with a loop to isolate colonies, you want to backtrack many times across the surface to distribute the sample as evenly as possible. Rotate the plate 90 degrees and repeat. Rotate the plate 45

degrees and repeat. Do not sterilize the spreader between each turn of the plate.

4. Replace the cover on the plate, and wait several minutes until the liquid from the sample is absorbed into the agar. Secure the lid and turn the plate upside down, medium side up, before placing in the incubator.

5. Incubate (anaerobic if required) with medium side up at 86° F (30° C) for three days.

6. Record results, including number, type, size, and color of colonies observed.

Check Plates

Labs use plating for yeast culturing and for contamination testing of liquid samples, but you can also use plating to test your brewery environment. You can set open plates out and inspect any growth to determine how clean or dirty the air is in a particular area. We call these "check plates." Here is an example where this will be helpful.

One brewery reported gushing in some of its bottles, which sounds like a wild yeast contamination, but it had not tested the bottles thoroughly. We set out check plates in many areas of the brewing and bottling area and some outside. As with many small breweries, it kept most of the doors open (including the roll-up doors) all day. Most small breweries also do not put their bottling lines in a separate clean room, so they are subject to the outside environment. The outside plates showed huge levels of wild yeast, as did the inside plates. Swabbing the empty bottles and culturing the beer showed the same wild yeast as outside.

Materials
- WLN and WLD plates (see Wallerstein media section, pp. 242-244)
- Incubator

Procedure
1. Allow WLN and WLD plates to warm up.
2. Set aside a set of control plates. Do not open them, since they are to test the sterility of the plates.
3. Label one WLN plate and one WLD plate for each area to be tested, along with the current date.
4. Place the labeled WLN and WLD plates in areas such as the brewery,

fermentation area, lab area, yeast pitching area, bottling area, etc., with the covers removed and the surface exposed.

5. Leave each plate open for 60 minutes.

6. After 60 minutes, close and collect all plates, including the controls, and place in an incubator, medium side up, at 86° F (30° C) for three days.

7. Record results, including number, type, size, and color of colonies observed.

Swabbing

This is a more direct test than check plates. Instead of checking what falls onto the plate from the air, you streak a sterile cotton swab in an area, transfer to a plate, and see what grows. This is a great way to check the inside of hoses, tanks, gaskets, and heat exchangers.

Materials
- Media plates
- Sterile swabs
- Incubator

Procedure
1. Allow plates to warm to room temperature.

2. Label plates with the area swabbed and the date. Use WLD or SDA plates to test for bacteria. Use LCSM plates or other wild yeast plates to test for wild yeast.

3. Take a sterile cotton swab and streak a plate. Label this plate "Control." This ensures your swabs are sterile and the medium is good.

4. Take another sterile cotton swab, and swab the area to be tested.

5. Streak the appropriately labeled plates.

6. The same swab can be streaked onto two or more plates if multiple types of media are used.

7. Place in an incubator, medium side up, at 86° F (30° C) for three days.

8. Record results, including number, type, size, and color of colonies observed.

Tank Sampling

Often the beer you want to test is still in the fermentor. You want to obtain a clean sample to avoid any false readings in the lab. It is important that all personnel take samples using the same method. Lack of attention to cleaning and sanitizing can result in inconsistent microbial testing and contaminated fermentors.

The method is simple: Work as aseptically as possible. It is important that you ready your materials before heading out for collection. Remove all jewelry from hands and forearms and wash thoroughly. If possible, wear latex gloves and use isopropanol on your gloved hands. For best results, work within close proximity to a flame. You can use a portable gas flame to sterilize the sample point. Work as quickly as possible once you have opened your sterile container.

Materials
- Sterile collection vessels marked with sample type and date
- Cotton or foam sampling swabs
- 70% isopropanol or aseptic wipes
- Portable gas flame

Procedure
1. Have your sterile, labeled collection bottle nearby with the lid unscrewed (do not remove the lid yet).
2. Clean the inside of the spigot/faucet with a swab soaked with isopropanol. Repeat until spotlessly clean.
3. Use an antiseptic wipe or isopropanol to clean outside of faucet.
4. Flame the faucet with the portable flame, if possible.
5. Open the valve and let about 12 ounces (0.33 L) of beer flow through tap before collecting into the sterile bottle. Collect a minimum of 120 milliliters for complete microbial testing. Close the lid securely.
6. Repeat the cleaning procedure after sample collection, and take the samples back to the laboratory for processing. Processing might include membrane filtration or plating.

Forced Wort Test
The forced wort test is a simple and very effective way to check that the hot side of the brewing process is clean. After you have cooled the wort, you collect a small amount prior to pitching the yeast. You can take multiple samples at each step of the process to help isolate any problems

with the cold side. Once you have the samples, incubate them to see if any contamination grows. If you see growth soon, after one or two days, you know there was a contamination problem. Here is a basic procedure:

Materials
- Sterile wort collection vessel
- Incubator or warm location
- Shaker table (optional)

Procedure
1. Aseptically collect a wort sample from the fermentor prior to pitching the yeast.
2. Place in incubator at 86° F (30° C) for three days, on a shaker table if available.
3. Inspect for haze, bubbles, off-odors, starting on the first day.
4. Refer to Figure 6.11 for the results.

Duration	Result
1 day	Very dirty, clean heat exchanger and hoses. Beer will need to be dumped.
2-3 days	Major contamination. Need to clean problem, beer most likely will be affected. Do not collect yeast for re-use from this batch.
3-6 days	Mild contamination buildup, clean problem. Beer may or may not be affected.
7 or more	Very clean, keep up the good work

Figure 6.11: Forced wort test results.

You can also check the stability of the pitched wort, to see if the pitch or pitching process introduced any contamination.

Materials
- Sterile wort collection vessel
- Cycloheximide solution
- Incubator or warm location
- Shaker table (optional)

Procedure
1. Aseptically collect a wort sample from the fermentor after pitching the yeast.
2. Add 1 milliliter cycloheximide solution per 100 milliliters of sample. Clearly mark sample as poison.
3. Place in incubator at 86° F (30° C) for 3 days, on a shaker table if available.
4. Inspect for haze, bubbles, off-odors, but do not taste, as it is poisonous.
5. Refer to Figure 6.11 for the results and compare to non-pitched result.
6. Dispose of sample in a safe and proper manner.

You can run the same tests on packaged beer to check the stability of your packaging process. If you bottle beer, just set a couple aside at 86° F (30° C) and inspect their condition over time. You can also treat some samples with cycloheximide, but use extreme caution to prevent anyone from tasting the beer by accident.

Forced Ferment Test

You should consider performing a forced ferment test (also known as a forced attenuation test) for every beer. Once the wort is aerated, pitched, and ready for fermentation, you pull a wort sample in an aseptic manner. Pull a large enough sample to allow for at least one specific gravity test and any other tests you might want to run. You are going to force the fermentation to go to its maximum attenuation through high temperature and constant stirring. The result is usually a finishing gravity slightly lower than the main fermentation, which is why brewers once called this the Limit of Attenuation (LA) test.

Materials
- Sterile wort collection vessel
- Incubator or warm location
- Shaker table or stir plate (optional)

Procedure
1. Aseptically collect a sample of pitched wort from the fermentor.
2. Place on stir plate or shaker table, if you have one, at 80° F (27° C).
3. Once all activity stops, take a specific gravity reading. This is the minimum gravity, the limit of attenuation possible with that yeast and wort combination.

This test fermentation should reach final gravity faster than your main fermentation. You can use this information to help make decisions about your main fermentation. If the main fermentation appears to stop early, you will already know what level of attenuation was possible. If you need to make temperature adjustments on the main fermentation based on a percentage of attenuation, you will know what value represents 100 percent of attenuation.

Diacetyl Force

Large breweries measure diacetyl levels with gas chromatography (or as total VDK levels with a spectrophotometer). A gas chromatograph or spectrophotometer is beyond the scope of many small breweries and most homebrewers, but there is a simple, nonquantitative way to see if your beer has potential diacetyl. Diacetyl precursors turn into diacetyl via oxidation. You can force this conversion in the lab, using heat and oxygen to change flavorless precursors in your beer to diacetyl in a short time.

Materials
- Two glasses
- Aluminum foil
- Hot water bath
- Ice water bath
- Thermometer

Procedure
1. Heat the water bath to 140 to 160° F (60 to 71° C).
2. Collect beer into each glass and cover with aluminum foil.
3. Place one glass in the hot water bath, while keeping the other at room temperature.
4. After 10 to 20 minutes remove the beer from the hot bath, and cool to

the same temperature as the other sample. An ice water bath is effective for cooling.

5. Remove the aluminum foil and smell each sample. If you smell the buttery character of diacetyl in either or both samples, you know that your beer has the diacetyl precursor.

Room Temperature Beer	Heated Beer	Conclusion
Negative	Negative	No precursor present, beer is ready.
Negative	Positive	Precursor present, beer needs more time on yeast.
Positive	Positive	Beer has a lot of precursor or could be contaminated. If not a bacterial issue, the beer needs more time on the yeast.

Figure 6.12: Diacetyl force test results.

If diacetyl is present, do not transfer or package the beer. Leave it on the yeast and continue to check daily. Raising the temperature of the beer a few degrees will also increase the rate of diacetyl uptake. If you have already transferred the beer off the yeast, kraeusening or adding more actively fermenting yeast will help.

Broad Spectrum Method for VDK

If you do have access to a spectrophotometer, this method allows you to quantify the diacetyl levels in your beer.

Reagents
a) -Naphthol solution. Dissolve 4 grams -naphthol ($C_{10}H_7OH$) in 100 milliliters isopropanol, 99.6%. Add about 0.5 gram vegetable carbon, and shake mixture for about 30 minutes, then filter. Store filtrate in the dark in amber bottle.

b) KOH-creatine solution. Dissolve 0.3 gram creatine in 80 milliliters 40% KOH solution (aqueous) and filter. Store in a polyethylene container under refrigeration.

c) Diacetyl, stock solution. Prepare an aqueous solution containing 500 milligrams per liter. Store in an amber bottle in refrigerator.

d) Diacetyl, working solution. Prepare immediately before use by diluting 1 milliliter stock solution to 100 milliliters with water; concentration 5.0 milligrams per liter.

Apparatus

- Colorimeter or spectrophotometer
- Distillation equipment, preferably all glass
- Volumetric flasks, 10 ml
- Graduated cylinders, 50 ml
- Heating mantle for boiling flask

Calibration

Prepare a standard curve from 0.5, 1.0, 1.5, 3.0, and 4.0 milliliters of working diacetyl solution in 10 ml volumetric flasks. Add water to bring volume in each to approximately 5.0 milliliters. Use 5 milliliters water for reagent blank. Develop color as in step 2 below.

Procedure

1. Distill 100 milliliters decarbonated beer into a 50-milliliter graduated cylinder containing 5 milliliters water. Collect about 15 milliliters distillate and dilute to 25 milliliters with water. Pipette a 5-millimiter aliquot into a 10-milliliter volumetric flask.

2. Color development. Add 1 milliliter -naphthol solution (reagent a) to each flask and swirl. Add 0.5 milliliter KOH-creatine solution (reagent b) to no more than 4 or 5 flasks at a time. Fill to mark and shake vigorously for exactly 1 minute. Let stand, and measure absorbance at 530 nm against reagent blank between 5 and 6 minutes after shaking. Repeat this procedure until all samples have been measured.

3. Plot absorbance values for standards against milligrams per liter diacetyl. Read unknowns from the graph and calculate diacetyl content of beer.

Fermentation Trials

The purpose of a lab-scale fermentation trial is to mimic production fermentation on a much smaller scale; 1.5 liters is a size that works well. This test allows a brewer to experiment with a new yeast strain or multiple strains, not just for attenuation, but for fermentation rate and flavor compounds as well. You can run several tests at once without it becoming too cumbersome. Collect 1.5 liters of hot wort (boiled and hopped as usual), for each trial you want to conduct, in a large, sterile container. Chill the wort to the desired fermentation temperature, then oxygenate according to your normal brew house standards. You can also add a very small quantity of sterilized antifoam to the wort at this time to avoid foam-over. Transfer 1.5 liters of wort to vessels for fermentation using aseptic techniques.

You are now ready to pitch the yeast at their correct pitching rates. It is critical that you use as accurate a pitching rate as possible, since smaller-scale fermentations are more prone to errors in pitching rate. As with all fermentations, lab-scale or main production, you should record and monitor fermentation temperatures from pitching to finish. In addition, keep a record of daily gravity readings of each fermentation for seven days. Temperature control is the most important parameter to perfect; otherwise, the trial fermentation beer will not taste like the main fermentation beer. Graphing these gravity readings over time provides a visual comparison of attenuation among the different fermentations. Beyond that, you can analyze the resulting beer for such things as bittering and flavor compounds. This lab-scale method allows ample volume for the daily gravity readings, as well as post-fermentation analyses.

Yeast Strain Oxygen Demand

Yeast strains differ in their oxygen requirement. Some are stimulated by low levels of dissolved oxygen, while others require high levels of dissolved oxygen to reach proper attenuation (Jakobsen and Thorne, 1980). Very flocculent yeast strains tend to have a high oxygen demand (White Labs observations). Even if you find your yeast strain has a low oxygen demand during fermentation, the dissolved oxygen level may affect its ability to survive storage and the number of generations you can reuse it. Something else to keep in mind is that there is a correlation between oxygen demand and the type of propagation necessary. For example, yeast strains with a high oxygen demand need more oxygen during propagation in order to have a successful fermentation. You should run this test on your brewery strains to determine the oxygen needs for each. It is best to test at least six times, with yeast selected from different generations and storage conditions.

Materials
- Dissolved oxygen meter
- Stir plate
- Trial fermentation equipment

Procedure (Modified from Jakobsen and Thorne, 1980)
1. For each yeast strain, set up four trial fermentations.
2. Oxygenate each of the four trials to 0, 2, 5, and 10 ppm, respectively.
3. Pitch yeast at rate of 10 million/milliliter wort, as done in trial fermentations.
4. Take gravity readings every 24 hours for seven days.

- Either assume the 10 ppm test is the measure of 100 percent attenuation or perform an attenuation limit test. The aeration level, which results in 50 percent attenuation in two days, determines if the yeast has a low, medium, or high oxygen demand. You can also do this in a nonquantitative way, without fermentation trials, by varying the dissolved oxygen levels in different brews.
- Low, stimulated by less than 5 ppm
- Medium, stimulated by 5 ppm
- High, stimulated by 10 ppm or higher

O₂ Requirement	Minimum Oxygen Required to Reach 50 Percent Attenuation		
	2 ppm	5 ppm	10 ppm
High	failed to attenuate 50% in 2 days	failed to attenuate 50% in 2 days	reached 50% attenuation in 2 days
Medium	failed to attenuate 50% in 2 days	reached 50% attenuation in 2 days	
Low	reached 50% attenuation in 2 days		

Figure 6.13: Oxygen demand test results.

There is no definitive advice on how these oxygen demand levels equate to how much dissolved oxygen a strain requires in preparation for fermenting a batch of beer, but it can give you a good idea of what to try. If you are experimenting with a high-requirement strain, make sure you oxygenate adequately. If you are experimenting with a low-requirement strain, perhaps lowering your dissolved oxygen levels would develop the flavor profile you desire.

- High requirement, try 10 to 14 ppm
- Medium requirement, try 10 ppm
- Low requirement, try 7 to 10 ppm

Iodine Test for Glycogen

Yeast use glycogen as a carbohydrate storage compound, much the same as humans use fats. Yeast build up glycogen near the end of fermentation, as the lack of sugar starves them. Yeast use glycogen to live during storage, and they also depend on their glycogen reserves when you add them to wort. When you pitch yeast into wort, they use their glycogen for metabolism. Yeast with good glycogen reserves start fermentation faster. There are complicated methods (enzymatic) and simple methods (iodine color measured with a spectrophotometer) to quantify the amount of glycogen present.

Materials
- Visible spectrum spectrophotometer
- 1 cm cuvettes
- Pipettes

Procedure (Quain and Tubb, 1983)
1. Keep yeast samples on ice to prevent glycogen breakdown during assay.
2. Yeast concentration should be 4 milligrams per milliliter dry weight, or 20 to 25 milligrams per milliliter wet weight.
3. Mix fresh iodine/potassium iodide reagent using distilled water (iodine 1 mg/ml in potassium iodide 10 mg/ml).
4. Suspend yeast in reagent, and immediately measure absorbance at a wavelength of 660 nm.
5. Use unstained yeast as a blank.
6. Obtain glycogen concentration in mg/ml (x). Absorbance is proportional to glycogen concentration.

$$x = (y - 0.26)/1.48, \text{ with } y \text{ as absorbance.}$$

If you do not have a spectrophotometer, you can estimate glycogen visually. The reagent will stain cells rich in glycogen (approximately 1 mg/ml) very dark brown and cells low in glycogen (0.1 mg/ml) yellow.

Respiratory (Petite) Mutant Test

One of the most common brewer's yeast mutations is respiratory-deficient mutants, also known as petite mutation. This mutation changes the ability of the yeast to respire. The result is that they grow very small on aerobic plates (hence the name petite mutants). If the mutations accumulate to more than 1 percent of the yeast population, the result can be a poor fermentation performance and flavor problems such as phenolic and diacetyl.

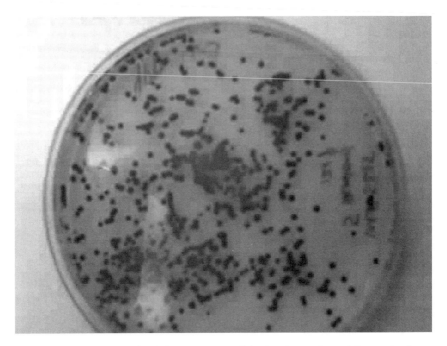

Figure 6.14: Respiratory (petite) mutant test. Colonies that stain a pink or red color are normal. Colonies that do not change color are respiratory deficient.

Materials

- Malt agar plates
- Agar
- 2 sterile 250 ml glass bottles
- Distilled water
- Triphenyltetrazolium chloride (TTC)
- NaH_2PO_4 (anhydrous, mol. wt. 120.0)
- Na_2HPO_4 (anhydrous, mol. wt. 141.96)

NOTE: You must wear gloves, goggles, and face mask when handling TTC.

Procedure

1. Dilute yeast sample to 500 to 1000 cells/milliliter. Plate 0.1 milliliter of this yeast solution onto a small malt agar plate. For reproducibility, make five plates for each yeast sample.
2. Let the plates incubate for two to three days at 80° F (27° C).
3. Prepare overlay solutions:

Solution A

Place in a sterile 500 ml bottle:

- 1.26 g NaH_2PO_4
- 1.16 g Na_2HPO_4
- 3 g agar
  Fill with distilled water up to the 100-milliliter mark, swirl contents, and place cap loosely.

Solution B

Place in another 500 ml bottle:

- 0.2 g TTC
  Fill with distilled water up to the 100-milliliter mark, swirl contents, and place cap loosely.

4. Autoclave or pressure-cook each solution at 250° F (121° C) for 15 minutes. Combine the two solutions when they reach about 131° F (55° C).
5. Overlay each plate with about 10 milliliters of the TTC solution, making sure the colonies are completely covered. Let the plates incubate for 1 to 3 hours at 80° F (27° C), and record the results immediately. Leaving the plates to incubate longer or putting the plates into cold storage to count later allows the TTC to oxidize and compromises the results of the test.
6. Colonies that stain a pink or red color are normal. Colonies that do not change color are respiratory deficient.
7. Count the number of stained and nonstained colonies to determine the percentage of respiratory mutants in the culture. An acceptable level is less than 1 percent.

Yeast Extract Peptone Dextrose Medium (YPD or YEPD)

You can prepare YPD either as a broth or as a solid medium. You will use YPD for plates and slants in some test procedures, although you can use malt-based media as well. For culturing and propagation, you will want to use a malt-based medium instead of YPD (see "Yeast Culturing," pp. 189-206). YPD does not contain maltose, so it is not an appropriate medium for growing yeast for fermentation.

Materials

- Yeast extract

- Agar
- Peptone
- Distilled water
- Dextrose
- Sterile bottle

Procedure for Solution
1. Weigh 10 grams yeast extract, 20 grams peptone and 10 grams dextrose into a sterile bottle.
2. Add distilled water to make 1 liter.
3. Close the cap tightly, and shake the contents well.
4. Loosen the cap, cover with foil, and write the date and medium type on the container.
5. Sterilize in an autoclave or pressure cooker, 250° F (121° C) for 15 minutes.
6. Let the medium cool before using.
7. Alternatively, you can add sterile dextrose after autoclaving to keep the carbohydrates from breaking down.

Procedure for Solid
1. Weigh 10 grams yeast extract, 20 grams peptone, 20 grams dextrose, and 20 grams agar into a sterile bottle.
2. Add distilled water to make 1 liter.
3. Close the cap tightly, and shake the contents well. Loosen the cap and microwave to dissolve the solids, being careful to avoid the medium boiling over. Be careful when handling the bottle, as it will be very hot.
4. Once the agar dissolves, cover cap with foil, and write the date and medium type on bottle.
5. Sterilize in an autoclave or pressure cooker, 250° F (121° C) for 15 minutes.
6. Let the medium cool to about 131° F (55° C) before using to pour plates.

Bacteria Tests

The number of detrimental organisms capable of destroying your beer is actually quite small, but the effects of these few can be horrendous. Due to the presence of hop resins (which act as antibacterial agents), low pH, high cooking temperatures, ethanol, and an anaerobic fermentation, beer is a hostile environment with limited resources for most organisms. However, there are a few organisms that thrive in beer. Although none of these can cause death or serious illness, they can do great damage to your beer.

Lactobacillus: The most common beer spoiling bacteria. *Lactobacillus* are resistant to hop compounds and will perform under anaerobic conditions. They abound in your mouth and on grain, which is one of the reasons you do not want to mill your grain where the dust can reach the cold side of your process. Evidence of *Lactobacillus* are a tart sourness similar to spoiled milk as well as possible diacetyl flavors. They usually create a haze similar to nonflocculent yeast.

Pediococcus: Sometimes found in the late stages of beer production, especially in lagers. They can be similar to *Lactobacillus* and will produce acidity, diacetyl flavors, and sometimes viscosity and ropiness.

B. coagulans and *B. stearothermophilus:* These lesser-known microorganisms can cause wort spoilage when a brewer leaves wort for long periods at higher temperatures (150 to 175° F , 65 to 80° C) and can create high levels of lactic acid.

Acetic acid bacteria: Acetobacter and *Gluconobacter* function mainly in aerobic conditions and oxidize ethanol to carbon dioxide and water, resulting in vinegar.

Obesumbacterium proteus: These bacteria are able to tolerate a wide pH range (4.4 to 9) but lack resistance to hop compounds. They are responsible for dimethyl sulfide, dimethyl disulfide, diacetyl, and fusel oils. These produce vegetative or cooked vegetable flavors.

Zymomonas: These bacteria can ferment glucose or fructose to ethanol and produce acetaldehyde and hydrogen sulfide. This can produce a rotten-egg aroma in the finished beer.

UBA Medium

Universal Beer Agar (UBA) is a medium containing nutrients and agar. You add beer to it during preparation, which purportedly makes UBA closer than other media to the natural environment found in a brewery. By using beer to prepare the medium, it becomes more selective for microorganisms that have adapted themselves to the presence of beer compounds, such as hops and alcohol. This reduces the chance of false positives from non-beer-spoiling organisms. You can also add cycloheximide (1 mg/L) to suppress yeast growth when testing yeast slurries for bacterial contamination.

Materials
- UBA medium
- Distilled water
- Beer
- Cycloheximide (optional)
- Autoclave or pressure cooker
- 500 ml Erlenmeyer
- Foam or cotton stopper

Procedure
1. Weigh out 5.5 grams of UBA into the Erlenmeyer.
2. Add 75 milliliters distilled water (and cycloheximide, if you wish to sup-press yeast growth). Close with a foam or cotton stopper, and bring the contents to a boil for 1 minute with constant agitation to dissolve.
3. While medium is hot, mix in 25 milliliters of beer without de-gassing.
4. Autoclave at 250° F (121° C) for 10 minutes. Higher temperatures or longer durations are detrimental to the medium.
5. After autoclaving you can either use for pour plates when it reaches 113 to 122° F (45 to 50° C) or pour 12- to 15-milliliter aliquots of the me-dium into sterile Petri dishes and allow to solidify. You can use the solidi-fied plates for other testing methods.
6. Store unused plates in the refrigerator and protect from daylight. The shelf life of prepared plates is approximately one week, and two months for medium stored in bottles.
7. Once samples are plated, close and invert the plates. Place in an in-cubator at 86° F (30° C) in either an anaerobic environment to detect beer-spoiling bacteria or an aerobic environment to detect yeast- and wort-spoiling bacteria.
8. Examine plates daily for three days for growth. Select identical and typi-cal colonies for further identification via gram staining or other methods.

HLP Medium

Hsu's Lactobacillus Pediococcus medium, as the name suggests, tests for the presence of Gram-positive lactic acid bacteria of the genera *Lactoba-cillus* and *Pediococcus*. HLP contains cycloheximide, which kills yeast but allows anaerobic bacteria to grow. Inoculating the medium while it is still in liquid form (113° F, 45° C) allows it to solidify around the sample, creating an anaerobic environment. HLP also contains oxygen scrubbers to rid the medium of any remaining oxygen. Anaerobic, heat resistant, and hop resistant, *Lactobacillus* and *Pediococcus* are the most common beer spoilers. This makes HLP one of the most popular media used in brewing laboratories.

Materials
- HLP medium
- Distilled water
- Agar
- Sterile pipettes
- Mechanical pipetter
- 16 x 150 mm sterile screw-cap culture tubes
- 500 ml Erlenmeyer
- Foam or cotton stopper
- Incubator

Procedure
CAUTION: Wear goggles, gloves, and face mask when weighing HLP.

1. Weigh out 7 grams HLP medium and 2 grams agar. Mix with 100 milliliters distilled water in the Erlenmeyer.
2. Close the flask with a permeable foam stopper or cotton plug.
3. Heat to boiling, swirling the contents frequently until the HLP dissolves completely.
4. Allow to cool in a hood or lab bench. If you are going to use the mixture at a later time, let it cool to room temperature, then place in cold storage for no more than two weeks.
5. If you will use the mixture right away, take a reading to assure it is at the correct temperature of 113° F (45° C) before pouring tubes.
6. Pipette 1 milliliter of the sample for testing into a sterile 16 x 150 mm screw-cap tube. Mark each tube with a sample number and date.
7. Transfer 17 milliliters HLP medium to each tube, and close the caps tightly.
8. Gently invert twice to distribute the sample evenly through the tube.
9. Place the tubes in an incubator at 86° F (30° C) for 48 hours.
10. Perform a preliminary count. *Lactobacillus* appear as white, inverted

teardrop-shaped colonies and *Pediococcus* appear as white spherical colonies.

11. Place back in the incubator at 86° F (30° C) for an additional 24 to 48 hours.
12. Perform a final count.

SDA Medium

You can use Schwarz Differential Agar (SDA), also known as Lee's Multi-Differential Agar (LMDA), to detect the presence of aerobic and/or anaerobic bacteria. SDA contains calcium carbonate ($CaCO_3$) to help identify acid-producing bacteria, bromocresol green to differentiate colony characteristics by color, and, optionally, cycloheximide to kill yeast growth. Acetic acid bacteria (*Acetobacter*, *Gluconobacter*) will display a halo zone around the colonies and will appear greenish blue on the underside. Because these organisms are often resistant to the negative effects of alcohol, acid, and hops, beer is a hospitable medium. Turbidity, ropiness, and off-flavors are results of even a small amount of *Acetobacter* or *Gluconobacter* contamination.

You can use the same medium under anaerobic conditions to detect *Lactobacillus* and *Pediococcus*. *Lactobacillus* colonies will display a halo zone and appear greenish-white with a dark green center and yellow underside. *Pediococcus* grow slower than the other organisms. They will appear smaller with a narrow halo zone.

Materials
- SDA medium
- Cycloheximide (optional)
- Distilled water
- Autoclave or pressure cooker
- Sterile pipettes
- Mechanical pipetter
- Sterile Petri dishes
- 500 ml Erlenmeyer
- Foam or cotton stopper
- Incubator

Procedure
1. Weigh out 8.3 grams SDA into a 500 ml Erlenmeyer.

2. Add 100 milliliters distilled water and 10 percent cycloheximide if you wish to suppress yeast growth. Close with a foam or cotton stopper and bring the contents to a boil for 1 minute with constant agitation to dissolve.

3. Autoclave at 250° F (121° C) for 10 minutes. Higher temperatures or longer durations are detrimental to the medium.

4. After autoclaving, swirl the flask frequently while it cools to keep the CaCO₃ suspended, but avoid creating foam.

5. Once the medium reaches 113° F (45° C), pour 12- to 15-milliliter aliquots of the medium into sterile Petri dishes and allow it to solidify. To insure even distribution of CaCO₃, avoid moving the dishes after you pour them.

6. If there is any foam on the surface after pouring, flame with a Bunsen burner to break the bubbles.

7. Once the plates become firm, invert and let dry overnight in an incubator at 86° F (30° C). Avoid drying hotter or longer than necessary.

8. Dilute the sample for testing to a concentration between 100 and 900 bacterial cells per milliliter. Your goal is to have about 25 to 50 colonies per plate. You may want to prepare several different dilutions to improve your chances of getting the right concentration.

9. Pipette 0.1 milliliter of the sample onto an SDA plate and spread with a sterile cell spreader.

10. Close and invert the plates. Place in an incubator at 86° F (30° C) in either an anaerobic environment to detect beer-spoiling bacteria or an aerobic environment to detect yeast- and wort-spoiling bacteria.

11. While you may see colonies forming earlier, it takes four to seven days for the bacterial colonies to develop enough to identify the organism.

MacConkey Medium

MacConkey is a differential medium that selects for Gram-negative bacteria (such as *Escherichia coli*) and inhibits the growth of Gram-positive bacteria due to crystal violet and bile salts. It contains two additives that make it differential: neutral red (a pH indicator) and lactose (a disaccharide).

Materials
- MacConkey medium
- Distilled water

- Autoclave or pressure cooker
- Sterile Petri dishes
- 500 ml Erlenmeyer
- Foam or cotton stopper
- Incubator
- 100 ml beer or water sample
- Membrane filtration apparatus
- Vacuum pump
- Filter pad (47 mm diameter)
- Membrane (0.45 micron pore size)
- Metal spatula or forceps
- Incubator

Procedure
1. Weigh out 5 grams MacConkey agar into the Erlenmeyer.
2. Add 100 milliliters distilled water. Close with a foam or cotton stopper and bring the contents to a boil for 1 minute with constant agitation to dissolve.
3. Autoclave at 250° F (121° C) for 15 minutes.
4. Once the medium reaches 113° F (45° C), pour 12- to 15-milliliter aliquots of it into sterile Petri dishes and allow it to solidify.
5. Follow the process for membrane filtration of the 100-milliliter sample.
6. Invert the plate and place in an incubator at 86° F (30° C). You can check the plate each day for growth. Usually it takes three to five days in the incubator for the enumeration of colonies. Lactose-fermenting colonies appear red to pink. Other bacteria form colorless colonies.

Gram Stain

Danish scientist Hans Christian Gram invented the Gram stain in 1884 in an effort to aid the taxonomy of bacteria. Gram staining allows you to separate unidentified bacteria into two groups: Gram-positive and Gram-negative. While the separation may not appear to be significant in the classification of bacteria, it has great value for brewing labs. Six of the approximately eighteen common brewery bacterial contaminants are Gram-positive. Although this does not provide a definitive identification of the bacteria, it is a useful tool in narrowing the field of possible beer spoilers.

The Gram stain procedure consists of a primary stain, a trapping agent, a decolorizing agent, and a counter-stain. Gram-positive cells retain the crystal violet stain and appear violet. Gram-negative cells do not retain the crystal violet stain and retain the pink safranin counterstain instead. While both Gram-positive and Gram-negative cells can take up the crystal violet dye, only the Gram-positive cells can retain it. The decolorizing agent partially destroys the Gram-negative cell wall, inhibiting its ability to retain the crystal violet dye and allowing the safranin to take hold instead.

In addition to bacterial identification aid, Gram staining increases the definition of cell structure and pattern. You can supplement Gram staining with other tests, such as catalase reaction and oxidase reaction, to pinpoint the microbe in question.

Materials
- Slides
- Rinse bottle filled with water
- Crystal violet
- Gram's iodine
- 95% ethyl alcohol
- Safranin

Preparing a Smear
1. Using an inoculation loop, transfer a drop of the culture to the slide. If the culture contains too much bacteria, the smear will be too dense, which makes good staining almost impossible.
2. The proper amount of bacteria will be a barely visible dot of material on the loop.
3. Spread the drop out to a diameter the size of a dime (about 18 mm) and allow to air dry.
4. Hold the slide with forceps or a clothespin, and fix it over a gentle flame for a couple of seconds. Keep the slide moving over the flame to avoid hot spots. This helps adhere the culture to the slide without burning it and causing morphological changes.

Procedure
1. Prepare a bacterial smear of the culture in question.
2. Using forceps or a clothespin to hold the slide, flood the smear with five

drops or so of crystal violet and wait for 60 seconds.

3. Pour off the stain and very gently rinse under the faucet or with a rinse bottle. You only want to rinse off the excess stain, not remove the smear from the slide. Do not rinse excessively.

4. Flood the slide with five drops or so of Gram's iodine for 60 seconds.

5. Pour off the iodine and rinse.

6. Decolorize by adding drops of 95% ethyl alcohol onto the smear until the solution runs clear. Wait too long or rinse too much, and you will remove too much stain from the cells. This is one of the most important steps. If you always get Gram-negative results even when staining Gram-positive bacteria, then you are overrinsing.

7. As soon as it runs clear, rinse immediately with water.

8. Flood slide with five drops or so of safranin counterstain for 30 seconds.

9. Pour off the counterstain and rinse.

10. Shake off the excess water or gently blot with paper towel and let air dry.

11. Examine under a microscope. Gram-positive is blue or purple and Gram-negative is pink or red.

Wild Yeast Tests

Just like bacteria, you can screen for wild yeast with specialized media, although it is more difficult to screen for wild yeast than it is bacteria. Wild yeast behave more like brewer's yeast, so a small amount of contamination from wild yeast may be difficult to find within a large brewer's yeast population. However, it is important to make the effort, as wild yeast can create plastic, phenolic, and Band-Aid-like flavors. There are several types of media that you can use to aid the search for wild yeast.

LWYM or LCSM

Lin's Wild Yeast Medium (LWYM) uses crystal violet to inhibit the growth of brewer's yeast while still allowing *Saccharomyces* wild yeast to grow. If you want to screen for non-*Saccharomyces* wild yeast, then Lin's Cupric Sulfate Medium (LCSM) uses cupric sulfate to allow non-*Saccharomyces* wild yeast growth. By plating on either of these media, you can determine if there is wild yeast in with your brewer's yeast. Certain brewer's yeast strains will still display microcolonies on wild yeast media, so it is important to know their typical morphology and be aware of any abnormal differences.

Materials
- LWYM or LCSM
- Distilled water
- Sterile pipettes
- Mechanical pipetter
- 16 x 150 mm sterile culture tubes
- 500 ml Erlenmeyer
- Foam or cotton stopper
- Incubator
- Autoclave or pressure cooker

Procedure
1. Measure 4 grams LWYM or LCSM into 100 milliliters of distilled water in a 500 ml Erlenmeyer flask.
2. Add 1 milliliter of crystal violet solution (LWYM) or cupric sulfate solution (LCSM).
3. Dissolve the medium by heating to a boil. Swirl frequently.
4. Autoclave or pressure cook at 250° F (121° C) for 15 minutes.
5. Pour sterile plates with 12- to 15-milliliter aliquots of the medium, and allow it to solidify.
6. Refrigerate LWYM plates for 24 to 48 hours before use, but use within five days. You can use LCSM plates immediately or refrigerate, but use them within three days.
7. Dilute the yeast culture to approximately 5 million cells per milliliter. Pipette 0.2 milliliter of the diluted sample onto LWYM or LCSM. Disperse the culture over the surface, using a sterile cell spreader.
8. Place in an incubator and hold at 82° F (28° C) for four to six days. You can assume any distinct colonies (ignore microcolonies) that form may be wild yeast.

Lysine Media

Lysine media uses L-Lysine to provide organisms with a nitrogen source. Most *Saccharomyces* yeast cannot use lysine as their only source of nitrogen, making them lysine-negative. Many other yeast strains (non-*Saccharomyces*) utilize lysine-N and grow on lysine medium, making them lysine-positive.

Materials
- Distilled water
- Yeast extract
- Lysine monohydrochloride
- Agar
- 500 ml Erlenmeyer
- Sterile 100 x 15 mm Petri plates
- Sterile pipette
- Sterile cell spreader
- Foam or cotton stopper
- Autoclave or pressure cooker
- Sterile filtration membrane

Procedure
1. Dissolve 2.35 grams yeast extract in 100 milliliters distilled water, and sterile filter.
2. Add 0.5 gram lysine and 4.0 grams agar to 100 milliliters distilled water, and autoclave at 250° F (121° C) for 15 minutes. While still liquid, add the liquid from the previous step.
3. Cool to 113 to 122° F (45 to 50° C). Thoroughly mix 1 milliliter of test sample with 12 to 15 milliliters of the lysine medium in a sterile plate and allow to solidify.
4. Dilute the yeast culture to approximately 5 million cells per milliliter. Pipette 0.2 milliliter of the diluted sample onto the plate. Spread evenly over the surface using a sterile cell spreader.
5. Incubate at 80° F (27° C) for two to six days, and determine the number of wild yeast per milliliter of the original sample.

Wallerstein Media

Wallerstein Laboratories Nutrient media come both with and without cycloheximide. Wallerstein Laboratories Differential medium (WLD) contains cycloheximide, which is an antibiotic that kills most brewing yeasts and mold while allowing common brewery bacteria to grow. Wallerstein Laboratories Nutrient (WLN) does not contain cycloheximide and is nonselective, allowing the growth of brewer's yeast, wild yeast, bacteria, and mold. Both WLN and WLD contain bromocresol green indicator, which will cause the media to lighten in color from blue to yellow or light green in the presence of acid-secreting bacteria.

You can also incubate Wallerstein plates aerobically and anaerobically. Aerobic conditions will help identify acetic acid and enteric bacteria, while anaerobic conditions will help identify *Lactobacillus* and *Pediococcus*.

Materials
- Distilled water
- WLN or WLD powdered medium
- 500 ml Erlenmeyer
- Sterile 100 x 15 mm Petri plates
- Foam or cotton stopper
- Autoclave or pressure cooker

Procedure
1. Weigh 8 grams WLN or WLD medium and place in 500 ml Erlenmeyer.
2. Add 100 milliliters distilled water, allow to soak for 10 minutes, and then swirl to mix. Close with a foam or cotton stopper, and bring the contents to a boil for 1 minute with constant agitation to dissolve.
3. Autoclave at 250° F (121° C) for 15 minutes.
4. Let the medium cool slightly (about 20 minutes) before pouring plates. Alternatively, once the medium has cooled, you can close the cap tightly and place it in cold storage for reheating and pouring later.
5. While the medium is cooling, mark the sterile plates with the medium type and date.
6. Pour sterile plates with 12- to 15-milliliter aliquots of the medium, and allow it to solidify.
7. Dilute the yeast culture to approximately 5 million cells per milliliter. Pipette 0.2 milliliter of the diluted sample onto the plate. Disperse the culture over the surface, using a sterile cell spreader.
8. Place in an incubator and hold 48 hours aerobically at 86° F (30° C) for bacteria or anaerobically at 80° F (27° C) for yeast.
9. Lactic acid bacteria colonies will grow larger anaerobically. The colonies will look the same, but will be smaller when grown aerobically. *Pediococcus* colonies appear yellowish-green and are smooth, while *Lactobacillus* colonies appear olive green and can be smooth or rough.
10. You will only see acetic acid bacteria (*Acetobacter, Gluconobacter*) on

aerobically grown plates. The colonies will appear blue-green in color, and the texture is smooth. The medium surrounding the colonies will change color also, due to the acid the bacteria produce.

11. Enteric bacteria (*Citrobacter, Enterobacter, Klebsiella, Obesumbacterium*) range from blue-green to yellow-green and are sometimes translucent. They have a smooth and slimy texture, but the medium around the colonies does not change color, since they do not produce acid.

Serial Dilution

Many times your lab work will require a specific concentration of yeast cells. For example, it is impossible to count cells without first getting the right concentration of yeast. Too little or too much, and you will not be able to get an accurate count. Of course, the amount of dilution needed depends upon the starting concentration and the desired final concentration. If you need to do more than a 1:10 dilution, it is best to do a serial dilution for accuracy.

Materials
- Sterile, capped 13 x 100 ml tubes with 9 milliliters of sterile water in each
- Sterile pipette
- Pipette pump

Procedure
1. Set up the test tubes in a rack for successive dilutions (depending on your desired dilution rate).
2. Label the dilution rate of each tube and loosen the caps.
3. Shake up the yeast and pipette 1 milliliter of yeast into the 9 mm water tube. Pump the pipette several times in the tube to mix up the yeast and water. This creates a 1:10 dilution.
4. Using the same pipette, remove 1 milliliter of this diluted yeast and place into the next water tube. This creates a 1:100 dilution.
5. The next dilution makes 1:1000, which is the usual dilution for counting yeast slurry.
6. You can continue with more dilutions if needed.

Cell Counting

One of the most common ways to count the number of yeast cells in a liquid suspension is with a microscope and hemocytometer. It is also convenient, because you can add dyes to the yeast sample and determine the viability at the same time.

Before you can perform a cell count, you need to have the correct concentration of yeast. Too few cells in suspension, and you will not see enough cells for an accurate count. Too many cells in suspension, and the hemocytometer field will be too crowded to get an accurate count.

Some yeast sources need more dilution than others. Here is a guideline for cell counting:

Beer	No dilution
Fermenting beer	1:10 or 1:100 dilution
Yeast slurry	1:1000 dilution

Figure 6.15: Common dilution requirements for various yeast sources.

Materials

- Microscope with 400X minimum magnification for counting yeast. You want built-in illumination, adjustable condenser with aperture diaphragm control, mechanical stage, and binocular eyepiece. Without x/y mechanical stage controls, it is nearly impossible to count cells. While a phase contrast microscope may be better for imaging the fine details, a far less expensive bright field microscope is more than adequate for counting cells.
- Hemocytometer
- Hemocytometer cover slip (thicker than standard cover slip)
- Fine-tip glass pipettes
- Handheld counter
- Transfer pipettes
- Kimwipes (or similar)
- Methylene blue solution (if also checking viability)

Sample Preparation

1. The most critical step of this procedure is preparing a properly diluted sample. A highly concentrated sample may be too difficult to count, and a very dilute sample may give erroneous results. You want less than 100 cells per microscope field (5 x 5 square) at 400X. Make sure you note your dilution factor (see "Serial Dilution," pp. 244).

2. When preparing the sample, you can use distilled water. Clumps of yeast also lead to inaccuracies. If you are working with a highly flocculent strain, first try shaking violently. If it still will not break apart, you might need to use a 0.5 percent H_2SO_4 solution instead of distilled water or add EDTA, which will bind calcium and will allow the yeast to separate. To use EDTA, centrifuge the yeast and remove the liquid. Add back the same volume of an EDTA solution (100 g/L, 0.268 M) and proceed as normal.

4. If you are combining cell counting with yeast cell viability testing, your final dilution step should be to mix 1 milliliter of your yeast sample with 1 milliliter of methylene blue solution. Mix and let it sit for about one or two minutes before filling the hemocytometer chamber. Again, make sure the sample is well mixed.

4. It is imperative that you mix your sample well (without introducing bubbles). Once you have prepared the correct dilution, mix the sample by inverting and/or shaking for several minutes. You may have to vent the sample to prevent pressure buildup.

5. It is important that the sample contains as few air bubbles as possible. De-gas if possible.

Procedure

1. Make certain that your hemocytometer is clean and dry before use. You can clean it with water. If needed, you can scrub the counting chamber gently with a lint-free towelette (Kimwipe), but proper rinsing after each use should prevent you from having to scrub the chamber.

2. Position a cover slip so that the glass covers both counting areas equally.

3. Place the tip of a glass pipette into the sample liquid, and let it fill via capillary action (drawn upwards automatically). Blot any excess from the tip on a paper towel before filling the hemocytometer chamber. Gently set the pipette tip on the edge of chamber in the etched cut and dispense (Figure 6.16). Be careful not to overfill the chamber; the sample

should not flow into the moat. If the chamber shows air bubbles, has any dry areas (underfilled), or is overflowing, you should clean the hemocytometer and start over.

Figure 6.16: Filling the hemocytometer.

4. Carefully place the hemocytometer on the microscope stage. Start at a low magnification to center the hemocytometer (Figure 6.20). Work up to 400X magnification, noting the distribution of yeast cells in the chamber. If the cells appear evenly distributed, then you can use the short cell count method. If cells appear grouped or clumped together, you may need to use the long cell count method or prepare another sample. If it looks like you have very few cells or more than 100 cells per small 5 x 5 grid, then you need to prepare a new sample. Ideally, there should be about 50 cells per small 5 x 5 grid.

5. You will be counting cells in the centrally located squares within the 1 mm^2 ruled area on the chamber (Figure 6.17). It is helpful to establish a counting protocol for all cell counts. For example, we do not count cells touching or lying on the top and right boundary lines, whereas we do count cells touching or lying on the bottom or left boundary lines (Figure 6.21). We count yeast cell buds emerging from mother cells only if the bud is at least one-half the size of the mother cell.

6. If performing viability counts, dead cells stain dark blue, as they cannot metabolize the intruding dye (Figure 6.22). Pale blue cells and budding cells that stain blue are not dead. If you are performing a cell count and viability count simultaneously, it is

Figure 6.17: Hemocytometer chamber and magnified counting grid.

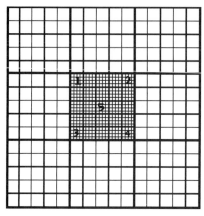

Figure 6.18: Counting grid, numbers added.

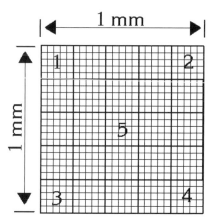

Figure 6.19: Counting grid magnified, numbers added.

best to count all cells (both live and dead) on the handheld counter and record noted dead cells on a written tally or a second counting device.

Counting Short Method, for Evenly Distributed Cells

1. Count the cells within the 5 numbered squares (Figures 6.18 and 6.19).
2. There are 25 of these smaller grids. To estimate the total number of cells in the entire grid multiply the 5 grids counted by 5.
3. The entire chamber holds a precise amount of liquid, 1/10,000 milliliter. To calculate how many cells would be in a milliliter, multiply the total cells in the grid by 10^4 (or 10,000).
4. The formula is:

Yeast cells/milliliter = counted cells x 5 x dilution factor x 10^4

For example, if you diluted the yeast by a factor of 200 and counted 220 cells within the 5 numbered squares, you would calculate:

Yeast cells/milliliter = 220 x 5 x 200 x 10,000 = 2,200,000,000 or 2.2 billion cells/milliliter

Counting Long Method, for Unevenly Distributed Cells

1. Count the cells within all 25 squares (Figures 6.18 and 6.19). This is the total number of cells in the entire grid.

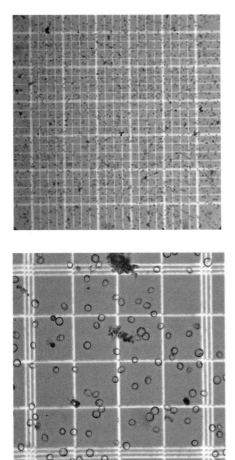

Figure 6.20: Entire hemocytometer chamber of 25 counting squares at 10X magnification. The cells are evenly distributed, and you can use the short method, counting only five of the squares.

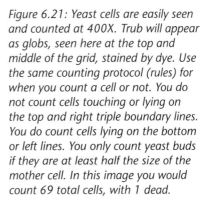

Figure 6.21: Yeast cells are easily seen and counted at 400X. Trub will appear as globs, seen here at the top and middle of the grid, stained by dye. Use the same counting protocol (rules) for when you count a cell or not. You do not count cells touching or lying on the top and right triple boundary lines. You do count cells lying on the bottom or left lines. You only count yeast buds if they are at least half the size of the mother cell. In this image you would count 69 total cells, with 1 dead.

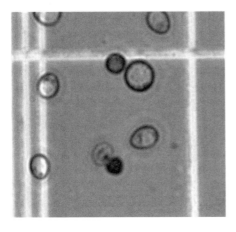

Figure 6.22: Dead cells stain dark blue. Cells that are still clear or pale blue are still alive (left of center). Budding cells may stain dark blue but are still alive (center). Budding cells are busy with growth metabolism and do not metabolize the dye.

2. The entire chamber holds a precise amount of liquid. To calculate how many cells would be in a milliliter, multiply the total cells in the grid by 10^4 (or 10,000).
3. The formula is:

Yeast cells/milliliter = counted cells x dilution factor x 10^4

For example, if you diluted the yeast by a factor of 200 and counted 1,100 cells within the 25 squares, you would calculate:

Yeast cells/milliliter = 1,100 x 200 x 10,000 = 2,200,000,000 or 2.2 billion cells/milliliter

Calculating Viability.

The formula for calculating viability:

Viability % = (total counted – dead cell count) / total counted x 100

Assuming we counted 35 dead out of our 1,100:

Viability % = (1,100 - 35) / 1,100 x 100 = 96.8%

Viability

The long-accepted method for viability testing is staining with methylene blue. While methylene blue is the most accepted method in the industry, most do not consider it a valid test when values fall below 90 percent, and some individuals prefer other dyes also described below. The alkaline conditions (10.6 pH) of the Alkaline Methylene Blue and Violet result in more rapid cell penetration and are said to provide a more realistic assessment of yeast viability. See "Cell Counting" (pp. 245-250) for more details on counting and calculating the viability percentage.

Methylene Blue (MB)

Methylene blue is available in many forms and grades. You can generally purchase it based on price and convenience. To prepare a stock solution from powder:

1. Weigh out 0.1 gram methylene blue and place in container.
2. Add distilled water to a final volume of 100 milliliters.
3. Swirl the bottle to dissolve the powder.
4. This is a 0.1 percent methylene blue solution.

Mix up or purchase a stock solution of methylene blue (0.1%). When diluting yeast for cell counts, add 1 milliliter of your yeast sample to 1 milliliter of methylene blue as your final step. Mix and let it sit for about one or two minutes before filling the hemocytometer chamber. Dead cells stain dark blue, as they cannot metabolize the intruding dye (Figure 6.22). Pale blue cells and budding cells that stain blue are not dead.

Citrate Methylene Blue (CMB)

1. Weigh out 2 grams of citric acid and place in container.
2. Add 10 milliliters of 0.1 percent methylene blue solution to the citric acid.
3. Add distilled water to make a total volume of 100 milliliters. This is a 0.01 percent solution.
4. Dilute the yeast sample with sterile deionized water to a concentration of 1×10^7 cells per milliliter. Add 0.5 milliliter of that yeast suspension to 0.5 milliliter CMB and gently agitate.
5. Count the cells microscopically after two minutes. Count dark blue cells as dead. Repeat test two more times and average the results.

Alkaline Methylene Blue (AMB)

1. Dilute methylene blue solution (0.1%) tenfold with a 0.1 M glycine buffer solution at 10.6 pH.
2. Add 0.5 milliliter yeast suspension (1×10^7 cells/ml) to 0.5 milliliter alkaline methylene blue staining solution.
3. Mix and incubate for 15 minutes at room temperature.
4. Count the cells microscopically. Count dark blue cells as dead. Pale blue and unstained cells are counted as living. Repeat test two more times and average the results.

Alkaline Methylene Violet (AMV)

Prepare AMV using the same method as with AMB, substituting methylene violet 3RAX for methylene blue. Consider dead cells displaying any variation of pink. Perform the test three times and average the results.

Standard Plate Count (SPC)

A nonstain method of testing viability is the standard plate count. You add a known quantity of yeast to a plate and count the colonies that result. For example, it you plate exactly 100 cells and 95 grow into colonies, that would be 95 percent viability. Labs rarely use this method because of the error associated with determining the number of cells plated.

To perform this test, dilute yeast with sterile deionized water to achieve a concentration of 1×10^3 cells per milliliter. Pipette 0.1 milliliter diluted yeast solution per plate onto three or more 100 x 15 mm nutrient agar plates and spread evenly. Incubate the plates at 80° F (27° C) for 42 hours. Count individual colonies on each plate, and use to calculate average viability as a percentage.

Vitality

There is no standard method for vitality testing. The industry continues to search for a fast, easy, reproducible method. Currently, the most popular method is the acid power test. The idea is that active yeast will drive the pH of a medium down (acidify it), so the faster the yeast acidifies the medium, the greater their vitality.

Acidification Power Test (AP)

Materials
- pH meter
- Deionized water
- 50 ml conical centrifuge tube
- Conical stir bar
- 20% glucose solution

Procedure

1. Calibrate your pH meter using the 2-buffer method before each series of assays.
2. Adjust the deionized water to about 6.5 pH.
3. Place 15 milliliters of sterile deionized water in a 50 ml conical centrifuge tube containing a conical stir bar.
4. Monitor the pH of the water while stirring constantly for five minutes.
5. At the end of five minutes, record the pH reading (AP0) and add 5 milliliters of rinsed and concentrated yeast slurry (1×10^9cells/ml) to the centrifuge tube.
6. Stir for 10 minutes and record the pH (AP10).
7. Immediately add 5 milliliters of 20 percent glucose.
8. Stir for 10 minutes and take a final pH reading (AP20). The acidification power is the difference between the AP20 and AP0 readings.
9. Repeat two more times and average the results.

Differentiation of Ale and Lager Yeast

There may be times when you do not know if a strain is an ale or a lager yeast. Perhaps you have acquired a new strain, or perhaps you want to make sure you have not cross-contaminated an ale and a lager culture. You can differentiate ale and lager strains by two methods, either the ability to grow at 99° F (37° C) or by the ability to grow on melibiose.

By Growth at 37° C

Lager yeast have a lower temperature tolerance than ale strains. Ale strains can grow at 99° F (37° C) but lager yeast cannot.

Materials

- Micropipette
- Sterile pipette tips
- Gloves
- Bunsen burner
- Lighter
- Cell spreader
- Large YPD plates
- Test tubes with 9 milliliters sterile water
- Incubators

Procedure

1. The first step differs depending on the type of sample. If the yeast is stored on a plate, put 5 to 10 yeast colonies in 9 milliliters of sterile water using aseptic techniques. If the yeast sample is in a malt solution, make a 1:10 dilution using aseptic technique.

2. Shake up the test tube so that no yeast is at bottom.

3. You will need to prepare two YPD plates per yeast sample: one for incubating at 77° F (25° C) and one at 99° F (37° C). Label the test tubes and YPD plates with the sample name or number and date.

4. Bring samples and YPD plates close to flame. Open lid and pipette 150 microliters of the yeast dilution onto each YPD plate.

5. Spread the yeast dilution evenly on the plate. (Make sure to use a sterilized cell spreader.)

6. Repeat this procedure for all samples.

7. Let the plates dry for about an hour. Place one YPD plate in a 99° F (37° C) incubator and the other in a 77° F (25° C) incubator for three days.

8. Record results for growth, or no growth, at both temperatures. Both ale and lager yeast can grow at 77° F (25° C), but only ale yeasts can grow at 99° F (37° C).

By Growth on Melibiose

Lager yeast can ferment the carbohydrate melibiose and ale yeast cannot. Many brewers speak of this as the ability to ferment raffinose, which is a sugar composed of melibiose and fructose.

Materials

- Yeast extract
- Peptone
- Glucose
- Distilled water
- Bromocresol green
- Screw-cap test tubes (150 x 12 mm)
- Durham tubes (60 x 5 mm)
- Melibiose
- Membrane filters, 0.45 µm pore size
- Incubator
- Balance

- Autoclave
- Inoculating loop
- Pipettes
- Isopropanol
- Sterile water

Procedure

1. Prepare a yeast extract-peptone fermentation broth by dissolving 4.5 grams yeast extract, 7.5 grams peptone and 30 milliliters bromocresol green in 1 liter of distilled water. Dispense 2-milliliter aliquots into 150 x 12 mm screw-cap test tubes, each containing an inverted 60 x 5 mm Durham tube. Put in autoclave at 250° F (121° C) for 15 minutes to sterilize.

2. Prepare a 12 percent melibiose solution by dissolving 12 grams melibiose in 100 milliliters of distilled water. Sterile filter the solution.

3. Prepare a 6 percent glucose solution by dissolving 6 grams glucose in 100 milliliters distilled water. Sterile filter the solution.

4. Take out the yeast plates for testing.

5. Sanitize lab bench and gloves using isopropanol. Get flame ready.

6. You are going to prepare three tubes for each strain to test: melibiose, glucose, and yeast extract-peptone.

7. Prepare 4 percent melibiose fermentation broth tubes. One at a time, bring each yeast extract-peptone fermentation broth tube close to flame. Pipette 1 milliliter of 12 percent melibiose solution into the tube. Close the cap and set aside.

8. Prepare 2 percent glucose fermentation broth tubes. Bring yeast extract-peptone fermentation broth tubes close to flame. Pipette 1 milliliter of the 6 percent glucose solution into the test tubes. This is your positive control.

9. Prepare yeast extract-peptone fermentation broth tubes. Bring yeast extract-peptone fermentation broth tubes close to flame. Pipette 1 milliliter of sterile water into the test tubes. This is your negative control.

10. Using a sterile inoculating loop, take 2 to 4 yeast colonies (depending on their size) off the plate.

11. Take one tube of each broth culture and carefully place the colonies into the broth. Make sure to flame the inoculating loop each time before going back to the plate for more colonies.

12. Place in incubator at 77° F (25° C).
13. Check on days 1, 2, 3, and 7. Record any changes of the indicator dye to yellow and the production of gas in the Durham tube. The negative control (yeast extract-peptone fermentation broth tube) should show no color change and no gas production. The positive control (glucose fermentation broth tube) should show a distinct change to yellow indicating acid production and gas production in the Durham tube. If these controls do not show these results, then the test is invalid.
14. It is the melibiose fermentation broth tubes that indicate if the strain is an ale or a lager yeast. If there is acid and gas production, then you can assume the strain is a lager yeast. If there is no indication of acid (yellow color) and no gas production (trapped in the Durham tube) then you can assume the strain is an ale yeast.

X-alpha-GAL Medium

This is another method to test yeast to see if a yeast sample has the ability to ferment melibiose. You will use X-alpha-GAL (5-Bromo-4-Chloro-3-indolyl alpha-D-galactoside), which is a chromogenic substrate for alpha-galactosidase. Alpha-galactosidase is the enzyme that makes it possible for a cell to utilize melibiose. Lager yeast have alpha-galactosidase activity, ale yeast do not.

Materials
- N,N-Dimethylformamide or dimethyl sulfoxide
- 5-Bromo-4-chloro-3-indolyl-alpha-D-galactoside (X-alpha-GAL)
- Glycerol
- D-galactose
- Yeast extract
- Bactopeptone
- Agar
- Ethanol
- Test tubes
- Hemocytometer
- Petri dishes
- Inoculating loop
- Micropipette
- Sterile pipette tips

- Gloves
- Reagent vial
- 2-liter flask
- Distilled water
- Bunsen burner
- Cell spreader
- Large YPD plates
- Microscope

Procedure

1. Prepare X-alpha-GAL stock solution by dissolving 25 milligrams X-alpha-GAL with 1.25 milliliters N,N-dimethylformamide or dimethyl sulfoxide in a reagent vial. Store at 39° F (4° C) in the dark.
2. Sterilize lab bench and prepare flame.
3. Label each YPD agar plate with appropriate yeast sample name and date.
4. Pipette 100 microliters of X-alpha-GAL stock solution on each YPD agar plate. Spread evenly using cell spreader. Flame the spreader between each use. Allow the plate to stand in dark for 30 to 60 minutes.
5. Determine the cell count of the sample using a hemocytometer and a microscope.
6. Set up 9 milliliters water test tubes in a rack. Dilute yeast sample to 100 to 200 colonies per 100 microliters.
7. Bring a YPD plate and dilute sample close to the flame. Open the YPD plate, pipette 100 microliters, and spread evenly using a cell spreader. Repeat process for all yeast samples, flaming the spreader between each use.
8. Allow to dry. Incubate plates in the dark at 77° F (25° C) for 6 days.
9. Count the colonies. Record the number of blue-green colonies (lager) and the number of white colonies (ale).

Yeast Strain Differentiation

Giant Colony

It is difficult to tell individual ale or lager yeast strains from each other by appearance. One classic technique is to grow the yeast until they form a giant colony. In normal plating, you grow yeast on plates for about two days, but if you grow them longer, the colonies take on a different

Figure 6.23: Different strains display different giant colony morphologies.

appearance. It turns out that this is a strain-specific phenomenon; different strains display different giant colony morphologies. It is not an exact method, but you can tell that two giant colonies are different strains just by their appearance. By taking pictures of known strains after growing them up to giant colonies, you can use them as a reference later to help identify different strains (Figure 6.23).

Mutations also cause giant colonies to take on a different appearance, so this can be a useful method to ensure that mutations are not building up in a population of yeast.

Materials
- Yeast culture or slurry
- Sterile water and tubes
- Sterile pipettes
- WLN plates
- Cell spreader

Procedure
This giant colony protocol is a modified version of the traditional

methods, which can involve incubation times of 30 days and specialized media. This requires a 7-day incubation and a WLN medium.

1. Use serial dilution to dilute yeast sample to 100 cells per milliliter.
2. Under the flame, sterile transfer 30 microliters of the diluted yeast slurry to the center of a WLN plate. Your goal is to plate only 1 to 3 cells.
3. Using a sterilized cell spreader, spread the culture around the plate.
4. Place in an 82° F (28° C) incubator.
5. Allow growth for 5 to 7 days or until giant colonies form.

Multi-Strain Drift

WLN medium contains bromocresol green, which is a dye that *Saccharomyces* yeast take up and do not normally metabolize. The medium is initially blue-green and becomes clear as the developing yeast colonies take up the dye. Different strains take up the dye in different ways, and you can use this knowledge to differentiate the strains in the culture.

Materials
- Yeast culture or slurry
- Sterile water and tubes
- Sterile pipettes
- WLN plates
- Cell spreader

Procedure
1. Use serial dilution to dilute yeast sample to 500 to 1,000 cells per milliliter.
2. Transfer 0.1 milliliter of this yeast solution onto WLN plate and spread with a sterilized cell spreader.
3. Let the plates incubate for 2 to 3 days at 80° F (27° C).
4. Inspect the colonies carefully to determine the number of strains present and relative percentages in the culture. The differences can be quite subtle, so you may need to use other tests to differentiate strains. If you started with two strains in equal amounts, the culture should show an equal mix of two different-looking colonies. If your mixed strain culture has substantially changed composition, you should consider starting a new culture.

7

Troubleshooting

Sometimes, despite a brewer's best efforts at doing everything right, fermentation just does not work out as planned. We feel it is better if you understand why a problem occurred, so instead of handing you just a solution in this section, we also offer up suggestions on how to think about the source of common fermentation problems.

Slow, Stuck, and Incomplete Fermentation

Fermentation Does Not Start

In most cases, it is rare to have a fermentation that never starts, unless the brewer made a serious mistake. Generally, when a brewer thinks fermentation is not going to start, it is just that the start is delayed. If this is an ale and it has been less than 18 hours since pitching, or if it is a lager less than 36 hours, then it is really too early to assume that fermentation did not start. If it eventually starts, you might want to review the information in this section on fermentations that are slow to start.

There are several possible causes for fermentation completely failing to start, but the most common center around yeast health or wort temperature. If the vast majority of the yeast is dead, or the temperature is so low or so high that the yeast was not able to get started, then you may have a fermentation that fails to start. Before taking any other action, inspect the fermentor for any signs of a kraeusen ring above the surface of the beer, and take both gravity and pH readings. It is not unheard of that fermentation occurred so quickly that it went unnoticed by the brewer. If the specific gravity of the beer has dropped, but not to normal attenuation levels, and you see no activity, then review the information on incomplete fermentation. If the specific gravity remains the same as it was at pitching, but the pH has dropped 0.5 to 0.8, then it is likely that fermentation is under way, even though there may be no visible sign. In this case you will most likely want to review your procedures for determining pitching rates, oxygen levels, and yeast health.

If there is no gravity change or pH change over the times indicated, it is time to pitch additional yeast. Ideally, you would pitch yeast already active and at the height of fermentation from another batch of beer. If you do not have that yeast available, then another stored slurry, lab propagation, package of liquid yeast, or rehydrated dry yeast is acceptable. If the source is the same as the previous pitch, confirm that the yeast is viable before pitching again. This can be as simple as putting some yeast in a small volume of wort at a warm temperature (80° F, 27° C) to see if it will ferment. You will also want to oxygenate the wort again. There is no need to worry about oxidation and staling at this point, as the damage was done with the first dose of oxygen if the yeast did not consume it. This second pitch of yeast is going to utilize the second dose of oxygen.

Once you get fermentation started, you will want to determine exactly what went wrong. Consider the following possibilities:

1. Was the yeast dead, or did it have very low viability or vitality before you pitched?
   a. Did you check the health of the yeast?
   b. What was the source of the yeast?
   c. How was it transported, stored, and handled before pitching? Freezing yeast packages, starters, or slurries is more common than you might think.

2. Was it the wort that killed the yeast?
   a. Could the wort temperature have been as high as 90° F (32° C)?
   b. Is it possible that the wort froze at some point?

   c. While unlikely, could it be that the malt was contaminated with my-cotoxins? Malt stored in hot, humid areas can reach unacceptable levels. See "Malt Contamination," p. 278.

   d. Could there have been some other source of contamination, in levels high enough to damage or inhibit the yeast?

3. Could conditions have been so unfavorable to yeast growth that the yeast could not get started at all?

   a. This is fairly rare as well, as long as you are following the general guidelines and pitching healthy yeast. Given enough time, they will make some headway.

   b. Was the temperature excessively cold? Very low temperatures may prevent yeast from becoming active, especially if they were taken in a dormant state from a cold environment and pitched into cold wort. Unless you are very familiar with a strain and its temperature needs, stick to the recommended temperature ranges for a strain. You may not notice a small drop in temperature, but yeast is far more sensitive to temperature changes.

   c. Did you provide enough oxygen for the yeast?

   d. Was the wort sufficient in nutrients for the yeast? Using distilled water as a brew source without adding back mineral salts, or making wort with large percentages of nonmalt sugars, can prevent the yeast from growing.

4. Has trub trapped the yeast at the bottom of the fermentor? Very flocculent English strains pitched into wort with large amounts of break material and hops can prevent the yeast from starting. Consider limiting the amount of material carried over to the fermentor. If you think this is the cause, agitate the fermentor every 15 minutes for the first several hours post-pitch.

No Activity After "X" Hours

First of all, do not panic. Many brewers, especially homebrewers, put too much emphasis on seeing a very short lag phase, often to the detriment of beer flavor. Remember that an appropriate amount and rate of yeast growth is vital to developing beer flavor. Check the following parameters:

1. Have you waited an appropriate amount of time? A lag phase of twelve hours for an ale and longer for a lager is quite normal. The colder lager temperature causes lower yeast metabolism.
2. If it is a lager, have more patience. The colder the liquid, the more carbon dioxide it takes before the beer reaches the saturation point and bubbles start to form and rise to the surface. If you are working with a fermentor that allows you to see the surface of the beer, get close to the surface and shine a strong flashlight on the beer at a low angle. If there are any tiny bubbles starting, you will see a sparkling at the surface.
3. Check your fermentation temperature, and make sure you are measuring the temperature of the beer accurately. If so, is the temperature in a range acceptable to the yeast? Consider raising the temperature, especially if you are already 24 hours into fermentation.

Once you have resolved the problem, determine why it occurred in the first place:

1. Did you start with a healthy pitch of yeast in the proper quantity for the batch of beer?
2. Was your propagation or storage procedure sound, favoring the health of the yeast, not just the cell count?
3. Did you provide the oxygen, pitching rate, and nutrients that the yeast need for proper growth and fermentation?
4. Also, consider the initial wort temperature. While there is some benefit to starting at a slightly lower fermentation temperature and allowing the temperature to rise over the first day or two, this is only valid for very healthy yeast in wort supplying proper nutrition and oxygen levels. If you are not providing those conditions, then it is better to start with a warmer fermentation temperature.
5. Has mutation in your harvested or propagated yeast caused changes in behavior?

Fermentation Does Not End

Fermentations that do not end tend to have several causes: poor initial yeast health, poor yeast environment, low pitching rates, or contamination. Before taking any action, take a specific gravity reading and compare it to your forced ferment test results (pp. 222-223). If the beer is at a lower gravity than the force test, then there is a bacterial or wild yeast contamination. More than likely, the beer should be dumped, though it might still be drinkable for a short time, depending on the type of contaminating organism.

If the specific gravity reading is close to or matching the force test, then it may just be a case of misinterpreting the evolution of carbon dioxide as fermentation. Just because an airlock, bubbler, or blowoff hose is bubbling very slowly, that does not mean that the beer is still fermenting. If you are warming the beer, it will cause the CO_2 saturation point of the beer to change, and CO_2 will come out of solution. The same goes for any sort of movement or vibration, which can also cause a saturated solution to bubble, just like shaking a soda.

If the specific gravity is much higher than the force test indicates, then fermentation may indeed be still progressing slowly. If you did not do a force test, then you cannot be certain the beer has not reached the proper terminal gravity for that wort. Even though a recipe may suggest what terminal gravity your beer should reach, it is still quite dependent on your wort production process.

If there is still active yeast, raise the fermentation temperature by a minimum of 5° F (3° C) to increase the metabolic rate of the yeast. You might also rouse the yeast or pitch some additional yeast that is at the peak of its fermentation activity. If that does not help, you can consider the addition of more oxygen as well. See the "Attenuation" troubleshooting section (pp. 272-275) for more ideas.

Fermentation Seems Incomplete

Refer to the "Attenuation" troubleshooting section (pp. 272-275)

Flocculation Changes

Flocculation changes in yeast cultures can happen quickly and may be an indicator of many other yeast health issues and problem fermentations. One of the most common causes of change in flocculation is selective pressure by the brewer. If your yeast harvesting and re-use always favors the most flocculent or least flocculent yeast, you will find that the yeast population quickly shifts towards containing only those cells. When you see a change, suspect yourself as the most likely cause.

The next likely cause of flocculation changes is yeast mutation. Mutations typically increase with each generation and can result in physiological changes in the yeast that inhibit flocculation. For instance, respiratory mutant yeast (petite mutant) is less flocculent than yeast without that mutation. If the yeast is high in petite mutants, then the brewer is usually at fault.

Other possible reasons for lack of flocculation include high levels of sugar remaining in the beer, insufficient turbulence in the fermentor during fermentation (possibly fermentor design or low fermentation vigor), and calcium deficiency. Calcium plays a key role in yeast cell flocculation. While it only takes a tiny amount of calcium for flocculation to occur (levels lower than 10^{-8} molar may prevent flocculation), ensuring a minimum fifty parts per million of calcium in your brewing water will prevent calcium-related flocculation issues. If you are making up your own water from distilled water or reverse osmosis treatment, this might be the issue.

One reason for premature yeast flocculation may be malt related. Although researchers have yet to determine the exact cause, there is a potential link between poorly modified malt, contaminated barley, and flocculation. Research has shown that fungal malt contamination can create co-factors that bind to yeast cells and cause them to drop out of solution prematurely. This continues to be the focus of much of the current brewing research related to flocculation patterns.

Excessively low or high temperatures can also affect flocculation, so keep that in mind as well.

Flavors and Aromas

There can be a number of causes for fermentation flavor and aroma problems, ranging from contamination to temperature control and more. It is important to know and control all of your fermentation parameters to achieve consistent growth and fermentation rates. You should know how much yeast you are pitching and how much growth you are achieving by measuring the amount of yeast at the end of fermentation. That is a big step toward consistency of fermentation.

Fruity Character and Fusel Alcohols

The most common reason for high levels of hot alcohols and esters, especially for homebrewers, is insufficient temperature control. For some yeast strains, a one- or two-degree change in temperature can cause large differences in metabolic by-product production.

Many other factors influence ester and fusel production, whether you are striving for an increase or decrease in their concentrations. Review the section on "Optimizing Fermentation Flavor" (pp. 103-107) and especially Figure 4.18, which shows how fermentation factors affect these flavor and aroma compounds.

Sulfur

It is important to ensure vigorous fermentation and let fermentation go to completion before capping the fermentor. Some brewers like to cap the fermentor near the end of fermentation to carbonate the beer by trapping the remaining CO_2. By doing this, the brewer also traps any sulfur in the beer, which will not go away without extraordinary efforts. This applies to both ale and lager brewing. It takes about 24 hours post-fermentation at fermentation temperature for the evolution of CO_2 to scrub out all of the sulfur.

If you find that you have a kegged beer with substantial sulfur, you can force carbonate the beer, then bleed off the pressure once an hour during a day, recarbonating the beer each night. After two or three days, check the character of the beer again. If there is still a need for sulfur reduction, continue until reduced to acceptable levels. Keep in mind that you are foaming the beer by using this process, and it can affect the head retention if you carry this on for many days.

Phenols

Some brewer's yeast strains and most native yeast produce aromatic phenolic compounds through a decarboxylation reaction of the phenolic acids naturally found in malt, such as ferulic acid.

Unintended phenolic flavors are most often a consequence of wild yeast contamination, whether it is from native yeast or cross-contamination from other strains used in the brewery. Generally, if the source was native yeast, it will also result in superattenuation of the beer. Native yeast contamination also tends to result in very dusty yeast that refuses to flocculate. Under normal conditions, mutation in nonphenolic brewer's yeast should not be a problem, though it is another possible source of phenolic off-flavors, and it would be an indicator that it is time to re-culture the pitching yeast. Often brewers assume mutation was the cause, when it was more likely that they introduced phenolic yeast somewhere in their process.

It is also possible for other wort spoilage organisms to produce phenolic compounds. Overall, it is a good idea to scrutinize your sanitation and cleaning processes if you encounter unintended phenols in your beer.

When working with phenolic-producing yeast, the amount of phenolic compounds the yeast produce is related to cell health and growth rates. Generally speaking, factors that increase growth increase the production of phenolic compounds.

Keep in mind that chlorine present in brewing water or introduced through chlorinated sanitizers or cleaners will combine with malt phenols to create chlorophenols. These can produce powerful medicinal flavors and aromas. Do not confuse this with a yeast problem.

Acetaldehyde

Acetaldehyde is an intermediate step in the production of ethanol. In a healthy fermentation allowed to run to completion, the yeast will eventually take up and convert the acetaldehyde. There are several reasons for high levels of acetaldehyde:

- Removing the beer from the yeast early, before it has completed fermentation.
- The oxidation of ethanol after fermentation is complete.
- The conversion of ethanol to vinegar by acetic acid bacteria, though this is accompanied by obvious vinegar character.
- Fermentation parameters that encourage excessively fast fermentation, such as overpitching and high fermentation temperatures.

Diacetyl

Diacetyl is a natural part of fermentation, and certain strains produce more than others. However, yeast naturally metabolize the diacetyl into flavorless compounds during active fermentation. Several factors determine the amount of diacetyl that remains after fermentation:

- Incomplete fermentation can leave high levels of diacetyl in the beer, because there was insufficient contact time between the yeast and wort to take up the diacetyl produced during fermentation.

- A warmer temperature at the beginning of fermentation, while the yeast is growing, creates higher levels of diacetyl precursor. If you follow this with lackluster fermentation, perhaps by lowering temperatures, it results in higher levels of diacetyl at the end of fermentation. This is a common pattern for many homebrewers—pitching yeast warm to make up for low cell counts or poor yeast health and then allowing the beer to ferment cooler as yeast activity falls off. Healthy yeast given adequate time and temperature at the end of fermentation results in beer with very low diacetyl levels.
- Insufficient aeration at pitching.
- Some bacteria produce diacetyl. Lactic acid bacteria also produce lactic acid, sometimes creating a rancid butter taste. Some small breweries and many homebrewers have a difficult time bottling beer in a manner that eliminates lactic acid bacteria. This is one reason why a brewery can bottle great-tasting beer, only to have it develop pressure, sourness, and diacetyl flavors in as little as eight weeks.

Sour

Bacterial contamination is the most common cause of acidic flavors and aromas in beer. Brewers will most often run into either lactic acid bacteria or acetic acid bacteria. *Lactobacillus* generally produces a tart, sour characteristic in beer, while *Acetobacter* produces vinegarlike flavors. There are other organisms, such as *Brettanomyces*, which can produce acetic acid under specific conditions.

If your beer is souring, review the contamination tests in the lab section to help determine where in your process you are introducing the spoilage organisms and take appropriate steps to resolve the problem.

Overly Sweet

Poor recipe formulation is responsible for many too sweet beers, but what do you look for when a trusted recipe turns out too sweet? Most often when a beer turns out overly sweet, it is an attenuation problem. When a forced ferment test shows that it is not an attenuation issue, then there are a few other possible causes.

While it may not make for an overly sweet beer, one issue that brewers often ignore is that the surface area of the yeast cells in fermentation significantly affects the IBU level. Generally speaking, the greater the total cell surface material, the lower the amount of isomerized alpha acids that make it to the finished beer. Yeast pitching rate, yeast growth rate, strain, yeast health, pitching generation, and other factors result in more or fewer IBUs in the finished beer. The brewer should strive for consistent pitching rates, consistent growth rates, and excellent yeast health on every batch of beer. By controlling these factors, adjustments to your recipe have a more controlled impact on the bittering/sweetness ratio.

Another possible explanation is that some alcohols have a sweet character, and those alcohols could be producing the sweet flavors. However, when this is the cause, tasting the beer gives an initial sweetness that fades. It does not produce a cloying sweetness. If you taste an upfront sweetness that fades and leaves a drier beer sensation. it is indicative of alcohol-related sweetness.

Cloying sweetness is indicative of underattenuation or poor recipe formulation. Beers that are too sweet but not cloying could be from recipe issues or the yeast taking out more bittering compounds than anticipated. For underattenuation problems, refer to "Attenuation."

Overly Dry

As with beers that are too sweet, poor recipe formulation is probably one of the most common problems. However, if you are working with a trusted recipe and have a problem with excessive dry beer character, then there are a few other possibilities. Again, a forced ferment test is a good tool in figuring out the source of the problem. Often bacterial or other contaminating organisms can cause a beer to overattenuate.

If the beer is not overattenuating, then it might be a process related issue:

- Improper pH during mash and runoff/sparging.
- Changes in water chemistry? Often water suppliers provide different water during different seasons.
- Changes in malt supply.

Keep in mind that for the most part the mash temperature does not determine the sweetness of a beer. The longer-chain sugars are not very sweet. If the yeast have fermented out a high-mash- temperature beer completely, then the finishing gravity of the beer can be quite high, but the overall character of the beer can be quite dry. Conversely, a beer with a low finishing gravity can turn out far sweeter. There are many factors, including yeast cell surface area and the alcohols produced during fermentation, that affect the final character of the beer.

Autolysis

For most homebrewers working with wide-bottom fermentors and healthy yeast, autolysis should not be much of an issue. Some strains are subject to autolysis faster than others, but overall, if you keep the beer/ yeast at reasonable temperatures and harvest the yeast in a reasonable amount of time, you should not experience any problems with autolysis.

The same is not true for commercial brewers working on a much larger scale. Very tall fermentors that concentrate yeast tightly in a cone tend to increase the rate of autolysis. If this represents your setup, make sure you provide adequate cooling to the cone (or top of the fermentor, if top cropping) and harvest your yeast as soon as possible after it has done its job.

One factor that may affect both homebrewers and professionals is packaging beer with excessive amounts of yeast. It only requires 1 million cells per milliliter to carbonate a beer properly. More than that will eventually produce higher levels of autolysis flavors in your beer.

Carbonation

Lack of Carbonation

It does not take much yeast to carbonate a beer. However, for consistent, timely carbonation you want to use healthy yeast in the proper quantity at consistent temperatures. If you are working with high-alcohol beers, it is beneficial to filter out the yeast and repitch with fresh, active yeast for bottle carbonation.

- Use fresh yeast if possible.
- Ensure you have provided the appropriate amount of sugar, based on the temperature of the beer. See "Appendix D: Priming Rates and CO_2 Volumes" in Brewing Classic Styles by Jamil Zainasheff and John Palmer for useful charts to determine the amount of carbon dioxide present in a

given beer and the amount of priming required.

- Store bottles at a warm-enough temperature for carbonation, allowing space between bottles so that all of them carbonate the same.
- If chemically sanitizing the bottles, make sure to measure the sanitizer concentration. Do not guess when mixing solutions, and allow adequate drain time for the product you are using. Excessive concentrations of sanitizing products can affect yeast health and carbonation.

Overcarbonation

Overcarbonation is the result of either too much sugar present at packaging time or the presence of an organism that is able to consume complex carbohydrates and produce gas.

- Take into account the amount of dissolved CO_2 present in the beer when calculating the amount of sugar. See "Appendix D: Priming Rates and CO_2 Volumes" in *Brewing Classic Styles* for useful charts to determine the amount of CO_2 present in a given beer and the amount of priming required.
- Your forced ferment test should give you a good idea of whether your beer has attenuated fully prior to packaging.
- If the problem is contamination, usually it will result in a change in beer flavor as well as excessive carbonation.

Attenuation

Many times a brewer sets his expectation of attenuation based on a recipe or the attenuation values given for a particular yeast strain. This may or may not be realistic. Regardless of what you do to prepare your yeast for fermentation, the fact is that wort composition trumps all when it comes to getting yeast to attenuate a desired amount. If you perform a forced ferment test, you will know the maximum level of attenuation you should expect for that wort. If your fermentation test shows that the beer will only attenuate down to 1.020 (5 °P) with the yeast you are using, then expecting it to drop to 1.012 (3 °P) is unrealistic. By the same logic, if your batch of beer drops below 1.020 (5 °P), you have some sort of contamination problem such as wild yeast or bacteria. If you find yourself with attenuation problems, the forced ferment test is a valuable tool.

Low Attenuation

It is common for fermentation of the main batch to fall a point or two short of the maximum attenuation shown by the forced ferment test. The higher the starting gravity, the further away from the maximum attenuation your beer will most likely end up. If the beer falls considerably short of the expected attenuation, and you have eliminated wort fermentability as the issue, then there was some sort of fermentation problem. Investigate the following possibilities:

- Fermentation temperature was too low, and the yeast was not active enough to complete fermentation. It is also important to avoid temperature swings, especially at the beginning during lag phase and as fermentation nears the end. Yeast are very sensitive to small changes in temperature. When the yeast start to slow down in fermentation speed, they will produce less heat, and if the temperature is too low, they will stop/slow down suddenly, making it very difficult to reach terminal gravity.
- Pitching rate was too low, so there were not enough cells to complete fermentation. Without enough cells to perform the fermentation, the yeast cells in solution have to work harder than usual in order to complete the job. These cells get tired and overworked and will often quit before they are finished. Yeast in beer fermentation rarely achieve more than three- to fourfold growth.
- Chronic overpitching can also result in poor attenuation even in the first generation. Generally, fermentation will begin quickly and finish normally, but successive generations will begin to exhibit health issues. Viability declines over time, and the population overall gets sluggish, since fermentation is producing few new cells.
- Lack of oxygen at the beginning of fermentation restricted growth and impacted cell health. Remember that high-gravity beers might benefit from an additional dose of oxygen around the 12-hour mark. As with incorrect pitching rates, the impact of chronic underoxygenation can be more apparent in successive generations, as the yeast are not equipped with the proper building blocks for synthesizing strong lipids for cell reproduction and growth. This can also contribute to low yield when harvesting yeast.

- Yeast mutation can also affect attenuation. Generally, the forced ferment test should reveal these problems, but it is possible that the mutation does not affect the stirred, warm test, but still has an effect on the main fermentation.
- Poor yeast health and lack of critical nutrients such as zinc can cause fermentation to stall before it reaches terminal gravity.
- Improper mixing in the fermentor can result in stratification and underattenuation. When either multi-filling a fermentor or diluting highly concentrated wort, you need to mix the two solutions properly. High speed filling and directing the incoming wort from the bottom of the fermentor up instead of top down will help mix the two.
- If you are reusing your yeast and harvesting it too early, you may be putting selective pressure on the population, causing underattenuation. The yeast that drop first are the least attenuative of the population. If your process favors them, then the pitch will become less and less attenuative over time. You can also negatively affect yeast health by leaving the yeast in the beer for long periods of time, and that can also affect attenuation of future batches.

Here are some common methods brewers use to try to drive a beer to attenuate a bit more:

- Rouse the yeast. Either carefully blow carbon dioxide up through the bottom of the fermentation tank, or when using a smaller homebrew fermentor, you can tilt it on edge and swirl the beer. This should get some yeast back up into the beer, and it will drive off CO_2, which may be inhibiting the yeast.
- Transfer the beer or the yeast. Transferring the beer or taking yeast out of the bottom and pitching it back in up top does the same things as rousing the yeast, but it also adds some oxygen and ensures the yeast and remaining wort sugars are evenly mixed.
- Increase the temperature. Higher temperatures increase yeast activity. Within reasonable limits, this is one of the best ways to help the yeast reach the target final gravity.
- Add more yeast. Many brewers ask if they can just toss in some dried Champagne yeast to finish out fermentation. Those who say it works were probably dealing with a beer that had large amounts of simple

sugars remaining, as Champagne yeast will not consume the longer wort sugars. You can add more brewer's yeast, but it is hard to restart a fermentation that stops. A partially fermented beer is not a yeast-friendly place, as it has alcohol and there is no oxygen, not enough nutrients, and not enough sugar. Only add yeast that is at its peak of activity. Add the yeast to a small bit of wort, let it reach high kraeusen, and then toss the whole thing into the beer. If you add enough yeast at their peak of activity, you should not need to add oxygen to the beer.

- Add enzymes. If the problem was with the wort sugar composition, this will often help. However, if it is a fermentation problem then this will not help.

High Attenuation

If your beer attenuates more than the maximum shown by the forced ferment test, you have a contamination problem. It is imperative that you locate the source of the contamination and eliminate it from your brewery. Turning a blind eye does not solve the problem. Review the laboratory section for information on how to go about testing your yeast and your brewery environment.

Yeast Storage Problems

Declining or Low Yeast Viability

Another big issue for brewers is declining viability in harvested yeast slurry. There are two fundamental reasons for a loss of viability. It is either that the yeast was in poor health at the time of harvest, or that the storage conditions were less than ideal.

Poor health at harvesting has many of the same root causes as slow fermentation: overpitching, low dissolved oxygen, and low initial viability. If the fermentation was normal and strong, then chances are the yeast were healthy at the end of fermentation. However, your actions after fermentation could have caused a loss of viability.

If you do not collect the yeast quickly enough from the fermentor, it can put a great deal of stress on the cells, including alcohol, pH, and hydrostatic stress. For optimal health, you should collect ale yeast 24 hours after the end of fermentation and lager yeast within three to five days.

Many times when small breweries upgrade fermentor size, they begin noticing viability issues with harvested yeast. This can be because the larger and taller the fermentor, the higher osmotic stress on the yeast. In addition, keeping yeast cool while in the fermentor can be an issue. Often cone cooling is inadequate, or with top-cropping yeast, the upper part of the fermentor may not be cool enough, resulting in stressful temperatures for the yeast.

If you are sure you harvested healthy yeast, then the issue is with your yeast storage practices.

Inadequate Shelf Life

First, make sure you have the right expectations of how long you can store yeast and still use it for a quality fermentation. If the yeast is in good health at the end of an average-gravity, average-hop rate fermentation, then you can usually store yeast for two weeks and reuse it without difficulty. After that, the results will always be highly variable. Keep the following in mind while storing yeast:

- Carbon dioxide pressure, even a small amount, is bad for the yeast while in storage. CO_2 damages yeast cell walls and can easily build up with yeast in storage.
- In most cases, lower storage temperatures result in longer shelf life, unless you accidentally freeze the yeast. A cold spell can cause yeast storage temperatures to dip below freezing. This is especially true when using older refrigerators that might not be able to keep up with demand during the day. As the ambient temperature drops, so does the refrigerator temperature. In this case, it is better to store your yeast a few degrees warmer, if there is a danger of accidental freezing.
- In some cases, you should not reuse yeast from high-alcohol or very high-IBU beers, which stress the yeast and impact viability.
- Holding the yeast in the beer for an additional eight to 12 hours after fermentation allows them to build their glycogen reserves before storage.
- Is the storage equipment clean and sanitary? This includes keeping them free from chemical contaminants and high levels of sanitizers that might impact yeast health.

Washing Problems

The most common problem with acid washing or chlorine dioxide washing is either using the wrong pH or the wrong concentration. You need to measure the pH accurately. It is worth investing in a decent pH meter and the calibration solutions to ensure you get the right pH.

Rinsing Problems

The most common mistake made when rinsing yeast is not using a large-enough volume of water or not knowing which layer is the yeast. If you do not use at least three to four times as much water as yeast solids, the slurry will be too dense to allow the heavier bits to drop to the bottom in a reasonable amount of time. The thinner the slurry, the better the separation.

Do not mistake the thinner layer on top as yeast. There might be some cells in there, but it is mostly proteins and perhaps other lightweight cell material, which you can discard.

Transportation Problems

Most issues with transportation center around temperature. Start with the healthiest yeast possible, monitor the temperature, and test the yeast at the receiving end.

Propagation/Starter Problems

If you start with a healthy colony of yeast and provide the correct inputs of sugar, nutrients, oxygen, and temperature, propagation should always proceed normally. Novices in propagation often wonder why they see no bubbles on the surface of a stirred or shaken vessel. The answer is that the stirring is effective at driving off any excess CO_2 as it forms and larger, visible bubbles are rare. Pay attention to the color and opacity of the propagation. If it becomes cloudy, that is caused by an increase in the population. Keep the following in mind:

- Start from a healthy yeast source. If you begin with a mutated culture, the resulting propagation may retain that mutation. It is possible for the nonmutated cells to outcompete the mutated ones, but there is no guarantee. If in doubt, use pure culture techniques to start over.
- Use only sugar sources high in maltose. Use a malt-based source, which

provides critical nutrients for the yeast. Growing yeast in simple sugar results in yeast that cannot ferment maltose.

- Supply aeration and an appropriate nutrient mix that includes zinc.
- Propagate yeast warm, around 72° F (22° C).
- Use a stir plate, orbital shaker, or frequently shake the vessel to drive off CO_2 and help mix the yeast with the remaining sugars.

Malt Contamination

Malt has a fair number of organisms on its surface, such as *Lactobacillus*. The boil kills the vast majority of these organisms, and the brewer need not worry. However, there are molds and fungi that may produce myco-toxins that will survive the boil. This is rarely a problem with the malt as it comes from the maltster, but rather is caused by poor storage conditions at the brewery. Hot, humid climates are especially problematic and can cause rapid mold growth and high levels of mycotoxins. While the mash eliminates a large portion of mycotoxins present, the mycotoxins that reach the boil kettle are not denatured. Mycotoxins such as trichot-hecenes (Flannigan, et al., 1985) inhibit *Saccharomyces cerevisiae* growth, which in turn can affect attenuation. Various toxins can also interact with the yeast cell wall and affect flocculation. This is exactly what these toxins are supposed to do in nature: help an organism outcompete yeast.

Troubleshooting Charts

Performance Problems

Factor	Problem		
	Slow/Stuck/ Incomplete Fermentation	Declining/Low Viability	Flocculation Changes
FAN/amino acid deficiency	•		
Mineral (Zn, Ca, etc.) deficiency	•		•
Contamination—wild yeast or bacteria	•		•
Underpitching	•		

Factor	Problem		
	Slow/Stuck/ Incomplete Fermentation	Declining/Low Viability	Flocculation Changes
Overpitching	+ (over several generations)	•	
Low dissolved oxygen	•	•	•
High dissolved oxygen		•	
High-gravity wort	•	•	
High ethanol concentration (>9%)	•	•	
Incorrect fermentation temperature	•		
Vacillating fermentation temperature	•		
Reused yeast collected too late		✔	
Reused yeast collected too early	•		•
Insufficient cooling of fermentor cone		•	
CO_2 buildup in fermentor	•	•	
Incomplete mixing of fermentor	•	•	
Yeast mutation	•		•
Dehydration of yeast	•	•	•
Malt in poor condition, undermodified	•		
Malt microorganism contamination	•		•
*Poor yeast health—low viability/vitality	✔	•	

*Figure 7.1: A '•' indicates the Factor is a potential cause of the Problem. A '✔' indicates the Factor is the most common cause of the Problem. * Many factors lead to poor yeast health, such as mineral deficiency, overpitching, low DO, high-gravity wort, high ethanol concentration, delayed yeast collection, insufficient cooling of fermentor cone, CO_2 buildup in fermentor, incomplete mixing of fermentor.*

Flavor Problems

Factor	Problem				
	Esters	Fusel Alcohols	Sulfur	Acetaldehyde	Autolysis
FAN/amino acid deficiency	+		•		
Mineral (Zn, Ca, etc.) deficiency	•	•		•	•
Contamination—wild yeast or bacteria	•	•	•	•	
Underpitching	+	++	+	+	•
Overpitching	-			+	+
Low dissolved oxygen	+	-			
High dissolved oxygen	-	+		•	
High-gravity wort	+	+			
High ethanol concentration (>9%)	+	+			•
Incorrect fermentation temperature	+ or -	+ or -	•	•	
Vacillating fermentation temperature				•	

Factor	Problem				
	Esters	Fusel Alcohols	Sulfur	Acetaldehyde	Autolysis
Reused yeast collection too late					•
Reused yeast collected too early				•	
Insufficient cooling of fermentor cone					+
CO_2 buildup in fermentor	-	-	+		
Incomplete mixing of fermentor					
Yeast mutation					
Dehydration of yeast	+	•	•	•	•
Malt in poor condition, undermodified					
Malt contamination					
*Poor yeast health—low viability/vitality			•		•

Figure 7.2: A '•' indicates the Factor is a potential cause of Problem. A '+' indicates the Factor causes an increase and '-' indicates a decrease. * Many factors lead to poor yeast health, such as mineral deficiency, overpitching, low DO, high-gravity wort, high ethanol concentration, delayed yeast collection, insufficient cooling of fermentor cone, CO_2 buildup in fermentor, incomplete mixing of fermentor.

Flavor Problems (continued)

Factor	Problem			
	Phenols	Over-carbonation	Lactic Acid	Diacetyl
FAN/amino acid deficiency				+
Mineral (Zn, Ca, etc.) deficiency				
Contamination—wild yeast or bacteria	•	•	+	•
Underpitching	+			+
Overpitching				
Low dissolved oxygen				
High dissolved oxygen				
High-gravity wort				
High ethanol concentration (>9%)				
Incorrect fermentation temperature				•
Vacillating fermentation temperature				•

Factor	Problem			
	Phenols	Over-carbonation	Lactic Acid	Diacetyl
Reused yeast collection too late				
Reused yeast collected too early				•
Insufficient cooling of fermentor cone				
CO$_2$ buildup in fermentor		•		-
Incomplete mixing of fermentor				•
Yeast mutation	•			•
Dehydration of yeast				•
Malt in poor condition, undermodified				
Malt contamination		•		
*Poor yeast health—low viability/vitality				•

*Figure 7.3: A '•' indicates the Factor is a potential cause of Problem. A '+' indicates the Factor causes an increase and '-' indicates a decrease. * Many factors lead to poor yeast health, such as: mineral deficiency, overpitching, low DO, high-gravity wort, high ethanol concentration, delayed yeast collection, insufficient cooling of fermentor cone, CO$_2$ buildup in fermentor, incomplete mixing of fermentor.*

List of Figures

References

Foreword

Schlenk, F. "Early Research on Fermentation—A Story of Missed Opportunities." In A. Cornish-Bowden, *New Beer in an Old Bottle: Eduard Buchner and the Growth of Biochemical Knowledge.* Valencia, Spain: Universitat de València, 1997, 43–50.

Part 1

De Clerck, J. *A Textbook of Brewing,* vol. 2. London: Chapman & Hall, 1958, 426-429.

Part 2

Bamforth, C. "Beer Flavour: Esters." *Brewers Guardian* 130, no. 9 (2001), 32-34.

Bamforth, C. "Beer Flavour: Sulphur Substances." *Brewers Guardian* 130, no. 10 (2001), 20-23.

Boulton, C., and D. Quain. *Brewing Yeast and Fermentation.* Oxford, U.K: Blackwell Science Ltd., 2001.

Briggs, D.E., J.S. Hough, R. Stevens, and T.W. Young. *Malting & Brewing Science,* vol. 1. London: Chapman & Hall, 1981.

Casey, G. "Yeast Selection in Brewing." In C.J. Panchal, *Yeast Strain Selection.* New York: Marcel Dekker, 1990, 65-111.

Fugii, T. "Effect of Aeration and Unsaturated Fatty Acids on Expression of the *Saccharomyces cerevisia* Alcohol Acetyltransferase Gene." *Applied and Environmental Microbiology* 63, no. 3 (1997), 910-915.

Hazen, K.C., and B.W. Hazen. "Surface Hydrophobic and Hydrophilic Protein Alterations in *Candida Albicans.*" *FEMS Microbiology Letters* 107 (1993), 83-88.

Kruger, L. "Yeast Metabolism and Its Effect on Flavour: Part 2." *Brewers Guardian* 127 (1998), 27-30.

Mathewson, P.R. *Enzymes.* Eagan Press, 1998, 1-10.

Meilgaard, M.C. "Flavor Chemistry of Beer: Part II: Flavor and Threshold of 239 Aroma Volatiles." *MBAA Technical Quarterly* 12 (1975), 151-168.

Mussche, R.A. and F.R. Mussche. "Flavours in Beer." 2008 Craft Brewers Conference, Chicago.

Pasteur, L. *Studies on Fermentations, The Disease of Beer, Their Causes, and the Means of Preventing Them.* London: MacMillan and Co., 1879. Reprint. BeerBooks.com, 2005.

Quain, D.E., and R.S. Tubb. "A Rapid and Simple Method for the Determination of Glycogen in Yeast." *Journal of the Institute of Brewing* 89 (1983), 38-40.

Smart, K.A. "Flocculation and Adhesion." *European Brewery Convention 1999 Monograph* 28. Nurenberg: Fachverlag Hans Carl, 2000, 16-29.

Walker, G.M. *Yeast Physiology and Biotechnology*. New York: John Wiley & Sons, 1998.

Zoecklein, B.W., K.C. Fugelsang, B.H. Gump, and F.S. Nury. *Wine Anaylsis and Production*. Gaithersburg, Md.: Aspen Publishers, 1999, 101.

Part 3

Aguilar Uscanga, M.G., M.L. Delia, and P. Strehaiano. *Applied Microbiology and Biotechnology*, vol. 61, no.2 (2003).

Boulton and Quain, *Brewing Yeast and Fermentation*.

Casey, "Yeast Selection in Brewing."

Fix, G.J. and L.A. Fix. *An Analysis of Brewing Techniques*. Boulder, Colo.: Brewers Publications, 1997, 57-65.

Mussche and Mussche, "Flavours in Beer."

Prahl, T. Apple Wine Fermentation – Using Indigenous Yeasts as Starter Cultures (2009) 27-28.

Quain, D. "Yeast Supply—the Challenge of Zero Defects." Proceedings of the 25th European Brewery Convention (1995), 309-318.

Shimwell, J.L. *American Brewer* 1947, no. 80, 21-22, 56-57.

Part 4

Boulton, C.A., A.R. Jones, E. Hinchliffe. "Yeast Physiological Condition and Fermentation Performance." Proceedings for the 23rd European Brewing Congress (1991), 385-392.

Boulton, C.A., and D.E. Quain. "Yeast, Oxygen, and the Control of Brewery Fermentations." Proceedings of the 21st European Brewing Convention (1987), 401-408.

D'Amore, T., G. Celotto, and G.G.Stewart. "Advances in the Fermentation of High Gravity Wort." Proceedings of the European Brewery Convention Congress (1991), 337-344.

De Clerck, *A Textbook of Brewing.*

Fix and Fix, *An Analysis of Brewing Techniques,* 75-81.

Grossman, K. Seminar. University of California at Davis, Oct. 3, 2009.

Hull, G. "Olive Oil Addition to Yeast as an Alternative to Wort Aeration." *MBAA Technical Quarterly* 45, no. 1 (2008), 17-23.

Jones H.L., A. Margaritis, and R.J. Stewart. "The Combined Effects of Oxygen Supply Strategy, Inoculum Size and Temperature Profile on Very High Gravity Beer Fermentation by *Saccharomyces Cerevisiae.*" *Journal of the Institute of Brewing* 113, no. 2 (2007), 168-184.

Laere, S.D., K.J. Verstrepen, J.M. Thevelein, P. Vandijck, and F.R. Delvaux. "Formation of Higher Alcohols and Their Acetate Esters." *Cerevisia, Belgian Journal of Brewing and Biotechnology,* vol. 33, no. 2 (2008), 65-81.

Landschoot, A.V., N. Vanbeneden, D.Vanderputten, and G. Derdelinckx. "Extract for the Refermentation of Beer in Bottles." *Cerevisia, Belgian Journal of Brewing and Biotechnology,* vol. 32, no. 2 (2007), 120-129.

Mclaren, J.I., T. Fishborn, F. Briem, J. Englmann, and E.Geiger. "Zinc Problem Solved?" *Brauwelt International,* vol. 19, no. 1 (2001), 60-63.

Meilgaard, "Flavor Chemistry of Beer: Part II."

O'Connor-Cox, E.S.C. and W.M. Ingledew. "Effect of the Timing of Oxygenation on Very High Gravity Brewing Fermentations." *Journal of the American Society of Brewing Chemists* 48, no. 1 (1990), 26-32.

Parker, N. "Are Craft Brewers Underaerating Their Wort?" *MBAA Technical Quarterly* 45 no. 4 (2008), 352-354.

Priest, F.G., and I. Campbell. *Brewing Microbiology*, 3rd ed. New York: Kluwer Academic/Plenum Publishers, 2003, 22-42.

Reed, G., and T.W. Nagodawithana. *Yeast Technology*, 2nd ed. New York: Van Nostrand Reinhold, 1991.

Saison, D., D. De Schuttera, B. Uyttenhovea, F. Delvauxa, and F.R. Delvauxa. "Contribution of Staling Compounds to the Aged Flavour of Lager Beer by Studying Their Flavour Thresholds." *Food Chemistry*, vol. 114, no. 4 (June 15, 2009), 1206-1215.

Shinabarger, D.L., G.A. Kessler, and L.W. Parks. "Regulation by Heme of Sterol Uptake in *Saccharomyces Cerevisiae.*" *Steroids* 53 (1989), 607-623.

Takacs, P. and J.J. Hackbarth. "Oxygen-Enhanced Fermentation." *MBAA Technical Quarterly* 44 (2007), 104-107.

Walker, G.M. "Role of Metal Ions in Brewing Yeast Fermentation Performance." *Brewing Yeast Fermentation Performance,* Oxford, U.K.: Blackwell Science Ltd., 2000, 86-91.

Part 5
Fernandez, J.L., and W.J. Simpson. *Journal of Applied Bacteriology* 75 (1993), 369.

Haddad, S., and C. Lindegren. "A Method for Determining the Weight of an Individual Yeast Cell." *Applied Microbiology* 1, no.3, (1953), 153-156.

Lenoel, M., J.P. Meuier, M. Moll, and N. Midoux. "Improved System for Stabilizing Yeast Fermenting Power During Storage." Proceedings of the 21st European Brewing Congress, 1987, 425-432.

Nielsen, O. "Control of the Yeast Propagation Process: How to Optimize Oxygen Supply and Minimize Stress." *MBAA Technical Quarterly,* vol. 42, no. 2 (2005), 128-132.

Part 6

American Society of Brewing Chemists. *Methods of Analysis,* revised 8th ed. Yeast-3. St. Paul, Minn.: ASBC, 1992.

Hulse, G., G. Bihl, G. Morakile, and B. Axcell. "Optimisation of Storage and Propagation for Consistent Lager Fermentations." In K. Smart, *Brewing Yeast Fermentation Performance.* Oxford, U.K.: Blackwell Science, 2000, 161-169.

Jakobsen, M., and R.W. Thorne. "Oxygen Requirements of Brewing Strains of *Saccharomyces Uvarum*—Bottom Fermenting Yeast." *Journal of the Institute of Brewing* 86 (1980), 284-287.

Kandror, O., N. Bretschneider, E. Kreydin, D. Cavalieri, and A.L. Goldberg. "Yeast Adapt to Near-Freezing Temperatures by STRE/Msn2,4-Dependent Induction of Trehalose Synthesis and Certain Molecular Chaperones." *Molecular Cell,* vol. 13, no. 6 (March 26, 2004), 771-781.

Quain and Tubb, 38-40.

Sidari, R. and A. Caridi. "Viability of Commercial Wine Yeasts During Freezer Storage in Glycerol-Based Media." *Folia Microbiology* 54, no. 3 (2009), 230–232.

Part 7

Flannigan, B., J.G. Morton, and R.J. Naylor. "Tricothecenes and Other Mycotoxins." New York: John Wiley & Sons, (1985), 171.

Kapral, D. "Stratified Fermentation—Causes and Corrective Action." *MBAA Technical Quarterly* 45, no. 2 (2008), 115-120.

Index

Numbers in **boldface** refer to illustrations, figures, and charts